The Final Words

of Jesus

and

Satan's Lies Today

by

James Jacob Prasch

First published in Great Britain in 1999
by
St Matthew Publishing Ltd
Copyright © James Jacob Prasch

ISBN 19015460 6 3

Scripture taken from the NEW AMERICAN STANDARD BIBLE © 1960, 1962, 1963, 1968, 1971, 1972, 1973, 1975, 1977, by The Lockman Foundation. Used by permission.

Cover design: Prototype Design
+44 (0)208 428 9885

Quotation from *Death in the City* by Francis Schaeffer used by permission.
published by IVP 1969 ISBN 0 85110 347 2

Printed by Clifford Frost Ltd, Lyon Road, Windsor Ave, Wimbledon SW19 2SE
+ (0)181 540 2396

St Matthew Publishing Ltd, 24 Geldart St, Cambridge CB1 2LX UK
Tel: +44 (0)1223 504871, Fax +44 (0)1223 512304
Email: PF.SMP@dial.pipex.com

Contents

Acknowledgements   4

PREFACE   5

INTRODUCTION   6

PART I

Chapter 1   One Jesus, Two Messiahs   9

Chapter 2   Midrash   19

Chapter 3   The Festal Calendar   29

Chapter 4   Interpreting Prophecy   37

Chapter 5   How the Church Lost Its Way   43

PART II the Lies

Chapter 6   Lie 1: Christian Zionism   55

Chapter 7   Lie 2: Restorationism   85

Chapter 8   Lie 3: Faith-Prosperity Gospel   171

Chapter 9   Lie 4: Gnosticism and the New Age   209

Chapter 10   Lie 5: Ecumenism   233

Postscript   241

Appendix   243

Index   247

Acknowledgements

This book has been long in preparation and would not now be available were it not the for the hard work of several people. Thanks goes to Portia Franklin who painstakingly researched the footnotes, wading through many volumes and many tapes, to Noel Poore who enabled the book to be set out in its current form.
Then to Alan Franklin and his wife for vetting the text and making many essential editorial corrections and comments.
Throughout David Lang has edited and re-edited the book at various stages in its development.
Neil Richardson proof read the text.

To all these and others who have to remain nameless our thanks are due.

To none of the above are to be attributed any errors.

To the only wise God, through Jesus Christ,
be the glory forever. Amen.
Romans 16:27

PREFACE

The Churches today are in very deep trouble. That is the reason for this book. All around us are problems and errors, disillusionment and pain among Christians who had sought to follow the Lord by following their leaders. This book attempts to address these matters head on. If it is outspoken it is because someone must speak out when things are so bad. For if the trumpet gives an uncertain sound, who shall get ready for battle? For a battle there is. A battle for the one unchanging gospel and a battle for the authority of Scripture in all matters of doctrine, faith and conduct.

The great difficulty for anyone trying to tackle such subjects is that they are like fungi in woodland. Round every rotting tree and sometimes on living trees as well, fungi seem to cling and grow and spread. Biologists tell us that many of these different growths are one rambling organism spreading its spores by nearly invisible underground threads throughout the whole wood. So, too, the current growths of error and deceit that at first seem to an observer separate problems, are all in fact connected 'underground' and are all related. Their roots go back to one central issue: misunderstanding of and disobedience to the Final Words of Jesus.

The book has been divided into two sections, of unequal length. The first addresses the Final Words of Jesus and how they ought to be understood. The author will introduce the concept of Midrashic interpretation of Scripture—almost certainly one of the main ways the early church approached God's written Word. In the second, much longer, section the author sets about tackling the problems we face today, tracking their connections back to early error and also trying to show how they influence one another.

By far the longest chapter is the one on Restorationism and 'Kingdom Now' theology. The author tackles the errors of Replacementism and Christian Zionism. He then tackles the money preachers and the new Gnosticism which has brought the New Age movement right into the churches. The ground covered is enormous in scope, but in the end the book will bring you back to the choice that God always lays before each one of us:

Choose this day whom you will serve.

Philip Foster, November 1999

INTRODUCTION

There is only one question that you need to ask concerning this book and only one question that you need to have answered. **Are the things in it true? Are they from the Word of God?**

The Final Words of Jesus

and

Satan's Lies Today

Part I

Chapter 1

One Jesus, Two Messiahs

The Final Words Of Jesus

'And gathering them together He commanded them not to leave Jerusalem, but to wait for what the Father had promised, "which", He said, "you heard of from Me; for John baptised with water but you shall be baptised with the Holy Spirit, not many days from now."

And so when they were come together, they were asking Him, saying, "Lord, is it at this time you are restoring the Kingdom to Israel?"

He said to them, "It is not for you to know times or epochs which the Father has fixed by His own authority;

but you shall receive power when the Holy Spirit has come upon you; and you shall be My witnesses both in Jerusalem and in all Judea and Samaria and even to the remotest part of the earth."'

Acts 1:4-8

One Messiah—Two Comings

In order to understand the Apostles' questions to Jesus and His answer the background of Acts 1 and 2 must be viewed from within the context of Jewish thought during the second Temple period—that is prior to the destruction of Jerusalem and the Temple in 70 AD. Central to any understanding is that to this day Judaism holds in tension two diverse portraits of the Messiah, which they attempt to marry together.

These are known as *Ha Moshiach Ben Yoseph*—Messiah the son of Joseph, and *Ha Moshiach Ben David*—Messiah the son of David. Later Talmudic literature goes to great lengths to reconcile the seemingly contradictory pictures of the Messianic Deliverer. The son of Joseph is popularly referred to as *Ben Ephraim* in Rabbinic thought and He is identified with the portrait of the suffering servant Messiah found in the fourth Servant Song of the Book of Isaiah chapters 52 and 53.

This 'son of Joseph' is that Messiah whose life is prefigured by Joseph the son of Jacob in the book of Genesis and the ministry of this Messiah in some way replays the life and experience of Joseph. There are at least thirty-five major parallels, even down to minute details between Joseph and Jesus of Nazareth, known in His day as *Rabbi Yeshua Ben Yosef* of Nazareth.

As Joseph was betrayed by his Jewish brothers into the hands of Gentiles and God turned that betrayal around and made it a way for all Israel and all the world to be saved; so too, Jesus was betrayed by His Jewish brothers into Gentile hands with the same result. Joseph was betrayed specifically by his brother *Yehuda*, or Judas, for twenty pieces of silver. Jesus as the Messiah, the son of Joseph, was also betrayed specifically by *Yehuda*, that is Judas, for thirty pieces of silver.

Joseph was taken from a place of condemnation to a place of exaltation in a single day as was Jesus in His resurrection. Joseph and Jesus were condemned with two criminals—one of whom lived while the other died. Upon his exaltation, every knee bowed to Joseph as every knee shall one day bow to Jesus.

All power and dominion was given to Joseph by Pharaoh the king of Egypt. Today the Jews understand God as the King of the universe and believe that He will give all power and dominion to their long awaited Messiah. Upon his exaltation, Joseph took a Gentile bride and figuratively, Jesus takes a Gentile bride—the Church. Joseph was not recognised by his Jewish brothers at his first coming, but at the second and then they wept over him. Similarly, Jesus was not recognised by His Jewish brothers, at his first coming but at the second when they too will weep.[1]

Joseph was falsely accused at an unfair trial, as was Jesus. Joseph's cloak was taken as proof that he was no longer in the pit as Jesus' burial cloak was taken as proof that He was no longer in the tomb. Joseph was despised without cause for his prophetic gift. So too Jesus was despised for who He claimed to be. Finally Joseph was the beloved of his father—as is Jesus.

Judaism understands that the Messiah will come in the character of Joseph and be typified by him. Yet there is another picture of the Messiah—the son of David. This Messiah would come in the character of Israel's great king and in some way His life and ministry would replay the experience and life of King David. For example David came as God's choice to replace the people's choice personified by King Saul.

This then is the background to the Apostles' questions. To this day Judaism is unable to explain the relationship between these two Messiahs. In retrospect, however, Christianity understands that it is rather **one** Messiah and **two** comings. At His first coming, Jesus is the son of Joseph, a suffering servant, fulfilling Isaiah 53 and Psalm 22 but in His second coming He is the son of David.

In His first coming, He fulfils the prophecy of Zechariah chapter 9:9 riding into Jerusalem on a donkey, but at His return He fulfils the prophecies of Zechariah chapters 12-14 when He comes as the Davidic conqueror. Even John the Baptist was unable to understand how Jesus could be both when he dispatched his disciples to ask Jesus if He was indeed the Messiah or if he should look for another.

Post-millennialism,
Hellenistic Perversion Of Jewish Faith

In fact Jesus did not fulfil all of the Old Testament's Messianic prophecies. At this time He has only literally fulfilled those pertaining to the son of Joseph. He is yet to accomplish those prophecies which relate to the son of David. It is in the light of this that the earliest literature of those closest to the Apostles maintained that apostolic Christianity was pre-millennial, seeing the need for Jesus to return and reign literally in the character of David from Jerusalem. Hence, from the original Jewish perspective of the Apostles and first century church, if there is no millennial reign it can be argued that Jesus is not the Messiah of the Jews and therefore neither is He the Christ of the church.

At the time of the events recorded in Acts 1:1-4 the Apostles were looking for Jesus to be that Davidic Messiah who would bring total fulfilment to all of their Messianic expectations and a complete fulfilment of all Messianic prophecy. Jesus' response was that this would happen in God's good time within the divine timetable. Their priority was to be fulfilment of and obedience to the great commission as detailed in Matt 28:27.

Palm Sunday—The Key To It All

What really happened on Palm Sunday? If Christians properly understood the Jewish background of the events surrounding the triumphal entry of Jesus into Jerusalem many of the greatest challenges and deceptions facing the church today could be understood and exposed for the unbiblical beliefs they are.

On Palm Sunday the procession into Jerusalem for the Pilgrim Feast of Passover commenced. The pilgrim throngs, representing Jews from throughout the Roman Empire, sang from the Hebrew festal liturgy now known as the *Maqzor*, Psalms 113-118. In Judaism these are known as the *Hallel Rabbah*—or the Great Praise—which even today remains an important part of the Passover liturgy or *Sidur*. Its climax is Psalm 118:22-29.

The Palm Sunday text found in Matthew chapter 21 refers to this twice. Once, in verse 9, when the crowds are singing "Hosanna to the Son of David", and secondly, in verse 42 when Jesus refers to Psalm 18:22, citing Himself as the stone which was rejected. The levitical choirs would lead the pilgrims down the cleft of the Mount of Olives, across the Kidron Valley, and through the East Gate of Jerusalem with Psalm 118 reaching its climax as the pilgrims heard "Hosanna! Hosanna!" meaning "Save Us, Save Us" and then they knew that the procession was approaching the Temple Mount.

> O Lord save us, we beseech Thee
> Give us prosperity
> Blessed is He Who cometh
> In the Name of the Lord -
> We bless You from the house
> Of the Lord.
>
> Psalm 118:25-26

and in Matthew 21:9 they said:

> Hosanna to the Son of David!
> Blessed is He who cometh
> In the Name of the Lord!

> *Baruch Ha Ba B'Shem Adonai*
> *Barachnu Hem Mi Beit Adonai*
> *Hodu L'Adonai Ki Tov*
> *Ki La Olam Chasdo*
> *Hoshanna, Hoshanna*
> *L' Ben David.*

During the choral climax on this pilgrim feast Jesus rode on a donkey at the front of the procession for his triumphal entry in fulfilment of the messianic prophecies of Zechariah chapter 9, and the Jews were cheering him as the Son of David, asking him for a salvation that would bring them prosperity, calling out to him: "Blessed is He Who Comes In The Name Of The Lord".

Yet a few days later in Matthew 23:39 Jesus tells the Jews that they will not see him again until they say to Him: "Blessed is he who comes in the name of the Lord." The same precise words they sang to Him a few days earlier. Now it seems Jesus acts as if Palm Sunday never happened! Why? Because it is in fact something properly reserved for a future time.

False Expectations Then And Now

There were three main reasons the Jews were not ready for Jesus to come the first time. They had a 'signs and wonders gospel', they had a 'kingdom now gospel' and they had a 'prosperity gospel'. As it says in Daniel chapter 7:21,22 the saints take full possession of the kingdom **after** the return of Christ—not **before**. His kingdom is not of this world. Yet the Jews wanted someone who would get rid of the Romans the way the Maccabees had disposed of the Greeks a century and a half earlier.

They were taken up by a false spirit of dominionism and triumphalism: almost exactly what we see throughout much of the church today. The Jews had no desire to know about a suffering servant Messiah, they simply wanted a dominionist 'kingdom now' messiah who would give them material prosperity. Having said that it must be understood that it is His purpose to bring material blessing, but at His second coming: as the Son of David and not at the first coming when He came to atone for our sins.

So they rejected the true Messiah because He would not tell them what they wanted to hear and they would not believe the truth that He gave them. Today the same errors of prosperity theology cause Christians to reject the true Messiah for the same reasons. Health, wealth and prosperity can only be fully realised at His return. Until then we may experience a foretaste of the coming blessings, but the message of the gospel is to pick up our cross and follow the Suffering Servant so that we will be ready for the return of the coming king.

We may now understand why Jesus told the Jews, "You will not see Me until you say, 'Blessed is He Who comes in the name of the Lord!'" They had said it to the Son of David, when they should have been saying it to the Son of Joseph. They should have embraced a suffering servant as opposed to looking for prosperity, and looked for a kingdom to come instead of a kingdom now. This is borne out by Zechariah chapter 12:10 which says that upon His return his own people, the Jews, will see the one they had pierced and know that the son of David is also the son of Joseph.

Jesus: A Messenger—Not A Showman

Palm Sunday was a day on which Jews would listen to famous rabbis having debates. Indeed, many of Jesus' encounters with the Pharisees take place against the background of these rabbinic debates which were customary during the pilgrim feasts.

Jesus' reputation had, however, gone before Him—including the accounts of His feeding thousands miraculously, healing the sick and raising the dead. The people wanted a display of what Jews call *nesim v'niflaoht,* an exhibition of signs and wonders. Jesus, however, refused to put on a show—as we read in Matthew chapter 21. Instead he drove the corrupt temple bureaucrats and religious leaders out of the temple. In other words, He performed the search for leaven in its truest sense. For before the lamb could be sacrificed at Passover the Temple had to be cleansed.

It was only after Jesus removed the leaven from His Father's house that He began to heal the lame and the blind (Matt 21:14). Jesus would not put on a show and would not elevate signs and wonders or the miraculous above His message of holiness and repentance.

Today we have major figures (particularly in the pentecostal and charismatic tradition such as Benny Hinn and others) who are doing the very thing Jesus refused to do. Indeed, as we shall see, Hinn voiced the view, held by many other 'faith teachers', that Jesus did not win the victory on the Cross when He said "it is finished", but rather that He became a satanic being in hell of one nature with satan and was born again in hell.[5] This is blasphemy and God will hold such men accountable for their words.

Conclusions

We find three false ideas of the Gospel being played out on Palm Sunday. The first was a 'kingdom now' theology which was dominionist and triumphalist along the same lines as what is promoted today in the belief systems of restorationism and dominionism.

Married to it is a dangerous emphasis on material prosperity, just the same as we found on Palm Sunday with the rejection of a crucified Messiah who beckons us to join Him on the cross before we will be able to join Him in His coming kingdom.

Thirdly, we see an over emphasis on signs and wonders of the kind that Jesus refused to allow His ministry to be reduced to: where power, exhibitions of the miraculous and showmanship are amplified over death to self, to the world and to the power of sin.

Most Jews of Jesus' day rejected Him because he would not deliver on their 'Kingdom' expectations of prosperity, dominionism, and signs and wonders exhibitionism. Instead, they were to follow a false messiah a generation later. His name was Simon Bar Cohba, falsely proclaimed as Messiah by Rabbi Akiva on the Second Jewish revolt circa 120AD. Rabbi Akiva and Bar Cohba typify the Antichrist and False Prophet. As Jesus said, "If another comes in My Name, him you will believe."[6] Bar Cohba led the Jews to a national holocaust as will the antichrist in the Great Tribulation. Rejecting the true Christ because most wanted a Messiah with a different message, they found a false one—and will do so again.

So will much of the Church, for precisely the same reasons. Many so-called evangelical, born-again Christians are caught up in dominionism, prosperity theology and signs and wonders theology. They are rejecting the true Christ and are already following false ones.

In Greek the definition of a false christ is someone with a false anointing[7] (although there will be an ultimate Beast as described in the Book of Revelation who will be the epitome of false anointing). Only the faithful remnant of Christians will be ready for the true

Jesus' return. Those following Benny Hinn, Morris Cerullo, Frederick Price, Rick Godwin, Paul Crouch, Jerry Saville, Larry Lee, Ed Cole, Marilyn Hickey, Ray Macauley, Oral Roberts, Kenneth Hagin, John Avanzini and Kenneth Copeland most certainly will not be ready.

Ultimately unsaved Jews, longing for a Messiah who will give them dominion and prosperity in this fallen world, will accept the Antichrist as they accepted Bar Cohba nearly two millennia ago.

Those Christians following triumphalism, chasing gifts and manifestations above the Giver, and believing word-faith prosperity might well follow the Antichrist also. If they want a show, this false Christ will put on one hell of a show for them.[8]

Notes on Ch.1

1. Zechariah 12:10.
2. 2 Samuel 7:13 & 16 (confirmed in Jeremiah 33:17).
3. Yalkuth, vol. II, page 79d, Nazir 32b. Also, Midrash Bereshith—Warsaw edition; "The Messiah is to exit in 33AD!"
4. John 4:10,13,14.
5. "He became one with the nature of Satan, so all those who had the nature of Satan can partake of the nature of God." ('Benny Hinn' program on TBN, 15 December 1990. Message entitled, 'The Person of Jesus', filmed at Orlando Christian Center on December 2, 1990. Videotape #TV-292).
   Kenneth Hagin, Kenneth Copeland and Freddy Price are among those who have developed these teachings; all were influenced by E.W. Kenyon.
6. John 5:43.
7. 2 Thessalonians 2:7-12.
8. Revelation 13:13.

Chapter 2

Midrash

The interpretation of scripture, and what happens when we do it, is called hermeneutics. Our approach to hermeneutics, or interpretation, will always be influenced, to a degree, by our world view, our own culture, and the pre-suppositions these things give us.

The interpretations used by Jewish rabbis like Jesus and Paul in the first century, were largely based on something called *Midrash*. The basic principles of *Midrash* are listed in the original seven points called *midoth* of Rabbi Hillel[1]. Rabbi Hillel was the grandfather of Rabbi Gamaliel who was the tutor of Saint Paul in the Pharisaic School of Hillel and who defended the rights of Jewish believers in the book of Acts.[2]

As the church became more Gentile after the gospel spread throughout the Greco-Roman world, it began to lose sight of its Jewish origins. People with a different world view, based usually on either the philosophies of Aristotle (called Aristotelianism) or Plato (called Platonism), began to re-define biblical truth on the basis of these Greek philosophies instead of explaining in Greek terms the Jewish philosophy that produced the gospel.

Centuries later the early Puritans recognised the limitations of protestant hermeneutics as did the later Plymouth Brethren who sought a proper understanding of Biblical typology. In much the same manner as early Methodism tried to restore mission to the church, realising the failures of Protestantism, so also the early Pentecostals tried to restore charismatic gifts while recognising the same failure to return fully to a New Testament Christianity.

The great Puritans John Robinson and John Lightfoot, were among the first to recognise the need to restore a Jewish approach to Biblical interpretation. They realised the need to handle allegory and typology properly along Midrashic lines without falling into the errors of misusing typology and allegory as seen in the Roman Catholic concept of *Sensus Plenior*, where it is claimed that the full sense of scripture can only be be understood by the Pope.[3] According to this doctrine it is only the Pontiff through the *magisterium*[4] (or committee) of the Roman church who can possibly understand the deeper meaning of scripture.

Midrash

It is my conviction that the internal evidence of the New Testament demonstrates that Jesus and the apostles employed a Midrashic hermeneutic as evidenced in the manner in which the New Testament often uses and explains the Old.

A Question Of Prophecy

Central to the issue of interpretation is not simply the use of Midrash in the New Testament alone, but rather how it functions in conjunction with the subject of prophecy. Western hermeneutics misunderstand the end times prophecy, seeing it merely in terms of prediction and fulfilment.

The ancient Jewish concept of prophecy saw it as a pattern being recapitulated. This idea is crucial in understanding the errors of dominionism and restorationism which argue that the last days are over, having all happened in a literal sense in 70 AD. At that time the second temple was destroyed in fulfilment of the prophecies of the Jewish prophet Daniel and also, later, those of Jesus in the Olivet discourse.

One way to understand the Jewish concept of prophecy is as thematic recapitulation, where a pattern of events replays the same theme repeatedly. For example one problem that western hermeneutics has never been able to answer satisfactorily is: how can Matthew be justified in quoting Hosea 11:1 out of all reasonable context as connected with his story of the nativity of Jesus in Matthew 2:15? The answer is pattern not just prediction.

Pattern, Not Just Prediction

The theme of the passage is that of "coming out of Egypt." Abraham—the father of all who believe—becomes an archetype; that is, his experience as patriarch is archetypal of his descendants coming out of Egypt—or in other words what happens to him, also happens to his descendants at a later date.

During a famine Abraham the patriarch stays temporarily in Egypt and following divine judgment on Pharaoh he leaves bringing wealth from Egypt before entering into the Promised Land. Many years later his descendants, the sons of Jacob, enter Egypt as the result of another famine and God's judgment again falls on Pharaoh. When they leave Egypt for the Promised Land, they bring the wealth of Egypt with them thus replaying the experience of the archetype Abraham and developing the theme of coming out of Egypt.

Similarly in 1 Corinthians 10 we Christians are told that we too have come out of Egypt, again replaying the same experience and further developing the same theme. Pharaoh was worshipped as God by the Egyptians who deified him and as such he becomes a metaphor for the Devil, the god of this world. Just as Moses made a covenant using blood which he sprinkled on the people, so Jesus, who was a prophet like Moses, makes a new covenant in His blood so covering His people. Egypt can now be seen as a symbol of the world, and just as Moses led the children of Israel through the Red Sea out of Egypt into the Promised Land, so Jesus leads us out of the world through baptism and into heaven.

In the book of Revelation we see the same judgements against Egypt replayed in the final judgements of God upon a sinful world. Just as Pharaoh's magicians were able to counterfeit the miracles of Moses and Aaron, so the Antichrist and False Prophet will counterfeit the miracles of Jesus and his witnesses.

The Song of Moses sung by Miriam in the Exodus narrative is sung again in Revelation where the destruction of Pharaoh and his army are seen as a type of the judgement of Satan and his demon cohorts. Therefore, just as Joseph's bones were brought out of

Egypt so the dead in Christ will rise first when we come out of the world together at Jesus' return.

Thus the Exodus of Jesus from Egypt in Matthew's nativity narrative fits precisely into the same pattern following the same theme. A wicked king is again judged—this time Herod—and the Messiah comes out of Egypt where he had fled in time of trouble. Here Jesus is pictured as the embodiment of Israel, in much the same way as the church is the Body of Christ. Old Testament citations such as "Israel, My Glory" and "Israel, My Firstborn" may now be understood for what they are—allusions to the Messiah.

Hence, as Abraham departed from Egypt, his physical descendants came out of Egypt in the Exodus. Then, his seed the Messiah comes out of Egypt, and we, His spiritual descendants, come out of 'Egypt'. Finally all of these Exodus events prefigure some aspect of the resurrection and rapture of the Church. As can be seen Jewish prophecies of this kind have multiple fulfilments with each fulfilment being a type revealing some aspect of their ultimate fulfilment. In fact in its simplest sense this is the basic principle of Midrash.

Approaching Matthew's nativity story from this Jewish perspective instead of a western one, we can understand how and why his words as found in the text of Hosea 11:1 apply to Jesus upon the death of Herod. We may understand how the phrase "out of Egypt I have called my son" is also valid as a prophecy about the Messiah who represents both the embodiment of Israel and the redemptive hope of Israel.

A further complication in relation to Midrash has been the misunderstanding and misuse of it by liberal theological writers. Midrash never uses typology or allegory as a basis for *doctrine*, only as illustration of it. A fundamental tenet of Midrash is the belief that scripture is literally the revelation of God to man. Yet in recent years, individuals from the liberal theological school have chosen to misuse it. It is also the case that prior to this, conservative scholars, perhaps perceiving that is was inevitable that Midrash could be misused by the liberal theological establishment, either avoided it, or tried to explain New Testament uses of Midrash as traditional typology.

James Barr, Oxford Professor of Hebrew, cites the New Testament's handling of the Old Testament to attack 'fundamentalism' with the argument that the apostles did not use the Bible literally.[5]

Dr Walter Kaiser, a conservative evangelical, in a cessasionist[6] evangelical reaction to this argument, correctly sought to argue that in Matthew's use of Hosea chapter 11:1, Matthew was using typology (with a historical correspondence between the Exodus and the return of Jews from Eygpt) and 'corporate solidarity' (a biblical literary technique where a person represents a group of people). Kaiser argues correctly that Matthew quotes Hosea's citation of a particular event in Jewish history but makes it significant for a specified situation. While Walter Kaiser never properly developed his argument by showing Matthew's use of Hosea chapter 11:1 as systematically coherent within the framework of second temple period Judaic understanding of Messianic and eschatological prophecy—he is correct in what he says. Unfortunately in his quest to defend doctrinal orthodoxy from heretical voices wrongly claiming a Midrashic basis for their positions, Dr. Kaiser did not recognise the incompatibility of Matthew's Jewish hermeneutic with the classical protestant methods of grammatical-historical exegesis which the Reformers derived from 16th century Christian humanism.

Some of the Puritan fathers made genuine efforts to return to a Judeo-Christian approach to scriptural interpretation. An essential tenet of early Puritan thinking was that the Reformation failed to go far enough in restoring Biblical Christianity and this extended into the area of hermeneutics. The Pilgrim chaplain John Robinson said, "There is more light in God's Word than we presently see". The Puritan scholar John Lightfoot composed a broad-based Midrashic commentary on the New Testament. However the English Restoration and the political quagmire in which the Puritans immersed themselves brought an end to what might have been a Renaissance of Judeo-Christian understanding of the Christian faith as the Apostles knew it.

In the 19th century the Plymouth Brethren tried to construct a model of biblical interpretation which emphasised typology from the viewpoint of Old Testament foreshadowings of the new covenant. They did this, however, not simply to better grasp how the old covenant pointed to Jesus and the church, but rather to illuminate the teachings of Jesus and the early church; that is, they used a typological understanding of the Old Testament to interpret and better understand and apply the New. This may have been the closest that the predominantly Gentile church has ever come to returning to its Jewish roots in the area of interpretation.

Since that time, most Judeo-Christian scholarship has focused more on the Judaic background of the gospels. This probably commenced with Jewish Christians such as Franz Delitzche and Alfred Edershein. Today the trend continues in the work of Arnold Fruchtenbaum and others. Such scholarship is vital.

The Place Of Theology

"Most theologians devote their lives to answering questions most people are not asking." C.S.Lewis

Did Jesus say to feed His sheep, or to feed the theologians? The majority of scholarly journals produced concerning the world of academic theology are submerged in a sea of theological debate as theologians respond to each other. Few of the many papers published are designed to equip the pastors with scholarly material of practical value in discipling their congregations. Almost none of it is directly relevant to the average person, be they saved or unsaved.

We do well to remember that when C.S. Lewis wrote books like *The Screwtape Letters*, *The Abolition of Man* and *Mere Christianity*, he was answering questions people *were* asking. Yet, although he was an Oxford don, the academic establishment was only willing to do a scholarly critique of his books from a literary point of view. It was not until 20 years after his death that theological journals even began to consider what he wrote as theology.

The best one can expect from theological journals is to find conservative evangelicals debunking the groundless presuppositions of liberal heretics. In academic circles, moreover, even the barrier between conservative and liberal can become very blurred. To traditional evangelicals Roman Catholicism is a theological anathema. Yet within academic circles Roman Catholic scholars can be regarded as fellow conservatives when compared to liberals both Protestant and Catholic. Very little of this debate contributes to carrying out the great commission of Jesus. Perhaps that tells us all we need to know.

Historically, most conservative Christian scholarship has correctly been a reaction against heresy. In the Apostolic church the issues were legalism, nomianism and judaisation. In the Patristic era it was wrong Christology (those with wrong views of the nature of Jesus) or Gnosticism against which the Church fathers reacted. During the Reformation the issues were justification and the authority of scripture, with the Reformers reacting against the heresy of the papacy. From the Enlightenment until the 1970s it was conservatives reacting against the liberal higher critics who tried to re-frame the Christian faith within the parameters of German rationalism. Now at the dawn of the 21st century the issues are again Gnosticism, Christology and, due to the growth of ecumenism and inter-faith trends, the definition of the gospel and the authority of the Bible. Reactive theology is essential, providing we recall that apostolic theology was also proactive. Paul, for instance, addressed the issue of the Mosaic law reactively in Galatians—refuting error, but proactively in Romans—not looking to refute error or deception, but to illuminating truth.

This book should not convey the impression that Midrash is simply a mechanism for refuting error. It is rather a general approach to interpretation that can be used to refute error (as with Paul's Midrash on Sarah and Hagar in Galatians chapter 4) or to uncover a deeper level of doctrinal truth (as in the epistle to the Hebrews where it is used as a commentary on Leviticus).

Another key in understanding Jewish Midrash is the need to determine whether or not a text contains a *pesher*, that is a real underlying meaning which does not contradict the obvious meaning but uses the obvious meaning to portray a deeper and more profound truth. Grammatical historical exegesis, which the Reformers derived from humanism, is a valid hermeneutic for interpreting the epistles, because the epistles themselves are simply inspired commentary on other scripture. When the epistles use typology, allegory or Midrash they either explain what it means (e.g. Galatians chapter 4) or assume that the readers already understand it from their own cultural point of reference (e.g. Jude's epistle).

None the less, in writing the epistles, the Apostles themselves plainly use Midrash. On what basis can the church today fail to do so, except to substitute models of our own invention for the ones that God has given us in His word through Apostolic example and more importantly the example of Christ?

Jesus is not only our perfect example of a pastor and an evangelist but he is also the perfect example of a teacher—prompting Paul to write in Corinthians, "Be imitators of me as I am of Christ." Traditional arguments maintained that it was acceptable for Jesus and the apostles to use such methods, but to protect the church from error humanistic approaches to exegesis were substituted for biblical ones. That is an error in itself.

Much more can be said on the subject of Midrash that extends beyond the scope of this book. The ancient rabbis had four methods of interpretation which form the Hebrew acronym *pardas* meaning 'orchard'. The *p* was the *peshut* (simple meaning) the *r* was the *remes* a numerical interpretation in effect related to something called *gamatria*. The *d* was the *drash* the exhoratory application and the *s* was the *sod* or secret meaning.

Thus, the Old Testament had as its *peshut* (from the Hebrew word *peshut* meaning simple) the situation that the Hebrew prophets were addressing for their own time. *Remes* would be found in interpretations of the Old Testament playing on numerical schemes as we see in the bi-sabbatarian (2×7) organisation of the ancestry of Jesus in Matthew's genealogy and the uses of words that convey numerical meanings that help illuminate what the words mean.

For instance, no Old Testament verse says "he shall be born a Nazarene", but 'Nazarene' comes from the Hebrew word *netzer*, meaning branch and there are multiple Old Testament prophecies which the rabbis attribute to the Messiah stating that he will be a righteous branch. Thus Matthew, within a Jewish framework, can handle the Old Testament in this fashion. Hebrew words are normally built around a three letter root called a *shoresh* which has a numerical equivalent (as for example we have in Roman numerals). Thus words are linked together not only etymologically, but also mathematically from which ancient Jewish exegesis would see a theological relationship.

The *d* of the *pardes* would simply be the homiletic exhortation of a prophetic message to the people. The *s* for *sod* is the secret meaning of all of the Old Testament writings is the revelation of the promised one, Jesus, who He would be and what He would do.

Notes on Ch.2

1.

    1. *Qal wahomer*: what applies in a less important case will certainly apply in a more important case.

    2. *Gezerah shawah*: verbal analogy from one verse to another; where the same words are applied to two separate cases it follows that the same considerations apply to both.

    3. *Binyan ab mikathub 'ehad*: building up a family from a single text; when the same phrase is found in a number of passages, then a consideration found in one of them applies to all of them.

    4. *Binyan ab mishene kethubim*: building up a family from two texts; a principle is established by relating two texts together; the principle can then be applied to other passages.

    5. *Kelal upherat*: the general and the particular; a general principle may be restricted by a particularisation of it in another verse; or conversely, a particular rule may be extended into a general principle.

    6. *Kayoze bo bemaqom 'aher*: as is found in another place; a difficulty in one text may be solved by comparing it with another which has points of general (though not necessarily verbal) similarity.

    7. *Dabar halamed me'inyano*: a meaning established by its context.

    Quoted from R.N.Longenecker, Biblical Exegesis in the Apostolic Period, Carlisle: Paternoster Press, first published in the UK in 1995. For further details and examples see J Bowker, The Targums and Rabbinic Literature, Cambridge: University Press, 1969:315. Also, J W Doeve, Jewish Hermeneutics in the Synoptic Gospels and Acts, Assen: Van gorcum, 1954:66-75. The listing of the seven middoth is found in Aboth de R Nathan 37, Tos. Sanh. 7.11, and the introduction to Sifra 3a, though some texts of Sifra omit the fourth.

2. Acts 5:34-39.

3. *Sensus Plenior* literally means 'a fuller sense' of the meaning of scripture.

4. The Magisterium consists of the Pope along with a governing body who claim to have the sole ability to interpret scripture.

5. More recent examples of this are found in the writings of Bishop John Shelby Spong, and in Michael Goulder's *Lectionary Hypothesis*.

6. The view taken by some people that spiritual gifts and miracles ceased with the end of the original Apostles' ministry.

Chapter 3

The Festal Calendar

The Festal Calendar Provides The Answer

A useful aid to understanding Midrash is found in the typology of the Jewish religious calendar which was an agricultural, civil and religious calendar based on the lunar year. God gave the Jews holidays to remind them of His past provisions for them. For example the Exodus is commemorated at Passover; and the Jews' sojourning in the wilderness when God provided for them is recalled at the Feast of Booths.

God wanted the Jews to recall the times He delivered and provided for them in the past in order that they might have faith in Him to provide and deliver them in the future. The holidays were also agricultural feasts on which the pagan nations gave thanks to Canaanite deities for rain and good harvests, but God wanted the Jews to thank the true God; hence their holidays and calendar became, in part, a polemic against paganism.

Above all else the calendar and holidays of the Jews were a typology of something theologians call *heilsgeschichte*, or salvation history. Each of the holidays corresponds to a redemptive event in God's plan of salvation. In His first coming as the Son of Joseph, the suffering servant Messiah, Jesus fulfils the spring holidays: these are Passover, the First Fruits and the Feast of Weeks or Pentecost. He will fulfil the autumn holidays when He returns as the Son of David.

As the calendar is also agricultural, we have two rainy seasons preparing the crops for harvest; there is a former and a latter rain. Rain produces something known in biblical Hebrew as *maim haim* or living water. In John chapter 7:38,39 during the Feast of Booths, Jesus told the Jewish people that He would give them living water, meaning of course, the coming of the Holy Spirit.

Like Passover (or *Pesach)* and Weeks, the Feast of Booths was a festival which drew Jews from all over the known world for a ritual called *Simcha Beit Ha Shoy'iva* where Jesus says He would give living water to those who thirst for it, much the same as he told the woman at the well[1] that He would give her living water. Isaiah chapter 44:3 similarly states that the outpouring of rain represents the outpouring of the Holy Spirit, as does Amos chapter 4:7.

The spring rain prepared the spring harvest. The three thousand Jews saved on the day of Pentecost, or the Feast of Weeks, are representative of the spring harvest; and the outpouring of the Holy Spirit that took place at Pentecost is representative of the spring rain.

In order to grasp the depths of these ideas, we must understand the calendar as shown on the next page.

The first and most important of the feasts is Passover which commences with the *Bedachot Hametz* or the Search for Leaven. In Biblical typology leaven represents sin because it puffs up and, just like yeast spores, its effects move from generation to generation. To this day in the Middle East oriental Jews and Arabs make bread by a sour-dough method: taking a lump of dough from the batter of one loaf of bread before it is baked and recycling it in subsequent loaves. The yeast spores multiply very quickly and move from generation to generation, as is the nature of sin.

In Mark chapter 8:15 Jesus warns his hearers to beware of the leaven of the Pharisees, and in Matthew's gospel the woman puts a pinch of leaven into the dough. Here leaven particularly represents sins of false doctrine. We need to understand that false doctrine is sin, because it also puffs up and tends to progress from generation to generation.

False doctrine is inevitably related to pride. So, to this day Jewish families need to purge the leaven from their houses before they can celebrate the Passover. Understanding that the Lord's Supper derives from Passover, Christians should similarly purge leaven from their houses before coming to the Lord's table.[2]

The Festal Calendar

Feast	Old Testament	New Testament	Meaning
Passover	Leviticus 23:5	1 Cor. 5:7	Jesus the Passover Lamb slain for our sins
First Fruits	Leviticus 23:10	1 Cor. 15:27	Resurrection
Weeks or Pentecost	Leviticus 23:16	Acts 2:1	Holy Spirit Outpoured
SUMMER—AGE OF THE GENTILE CHURCH			
Trumpets	Leviticus 23:24	Revelation 8:2	Great Tribulation
Atonement or Yom Kippur	Leviticus 25:9	Hebrews 9:1-14	Atonement and Return of Christ
Booths or Tabernacles	Leviticus 23:42 (Zech 14:16-18)	Revelation 20:4	Millennium

Passover And The Search For Leaven

The Sanhedrin were responsible for the purging of leaven from Jerusalem before the Passover Feast. However, when Jesus drove the moneychangers out of the Temple, it was He who performed the true purging of leaven at Passover time. Where the Sanhedrin had merely removed physical leaven, Jesus removed the actual leaven. Jews required a lamb without blemish to celebrate the Passover because to God one man without sin is worth all the men with sin.

That very day the Sanhedrin had inspected the lambs to see if they were suitable for sacrifice, that is, if the animals were without spot or blemish. So, Jesus the Lamb of God was also inspected by the Sanhedrin who, finding no sin in Him, neither spot nor blemish, judged that He too was worthy to be sacrificed for the sins of the people at this most fateful Passover.

The Sanhedrin, however, were engaged in bribery and corruption. There was graft and people turning the blood sacrifice into a business from which the religious leaders themselves profited. Judgement always begins in the house of God, thus Jesus purged the temple.

As we shall see the Jewish authorities wanted someone to get rid of the Romans; instead God got rid of them. God is always more concerned with the sin among His own people than he is with the sin of those who are not called by His name.

Today little has changed. The prosperity preachers have been publicly discredited—as in the case of Jim Bakker. They turn the ministry of the gospel into a business and profiteer on the blood of the Lamb to the exploitation of God's people. Today, just as at Jesus' triumphal entry, judgement still begins at the house of God. Jesus performed the purge for leaven by cleansing the temple and He is once again cleansing His temple today, purging hypocrisy and financial corruption within the church.

First Fruits And Pentecost

The third day after His crucifixion is the Feast of First Fruits, when the high priest would enter the Kidron Valley outside the East Gate of Jerusalem and, at sunrise, ceremonially harvest the first grain pushing up out of the earth in a symbolic ritual. All four gospels tell us that Jesus rose from the dead at precisely this same sunrise. The rising of the 'sun' thus becomes a metaphor for the rising of the Son. The very hour when the high priest was bringing the first fruit into the temple, Jesus was the first fruit of the resurrection entering the temple of God in the heavenlies as we read in the epistle to the Hebrews.[3]

The Song of Solomon is connected to the Passover in Jewish tradition. Its typology portrays Jesus as the bridegroom and the Church as His bride.[4] In chapter 4 the bridegroom is anointed for burial with myrrh and goes up to 'the mountain of myrrh' to offer a sacrifice for the bride, just as Jesus goes to 'the mountain of myrrh', also called Calvary, to die for His bride.

The Song of Solomon hinges around two dreams found in chapters 3 and 5. In chapter 3 the bride is ready for the bridegroom and it is her best dream. In chapter 5 she is not ready; she misses him, and it is her worst nightmare.

Drawing on what is read in the synagogues at Passover time, Jesus takes the Song of Solomon and explains it in Matthew chapter 25 in the parable of the wise and foolish virgins. The point of the parable is that some will be ready for His coming and others will not. The return of Christ will be either our best dream or our worst nightmare. Note that Jesus continually explains both the eschatological and messianic meanings of the liturgical texts used at Passover time in Judaism.

Forty days later at the Feast of Weeks—or Pentecost—the book of Ruth is read. It is the story of a wealthy and powerful Jewish man who takes a gentile bride just as Jesus takes the gentile church as His bride. Thus Pentecost, when Ruth is read in the synagogues, is the beginning of the age of the church preceded by a large harvest of Jewish souls.

No Rain—No Grain!

A long hot summer ensues in which Israel is agriculturally reliant upon the melting snowcaps of Mount Hermon and the rainfall already accumulated in the Sea of Galilee. It rains little during Middle Eastern summers and this helps us to understand, in part, the phenomenon of revival.

In Amos chapter 4:7 God said that He would pour out His rain on one city, but another city would remain in drought. The part not rained upon would dry up, hence we can see tremendous revivals today happening throughout the poorer nations of the world, while in the more wealthy nations there is drought—God's Spirit is not being poured out.

In the case of New Zealand, for instance, we can see tremendous growth with large numbers of people being saved among the native Maori people in a city like Rotorua, but practically none in a white European city like Christchurch. The world is full of examples like this. God's Spirit is poured out upon one city, while another suffers drought and, spiritually speaking, dries up.

In the autumn however, the autumn rains fall rapidly following a hot, sticky close of the summer called *Hamsin* when warm desert winds from the Arabian Peninsula blow through the Middle East making the end of the summer the most oppressively hot time of year. Then as if from nowhere, torrential rains commence and dried up riverbeds, called wadis, become flash flood zones. Vegetation and harvest follow quickly after a long hot summer of tending the fields.

The Holy Spirit similarly begins to fall powerfully in the last days. The fact that rain and harvest come in the beginning and then again at the end explains in large measure why the gifts of the spirit were in abundance in the early church and why they re-appear in the last days as per Peter's quotation of Joel chapter 2 on the day of Pentecost.[5] It also explains why there are large numbers of Jews saved in the early church corresponding to the spring harvest and then large numbers again at the close of the age.

The Millennium In The Feast Of Tabernacles

There are two further Autumn holidays—the Feast of Trumpets, which corresponds to the Tribulation period, followed by the Day of Atonement. The final holiday is the Feast of Booths or the Feast of Tabernacles which Jesus celebrated in John chapter 7 against the background of the *Simha Beit Ha Shoyava* ritual of pouring out Living Water from the Pool of Shiloah. This text draws on the imagery of Ezekiel chapter 47 (which Toronto experience advocates divorce from its Judaic context and turn into an argument for so called 'latter rain' doctrines).

During this festival the Jews recall their sojourn in the wilderness as they journeyed to the Promised Land by living in booths. So also Christians are to dwell in booths in this world, not making a permanent home in this life, but longing for a promised land in the kingdom of heaven. As we see in Zechariah chapter 14, upon the return of Christ, the Feast of Booths is celebrated when He establishes His kingdom.

The above explains why, at the Transfiguration, when Jesus appears with Moses and Elijah, Peter wanted to build three booths. He thought that this was the arrival of the Messianic kingdom and it was now time to begin the millennial reign. Peter did not understand the difference between the Son of Joseph and Son of David at this point. In Acts ch.1 the Apostles were still unable to understand the difference. That difference is **one** Messiah who comes **twice**. In His first coming Jesus is the suffering servant or *Ben Ephraim*—the Son of Joseph. In His return, He is the Son of David who will set up the millennial kingdom.

The *hallel rabbah* from Psalm 118 sung to Jesus on Palm Sunday however, was actually to be sung twice in the Jewish annual liturgy. It was to be sung with hands waving on Passover, but with palm branches or *lulavim* on the Feast of Booths.

On Palm Sunday the Jews of Jesus' day, however, began to sing it with palm branches at Passover time. They began to celebrate the Feast of Passover as if it were the Feast of Booths. They could not understand the concept of one Messiah who comes twice. It is in Zechariah chapter 9:9 that the Messiah comes meek and lowly riding on a donkey as the Son of Joseph. But it is in Zechariah chapter 12 when He comes as the conqueror in the spirit of King David. Those three chapters make the difference between true and false understanding of God's purposes.

Confusion Then And Now

The Jews tried to celebrate Passover as if it were the Feast of Booths. They began to celebrate the suffering servant Messiah who came to be an atonement for sin as if He were the conquering Messiah coming to set up the millennial kingdom. They sang "Hosanna" to the Son of David telling the Son of David, "Blessed is He who comes in the name of the Lord." In fact, they should have been saying, "Hosanna, save us—blessed is He who comes in the name of the Lord," to the son of Joseph.

The Jews had the right Messiah, yet they also had the wrong one. They understood about Jesus, yet they misunderstood Him completely. As we have seen they had made three basic mistakes on Palm Sunday: they had asked Jesus for prosperity; they were asking Him to set up His kingdom then and there; and they wanted Him to put on a show exhibiting signs and wonders. Nothing changes.

Notes on ch.3
1. John 4
2. Corinthians 11:27–29.
3. 1 Corinthians 15:20; Hebrews 9:11.
4. The Song of Solomon is choral poetry sung to this day in the synagogues at the Feast of Passover. We know from the gender and number of the original Hebrew text what the Bride is singing, what the Bridegroom is singing and what the witnesses to the relationship are singing. It is a poetic reflection of King Solomon's romance with the daughter of Jerusalem called the Shulamite. Solomon represents Jesus the Bridegroom, the Shulamite represents the Bride of Christ and the witnesses represent the *Tsavahot* or hosts of heaven.
5. Acts 2:17–21; Joel 2:28–32.

Chapter 4

Interpreting Prophecy

A Question Of Prophecy

Central to the issue of hermeneutics is not simply the use of Midrash in the New Testament alone, but rather how it functions in conjunction with the subject of prophecy. Western hermeneutics misunderstand eschatological prophecy treating it simply in terms of prediction and fulfilment.

The ancient Jewish concept of prophecy understood prophecy as a pattern being recapitulated. This idea becomes crucial in understanding the errors of Dominionism and Restorationism which basically argue that the last days are over and have happened in a literal sense in 70 AD when the second temple was destroyed in fulfilment of the prophecies of the Jewish prophet Daniel and also, later, of Jesus in the Olivet discourse.[1]

Prediction As Pattern In Eschatology

Pretorism is the preferred approach of liberals who may be said to hold the form of religion but deny the power thereof.[2] Because they cannot be sure of the existence of a God, let alone one who either knows the future or reveals it to men, they follow the pretorist approach. This says that prophetic predictions are events which have already happened inserted after the fact in the language of the future tense and made to seem like predictions.

In the liberal view of pretorism, Isaiah could not know that it would be a king named Cyrus who, two hundred years later, would show benevolence to the Jews. Therefore this automatically proves to the liberal mindset that Isaiah could not possibly have written Isaiah chapter 45 before the Babylonian captivity. Logically it follows that someone else (whom they call Deutero-Isaiah) wrote it after the captivity and attempted to make it appear as if the events were predicted.

The second argument is historicism which says that those prophetic events predicted by Jesus in the Olivet discourse[3] were fulfilled in the early church and had no future meaning; the last days being the events in 70 AD surrounding the destruction of the temple as recorded by Flavius Josephus and later written into church history by Eusebius. The Reformers tended towards a special variation of historicism which saw the Roman Papacy as the Abomination of Desolations and the Pope as the Antichrist. They thought the Pope's ascent had been restrained by Imperial Rome, but his power had increased after the Visigoth invasions and the collapse of the western Roman Empire.

Third, polemicism sees apocalyptic literature such as Revelation as merely designed to encourage the persecuted church during times of acute distress.

Finally, futurism perceives the events chronicled in Matthew chapters 24 and 25 and the book of Revelation as awaiting fulfilment at the return of Christ and in the events leading up to it.

How Jesus Handled Prophecy Of The Last Days

The origin of apocalyptic literature has its root in various Old Testament books like Zechariah. However it only developed as a literary genre in the intertestamental period as seen in First Maccabees and Second Maccabees in the *Apocrypha* where the story of the liberation of Jerusalem by the Maccabees against the forces of Antiochus Epiphanes is recorded as the first Hanukkah. This is the same festival celebrated by Jesus in John chapter 10 where it is called the Feast of Dedication.

Jesus took a prophecy which had already been fulfilled in the story of the Maccabees about Antiochus and the image in the temple[4] which Daniel had predicted and explained how the same thing would happen again within a specific context, seemingly ignoring the fact that it had already been fulfilled! That it had been he himself confirmed when he celebrated Hanukkah. Hence Jesus used pretorism—taking something that already happened—and spoke of it as a prediction.

Secondly, Jesus used polemicism. The apostle John was exiled on the Isle of Patmos during the persecutions at Ephesus under the reign of the Emperor Domitian. Although the early church allowed for the fact that Christ need not return in their lifetime, the popular expectation was that He would. By the end of the first century all the Apostles except for John had been martyred, Christ had not returned and the church was in a state of doubt and confusion. It was then that Jesus appeared to John during this time of crisis and gave him a message to be sent to seven churches in Asia to reassure them of the coming Messianic Kingdom.[5] This is what we know today as the book of Revelation.

However, as the Roman historian Josephus records and as Eusebius stressed, the early church in Jerusalem saw the events of 70 A.D. as a kind of parousia[6] expecting their flight from Jerusalem to be somehow synonymous with the End. That is to say when they fled Jerusalem under the leadership of Simeon, a cousin of Jesus who became pastor after the martyrdom of James, they thought their flight to Pela,[7] undertaken in obedience to the command of Jesus when they "saw Jerusalem surrounded by an army of Gentiles", would be immediately followed by the resurrection, the rapture and the return of Christ.

As Josephus records, the legions of the Roman General Titus set up pagan ensigns where the Holy of Holies[8] had stood and worshipped them.

Thus an 'abomination of desolation' (*Ha Shikutz ha meshomem* in Aramaic) had been set up. Similarly in the second century after the second destruction of Jerusalem by the Emperor Hadrian (following Bar Cochba's rebellion), a pagan city called Aeolina Capitolina was built with the temple of Jupiter on the temple mount in Jerusalem.[9]

Today, the Mosque of Omar, known as the Dome of the Rock, stands on the temple mount with a quotation from the Surrat in the Koran inscribed on its outer periphery stating: "God has no

Son"—yet another abomination. Hence there are multiple historical fulfilments of this prediction which validate historicism. Finally all of these things together typify or reveal some aspect of the ultimate future meaning spoken of by Paul in 2 Thessalonians chapter 2.

The Protestant Error In Understanding Prophecy

From a western protestant perspective, where exegesis is built solely upon grammatical-historical considerations, only one of the four approaches to eschatological prophecy can be true. But in terms of the Hebrew thought—which produced the Bible—all four, pretorism, historicism, polemicism and futurism are simultaneously true because the Jewish concept of prophecy is, as I have demonstrated, not mere prediction, but pattern with the same events being recapitulated and the same theme being progressively developed towards the goal of an ultimate fulfilment. That is to say there are multiple fulfilments of the same prophecy, and each one is a type, or shadow, revealing something about the ultimate fulfilment. In the same way, as we saw earlier, all the stories about coming out of Egypt point ultimately to the Resurrection and the Rapture.

The root problem of the Reformers' error in only restoring part of biblical Christianity in the areas of mission, hermeneutics and spiritual gifts, as well as their negation of the divine purposes for Israel prophetically, is based on their failure to understand the new covenant as it was first predicted in Jeremiah 31:31.

Given that the new covenant would not be like the covenant God made with their fathers, Jeremiah was up against the same problem later encountered by John the Baptist, Jesus and Paul. This was essentially the problem of a national covenant, which is to say, 'a state Church.'

The Jewish people of the days of Jeremiah believed themselves to be automatically in a right relationship to God because they were circumcised as infants and therefore part of a national covenant. Jeremiah predicted that this would no longer be the case, and the new covenant would require an individual response, based on the heart of stone being changed into a heart of flesh, with God's law being written on the hearts of those who responded to his grace as the author of salvation through the coming Messiah, who would Himself be the atonement for sin.

John the Baptist dealt with the same issue when he told the religious leaders that they were not truly Abraham's children simply because of biological birth or circumcision alone. He said the Messiah would come and put an end to this idea, once and for all. Then in the book of Romans Paul teaches that the Messiah has indeed done just that, not abolishing the Law, but fulfilling it and so inaugurating a new covenant to which people must respond as individuals. Hence, Jeremiah and John the Baptist predicted Jesus would do away with the state church and national covenant. In His death upon the cross and in his resurrection, Jesus does precisely this. This also becomes the thrust of Paul's message in Romans and Galatians.

Notes on ch.4
1. Matthew 24:15; Mark13:14; Daniel 9:27, 11:31, 12:11; 1 Maccabees 1:54.
2. 2 Timothy 3:5
3. Matthew 24, 25; Luke 21.
4. Matthew 24:15; Mark13:14; Daniel 9:27, 11:31, 12:11; 1 Maccabees 1:54.
5. Revelation 1:4-3:22.
6. Parousia, literally 'the coming'. The expectation of Christ's imminent return is often linked with destruction as in 2 Peter 3:3-9.
7. Recorded by Eusebius, H.E. III, 5.3. (*A New Eusebius*, Edited by J Stevenson. SPCK, London.1978 pp6-7). Pela was beyond the Jordan.
8. Holy of Holies, was the most sacred part of the tabernacle, only entered by the high priest and only once a year, on the great day of atonement. Exodus 26:33; Hebrews9:25.

9. When Constantine's nephew, Julian the Apostate, tried to rebuild a temple on the temple mount, and mysterious fires occurred, much like the pagan ensigns and the temple to Jupiter, this was seen as another Abomination of Desolation.

Chapter 5

How the Church Lost Its Way

How Much Did The Reformers Reform?

The Reformers, influenced by sixteenth century humanism, through the works of such figures as John Colet, Lefevure, and above all Erasmus of Rotterdam, sought to restore a Biblical Christianity. Indeed justification by faith and the authority of scripture, principles long struggled for by pre-reformation evangelicals such as Jan Huss, the Bohemian Brethren, the Waldenseans, the Albigenses, and to a degree John Wycliffe and the Lollards, were generally re-instituted by the Reformation.[1]

Yet, there were a wide number of crucial areas in apostolic thought which were either neglected or rejected by the Reformers (but which were often embraced by Anabaptist sects which were in most fundamental respects closer to Biblical Christianity than mainstream Protestantism).

These areas included a view of mission which called upon the church to take the gospel to unevangelised people. When Justinian Weltz, William Carey and others argued for the restoration of mission they came up against the non-mission theology of sixteenth century Protestantism and the anti-mission theology of extreme Calvinism. Another trait of first century Christianity rejected by the Reformers was the restoration of gifts of the Spirit which were seen as vital both in the early Wesleyan revivals and in twentieth century Pentecostalism.

Judaization—Satan's First Trick

The Church first began to go seriously wrong when, through the influence of Cyprian and Ambrose, Augustine developed the false doctrine of the 'visible' and the 'invisible' church. This became the way in which the Roman Emperor Constantine's reduction of Christianity into a religion of the state was theologically justified in defiance of the New Covenant, which was not intended to be like the covenant God made with their Jewish fathers—a national Church which people would enter upon birth into a religious culture.

Augustine began to argue that the church was made up of the converted and the unconverted, so just as the Jews circumcised everyone making them all members of the state religion, so Christendom began to sprinkle babies, calling that baptism, and making them all members of a state religion in the process.

Thus (as predicted by Jeremiah and John, and as confirmed to have happened by Paul) what Jesus came to abolish, Constantine and Augustine put back.

In order to genuinely reform the Church, returning it to New Testament Christianity, it was necessary to break the unscriptural marriage between Church and state and to remove the unbiblical practice of infant baptism which became the Christian equivalent of circumcising babies.

However, instead of abolishing the State-Church link and restoring believers' baptism where the Church would be the 'called-out ones' (as the Greek word for Church, *ecclesia*, actually means), the Reformers simply replaced a Roman Catholic State Church with a Protestant one continuing the same unscriptural practices as before.

Thus, not only did Constantine and Augustine put back what Christ died to remove, but Calvin, Luther and Zwingli also kept it as an integral part of Protestantism. Thus, the Reformation could be described as Augustine's doctrine of the church being challenged by his doctrine of grace.

The Reformers' mistake was that instead of returning to the four gospels, they went back to Augustine. Because of the influences of sixteenth century humanist scholarship on the Reformation, rather than retracing their path directly to the Scriptures, they focussed instead on what the later Church fathers said **about** the scriptures: reading the Bible through the prism of the errors of Augustine.

Remember that before Satan tried to paganise the Church in the aftermath of Constantine he tried to Judaize the Church through legalism. This was in an attempt to seduce Christianity back under the curse of the Law and to put it back under the old covenant—as we see in Galatians.[2]

In establishing a Christianised version of the state Church, Roman Catholicism and Protestantism did achieve what the Judaizers and Nomians failed to achieve in Galatia (thanks to the preaching of Paul), the re-establishment of a theocratic state. The Holy Roman Empire of the Middle Ages (which was neither holy nor Roman) was simply replaced by Protestant versions of it. Whether it was Zwingli's police state in Zurich with its massacre of the Baptists, or Calvin's theocratic police state in Geneva (which John Knox tried to imitate in Scotland) the results were the same.

In summary then: the Reformers did try to correct the Judaization of the Church as it was manifested in Medieval Roman Catholicism which in essence taught that salvation came through works, sacramental rituals, etc. The problem is not what the Reformers did, but rather what they did not do. They only understood one aspect of Judaism and hence, due to their failure to comprehend the New Covenant as Jeremiah predicted it in Jeremiah 31[3], they retained other aspects such as a State Church and initiation of the unconverted into membership through infant baptism.

Old Testament Theocracy In The Church

Luther stated: *Cuis Regio Euis Religio* ("whatever your government is, your religion should be"—be it Catholic or Protestant), and Hooker's statement that "a citizen of the Commonwealth is a member of the Church of England, and a member of the Church of England is a citizen of the Commonwealth" is once again a return to the old covenant and so an undoing of the new.

So as there were Jews who thought they were in a covenant

relationship with God because they were circumcised as babies, we now have the same situation where people baptised as babies think they are in a covenant relationship with God because they were sprinkled as infants. Thus, not only does Replacement Theology undermine God's purposes for Israel, it actually undermines His purposes for the Church.

We must also consider that the New Testament teaches specifically that the gospel is, by virtue of covenant relationship, available to the Jew first as the power of salvation.[4]

Thus, the results of **rejecting** the gospel are also incumbent upon the Jew first.[5] There is nothing in scripture which retracts either the availability of the gospel to the Jew first, nor the consequences of such rejection. If we are to transplant an Old Testament model from Israel to the Church, we must beware of its covenantal consequences: a tragic fact to which the history of the Church eloquently testifies. The theological term for this is Reconstructionism, a Christianised theology of the state which seeks to establish a political role for the Church in the affairs of secular government, again in open contradiction of Jesus' statement that His kingdom is "not of this world"[6]; remember, He refused political power when it was offered to Him.[7]

Reconstructionism, A Formula For Disaster

Reconstructionism has always brought both spiritual and moral death not only to the Church, but also to the states which have taken it on board. The bloody history of the Middle Ages and the Counter-Reformation give a sorry account of repeated repression, slaughter, and religious hypocrisy combined with political and financial corruption. The aftermath of the Reformation often did little more than replace Roman Catholic tyranny with Protestant dictatorship.

This is particularly true where strong reformed and Calvinistic influences from the church permeated the social fabric. Even in the twentieth century, the three Bible belts of the English speaking world—the American South, Northern Ireland, and South

Africa—each have an acute and bloody history of social injustice fostered by the influences of Calvinist ecclesiology and soteriology (doctrine of salvation) emphasising predestination and election which in each of these cases is then translated politically into divine fore-election.

In Northern Ireland it is the strict Presbyterian tradition owing its heritage to Calvin and Knox. In South Africa it is the Dutch Reformed Church with the same doctrinal presuppositions. In the American South, the Southern Baptists adopted a Calvinist line. So superiority over Catholics or blacks by divine election was translated into a political-economic model for suppression perpetrated with the support of the Church, based on a warped Protestant view of the gospel and what the Church is meant to be.

We must understand that Wesley's revivals in Britain were an Arminian reaction against the social and economic injustices of the Calvinist perspectives which poisoned society, government and their institutions with a formula for repression derived from these reformed models—that is a Judaized Christianity; a religion of the state that the gospel was never intended to be.

Indeed, from Constantine to Calvin, from Augustine to apartheid, whenever the Church has established itself as a political power, the result has always been death. Such political aspirations cause the very kinds of problems the New Testament was designed to get rid of—according to Jeremiah.[8]

This same Replacementism which underlies the abominations of medieval Roman Catholicism, and the subsequent failure of mainstream Protestantism—to say nothing of the dilemma of Israel—is what lies at the root of most of the dominionist eschatology we see surfacing today in Pentecostal and Charismatic circles—as will be shown.

A Truth Taken Too Far

It is quite possible to note the influences of the Reformation not only on the rise of capitalism but on the form it took with the Protestant work ethic (as explained by Max Weber). In medieval

Roman Catholicism, in order to serve God one needed to be a member of the Roman clergy. Protestantism, however, rediscovered the truth that Christians should do all things for the glory of God, hence a housewife or baker or doctor were all serving God and should therefore pursue their craft as unto the Lord. Idle hands were seen as the devil's workshop and Calvinism stressed the need for activity to prove our salvation (thus while Roman Catholicism advocated performing works in order to gain salvation, Calvinism pressed for works to prove they had it).

The Biblical emphasis on stewardship further helped engender the ideas of creating capital and prudent fiscal management. Similarly, the democratic concept of being dedicated to the rule of law was founded on biblical principles through the influences of Puritanism. But once again, we note that Puritanism degenerated into witch burning and oppression in the United States. Thus when George Whitfield arrived with the gospel in America, he said that he had been sent by God because the Puritan flame had burned too low to carry out the purposes of God.

We again point to the religious oppression that occurred in Zurich, Geneva, and elsewhere under Protestant versions of Erastianism, that is when the state rules the Church. We may certainly argue the need for the church to bring a moral influence into government, economy and society, but we cannot argue Biblically for the New Testament Church to become a political institution or that it be ideologically identified with any political or economic philosophy of man. As we have already seen, Jesus Himself absolutely refused to reduce the gospel to the political level.

When Truth Is Taken Too Far, It Becomes Error

We can apply biblical principles to various models of economy, society, and government, but theonomy is part of the Old Testament covenant for the Jews and the Deuteronomic legislation that God gave them as a nation. Its principles may be applied to the Church and indeed through the Church as an agent of moral seasoning, but its covenant cannot.

This new representation of old style Reconstructionism and Theonomic confusion is a logical partner for the errors of Dominionism. In fact this imbalance has become so extreme that Pat Robertson of the Christian Broadcasting Network is now popularly quoted as saying that the CBN will film the return of Christ!

Most Born Again Christians Are Not Protestants

Pentecostals, most charismatics, Baptists, Brethren, and other evangelical churches and denominations which are not state Churches, but follow what is called in Europe a 'non-conformist tradition', are not Protestant. Christians in churches which hold to a separation of Church and state, believers' baptism as opposed to sprinkling infants, and particularly those who believe in gifts of the Spirit, would not have even been called Protestants during the Reformation. At that time they would have been called Anabaptists and would have faced wholesale extermination at the hands of both the Protestant Reformers and the Roman Catholic church alike.

The New Judaizers: Reconstructionists

The influx of restorationist/dominionist theology into Pentecostal and Baptist churches, along with their a-millennial and post-millennial appendages, must be seen as representing not only the Protestantisation but the Judaisation of traditional, non-conformist Christianity.

It is therefore no coincidence that there is a trend towards Replacementism along with a leaning towards a-millennial and post-millennial theology and Dominionism in the very same Pentecostal and Baptist churches that once saw the restoration of Biblical pre-millennialism as an integral component for their *raison d'être*. Churches which saw it as their calling to restore these truths are now abandoning them in order to espouse the very errors they were set up to correct.

Was The Charismatic Movement Ever Of God?

I am positive that this movement was a genuine outpouring of God's Spirit, calling the Church to repent, and restore itself to a biblical foundation in Christ based upon God's Word. I am also sure that this failed to happen when the Word of God was left out in favour of feelings, emotion, and worship that was often more fleshly than spiritual. In their turn these things have finally led to tolerance of every strain of doctrine imaginable.

When renewal started people were driven first to the Word of God and from there into worship. In the 'charismaniac' Christianity that this renewal quickly became, experience was chosen over scripture; while the ministry of the Word was left out in favour of proceeding directly to 'worship'. No consideration was given to what God actually wanted to achieve by renewal because there was often not much foundation—and in some cases no foundation—in His Word.

We Blew It, God Didn't!

Thus, in place of the Word of God, it became only natural that charismatics would become the obvious bedfellows for restorationist and dominionist false prophets and false teachers. Having turned away from the Bible as the Word of God, they instead turned to false prophets like those I have previously named.

This is exactly what happened in the days of Jeremiah and Ezekiel and it is exactly what is going on today. The true prophets tried to point the people back to the Word, the false ones give them hype and false prediction. True prophets warned of judgement and stressed repentance and the authority of scripture; the false ones stress triumphalism, and 'words from the Lord' which invariably were not from Him at all. Once more, as scripture predicts would happen, we have neglected the grain and eaten the straw (Jeremiah chapter 23:28).

What blossomed in the charismatic movement has now begun to make headway into much of mainstream Pentecostalism. Ten years ago, the Assemblies of God lost thousands of members to the

Restorationist house churches in Great Britain. Today, those same doctrines are being trumpeted throughout British Pentecostalism.

The Cancer Spreads

It is true that traditional Pentecostalism lacked much talent in the area of Hebrew and Greek scholarship, but the older generation of Pentecostals did have a proper Biblical balance emphasising holiness, the authority of Scripture and the power of the Holy Spirit—real power, not hype!

The kinds of Pentecostal fire associated with aspects of the Sunderland revivals in England, the sunshine revivals in Australia, and the Azusa Street revivals in California are now burning throughout Latin America, Asia, Eastern Europe, and Africa, but have fizzled out in Britain, Western Europe, Australia, and most of North America.

Meanwhile the nonsense, the man–made doctrines, experiential theology, and hype disguised as power, all of which undermined the now-failed Charismatic Renewal, already permeate much of the declining Pentecostal denominations of America, Western Europe, and Australasia.

David Shearman has stated that the original languages of scripture are irrelevant but that only the English vernacular is important.[9] In 1994, Shearman, claiming to have a prophetic anointing of some kind, removed a bright canary yellow coloured jacket (which he wore as part of a bet) during his address to the Assemblies of God conference in England. He then invited those who wished for a prophetic anointing to come and touch his jacket in order to receive it. While many of the older generation of Pentecostal ministers, who had a traditional grounding in sound doctrine, the authority of scripture, and traditional pre-millennialism, expressed shock, younger ministers from the experience-oriented axis of British Pentecostalism came to get the 'anointing' from the jacket!

This is the kind of hocus-pocus that has left the churches which experienced the Charismatic Renewal today far worse off than before the renewal happened. It is with the same kind of madness that David Shearman and others of his persuasion are torpedoing what little is left of western Pentecostalism today.

Pentecostals now also reject grain and feed on straw, confusing anointing with hype and the doctrines of God with the arrogant boastings of foolish men who are devoid of the true power of the Holy Spirit and ignorant of the Word of God. Similar Triumphalism and experiential 'theology' are being imported from America and Britain into Australia by Phil Pringle. I repeat, none of this unscriptural nonsense has anything to do with the traditional Pentecostalism that once shook the world, and can do so once again if we throw out this rubbish and return to the Word of God.

New Age And New Rage

Efforts to stem or reverse the decline of evangelical Protestantism in the United States, Great Britain and Australia come hard on the heels of the Charismatic renewal which after 30 years has completely failed to deliver what it promised. Having neither stemmed the moral landslide nor re-invigorated the church, with the accompanying salvation of souls, it is now desperately grasping at any available trend or fad that will help create the illusion that God is once again on the move in the Protestant democracies. Not since the Jesus Movement of the late sixties and early seventies has there been a revival in the church where large numbers of unsaved people turned to Christ as a result. I say again the charismatic renewal has not even been able to slow the moral landslide in the Church itself, let alone in society.

Something that began as a move of God was rapidly undermined by compromise and substitution of Biblical theology with experiential theology. This experience-based Christianity coming as it did in the aftermath of the charismatic failure, is now even more loudly amplified. As with New Age religion, subjective experience instead of scripture has become the method of determining whether or not something is of God, instead of the objective truth of God's Word.

This is why when challenged about the unscriptural nature of an experience, people who claim to have received some kind of a blessing in Toronto or at Pensacola will ignorantly avoid the test of scripture and simply argue subjectively, "Well, I was blessed." In fact all that usually happened was that they were deceived or hypnotized.

Now such deceptions as 'The Laughing Revival' and the Pensacola phenomena are themselves incorporations of hypnotic induction and Kundalini Yoga into an experiential instead of biblical Christianity. Anglican clergyman Philip Foster has cited professional stage hypnotists to explain exactly how Toronto preachers used hypnotic techniques.[10] Again, the Indian evangelist to the Hindus, Thomas Chakko, has warned that Toronto manifestation are by and large Kundalini Yoga and New Age Eastern religion infiltrating the Church. Ironically, this is the very Hinduism out of which so many believers in India have been saved. Pentecostal Romany Gypsy believers who have seen videos of Rodney Howard-Browne and Kenneth Copeland warn that it is the very 'duckering' (use of the occult to get money out of people) out of which they were saved!

Notes for Ch.5

1. The Reformers were humanists and thus their exegetical approach is humanistic i.e. man- instead of God-centred. They applied grammatical-historical exegesis, whilst ignoring Second Temple Period Jewish hermeneutics, reducing understanding the Bible to a mere intellectual exercise. Therefore, the reformer's attempt at returning to Biblical Christianity was not wholly Biblical in all areas.

2. Galatians 5:1-12.

3. Jeremiah 31:31-34.

4. Romans 1:16.

5. Romans 2:9.

6. John 18:36.

7. On Palm Sunday he came humble and on a donkey as the son of Joseph, the suffering servant; declining the crowd's welcome of him as conquering king, a political leader who would overthrow the Romans; Matthew 21:4-11; Mark 11:8-10; Luke 19:35-44. Again, Jesus refused political power when tempted with it by the devil; Luke 4:5-8; Matthew 4:8-10.

8. Jeremiah 31:31-36; 32:37-41; 50:1-7.

9. "Instead of clever language about our understanding of the Greek we would be benefited by a simple adherence to the vernacular" Documented in a fax to Yacov Prasch on the 27 April 1994.

10. Philip Foster, 'Suggestibility, Hypnosis and Hysteria', pp61-82 (Peter Glover, ed., *The Signs and Wonders Movement—Exposed*, Day One Publications, Kent. 1996).

PART II

The Lies

Chapter 6

Lie 1: Christian Zionism

When the devil is unable to blind the Christian to the prophetic purposes of God concerning Israel and the Jews, his next deception is to divert Christians into the errors of Christian Zionism. I would preface matters by pointing out that there are valid evangelical organisations such as *Prayer for Israel* and *Christians Friends of Israel* in Great Britain which are both Christian and pro-Zionist. They are moderates, Christo-centric as opposed to Israel-centric, and therefore biblically balanced in their approach. They do stand for Israel's right to exist, warn of the dangers of Islam to Judeo/Christian civilisation, and work to point the Christian church back towards its Hebrew root. They do not, however, turn their backs on the local Israeli Body of Christ in order to placate the Rabbis and cultivate good relations with Israeli politicians. While these organisations are not evangelistic, they do stand with the Israeli Messianic believers in their quest to evangelise Israel, and the people in these organisations will often share their faith on a personal low key basis. Let me make it clear, my argument is with those organisations which have agreed to withhold the gospel to the Jewish people and in some cases have even taught against presenting it.

The Cross Of The Messiah, The Central Truth

The world in which we live is one where the cross of Jesus is being removed from its central place and put on the sidelines. There is one central truth in the Word of God; that is "Jesus Christ crucified, Christ risen and Christ coming again". Virtually every major deception of Satan will endeavour to subvert or divert attention away from the Cross, the empty tomb and the Mount of Olives, beginning with the Cross.

In Roman Catholicism the doctrine of the Mass stands in open contradiction to the teachings of the epistle to the Hebrews. Catholicism holds that the Mass is the same sacrifice as Calvary, where Jesus dies again. The book of Hebrews clearly teaches that His was the perfect sacrifice made once for all. So in Catholicism the cross is removed from its central place only to be replaced by a sacramental way of salvation (which is no salvation at all) instead of by the new birth achieved by the cross and the resurrection.

Similarly the root of Prosperity preaching derives from the heretical teachings of E.W.Kenyon who claimed that the victory was not won on the cross, but in hell when Jesus became one with Satan. That is supposedly when Jesus became a Satanic being of one nature with the devil. This blasphemous lie is abominably wicked in itself, yet because the cross of Jesus is not central to this detestable perversion of the gospel, neither can it be regarded as the central truth of our Christian lives.

Emphasis on living a crucified life is replaced by stressing what has been called 'name it and claim it' 'theology'; a false faith which is not faith at all, but rather faith in faith, where gimmicks designed in hell put money in the pockets of those who peddle such heresy. More seriously, they undermine the true gospel.

There are many truths in the Word of God. There is even a truth in the biblical principle of prosperity in such biblical texts as Deuteronomy 8, albeit not in the distorted ideas of Hagin and Copeland[1]. The fact is that whenever another truth, no matter how true that truth may be, becomes a central truth instead of the Cross of Jesus, that truth immediately becomes a lie.

God's purpose for Israel is one such truth. Those who reject her are in error and as we draw closer to the return of Christ they will likely fall into more serious error unless the Lord in His grace opens their eyes and hearts to the full meaning of His Word. However, when Israel, instead of the cross of Jesus, is made into the central truth, even Israel becomes a subject of error.

God's purpose for Israel is the redemption of Israel. Today when organisations, such as the International Christian Embassy, ask people to sign statements agreeing not to give Jewish people the gospel and not to give them the message of the cross of their Messiah—without whom they are on their way to eternal hell—they are denying God's purpose for Israel.

It is the Cross and all it stands for that is the central truth of the Christian message. It is the Cross of Jesus alone that is the truth upon which all other truths must be predicated and built. There is no other foundation except Christ crucified, Christ risen and Christ coming again. It is His Cross that is the prism through which we must read all other scripture.

God's True Purpose For Israel—Salvation!

God's purpose for returning the Jews to Israel is not, and never has been, an end in itself, but rather for their final salvation. The Jews are not being re-gathered to their ancient land to be blessed, but to face a terrible judgement—known in Jeremiah 30 as the time of Jacob's trouble (the Great Tribulation) in which they will be deceived into thinking the Antichrist is their Messiah (John chapter 5:43).

There is no blessing for the Jews apart from Jesus. The Jews are under the curse of the law, as Paul plainly states in Romans and Galatians.[2] As the Bible teaches, the law of God is indeed perfect,[3] but it brings an indictment against all mankind for their sins. Yet because the Jews were specifically chosen to bring the world the revelation of God, the indictment falls upon them first.[4]

The Curse Of The Law And Anti-semitism

The terrible tragedies of Jewish history—especially the centuries of anti-Semitism and genocide—are the outworkings of the curse of the law found in Deuteronomy 28 and Leviticus 26. The scattering among the nations, the inquisitions and the Holocaust is the Word of the Lord being fulfilled: that He would give them into the hands of their enemies. We must understand that anti-Semitism has its origin in Genesis 3:15 (as indeed does persecution of the Church).

I will put enmity between you and the woman,
between your seed and her seed; you will
bruise him in the heel, he will bruise you in the head.

Because Israel (represented by the woman, Eve) was to be the divine instrument of salvation bringing the scriptures, the Messiah, and the gospel to a lost and fallen world, Satan (represented by the serpent) desires to destroy the woman. At present the role of Israel is now equally applied to the Church, which is also incorporated into the woman. Thus anti-semitism and persecution of the Church are always related historically, theologically, and spiritually.

We might understand the dynamic relationship between anti-semitism and persecution of the Church like a coin. We can distinguish between heads and tails, but they are two sides of the same coin—we cannot separate them. They always go together.

In the first and second centuries the pagan emperors of Imperial Rome first turned on the Church, then turned on the Jews. The two groups most persecuted in European history by the dominant Roman Catholic church have been born-again Christians and Jews. It is probably no coincidence that Norwich in England, an area from which Jews were expelled during a pogrom, is the same location where non-conformist evangelicals were murdered by the established Church. Today, throughout the Moslem world, the two kinds of people most hated are Jews and Bible-believing Christians. In the old Soviet Empire the two groups of people most persecuted by the Communists were, again, Jews and born-again Christians.

The anti-semitism of Pharaoh,[5] Haman[6] and Amalek,[7] re-emerged into hellenised Christianity in the anti-Jewish teachings of John Chrysostom and later in the call for the mass extermination of the Jews by various Popes. Martin Luther was one of the worst offenders and preached that the German nation was to blame for failing to murder the Jews in order to prove that it was truly Christian.

In Deuteronomy chapter 18 Moses predicted that if the Jewish people would not accept the Messiah, who would be a prophet like Moses, God would require it of their hands. Daniel predicted that the Messiah would come and die before the second Temple was destroyed. Without the Temple it is no longer possible to practise Mosaic Judaism as God gave it in the Pentateuch. The Septuagint translated Leviticus 17 thus: "Without the shedding of blood, there is no forgiveness of sins." Thus, without a proper temple and priesthood, the law remains in effect, but Jews have no way to keep that law or atone for sin, other than through faith in Jesus as the Messiah who fulfilled the Law on their behalf.

Every Jew—Either Free Or Cursed By The Law

Every Jew is either under one covenant or another. They either accept Jesus as the Messiah who fulfilled the Law, or else they remain under its curse—an accursed people under the power of a curse that only the blood of the Messiah can break. We must therefore return now to the final words of Jesus. As we noted earlier the apostles asked Him about the restoration of the Kingdom. When would He be the Son of David? When would He re-establish the nation of Israel?

While incidentally confirming it would happen, Jesus explicitly warned them it was not their concern or priority, but God's. Their priority was to be the presentation of the gospel beginning in Jerusalem with the Jews, then throughout Judea to Samaria and ultimately to the ends of the earth. The final instruction Jesus gave the Church was to let God worry about restoring Israel, but that the Church should present the gospel of salvation to Israel.

In its defiance of the Word of God, and in its direct rebellion against the last command that Jesus gave us, some allegedly christian organisations (such as the International Christian Embassy,[8] and other Christian Zionists) are wilfully disobedient to the Lord's final command and are guilty of doing the very opposite of what He required.

Instead of the salvation of the Jews, which can only be achieved by giving them the gospel, their priority degenerates into the politics of national restoration and Zionism. This is as perverse and unbalanced on one side as the rejection of the prophetic significance of Israel is on the other.

At the largest Pentecostal rally in Europe, 'Mission London' (presided over by Morris Cerullo), the Founder of the International Christian Embassy, Jan Willem Van der Hoven, took the platform with Cerullo and taught Europe's Pentecostals that they were not called to preach the Gospel to Jews but only to comfort them. This distorts the text of Isaiah chapter 40 out of all reasonable context, perverting its theme and virtually reversing its meaning. This occurred after Cerullo was exposed on national British television for preaching "send £10 and see two Jews saved and as an added bonus two members of your family will be saved." This was, of course, highly detrimental to the cause of Jewish evangelism in Europe and also extremely damaging to the testimony to Jewish people in the Christian Church.

It was the International Christian Embassy which first introduced Morris Cerullo into Israel for their "Feast of Tabernacles Celebration".[9] Curiously, later, Cerullo distributed over one million booklets aimed at evangelising Jews in Israel. A number of Israeli pastors found the contents of the booklet called **Ha Shalom** to be a deplorable misrepresentation of the message of salvation, and in interviews many Israeli church leaders were unanimous in their condemnation of the fact that the booklets were distributed without any reference to the local Israeli Body of Christ, its congregations, its leaders, or the National Evangelism Committee.

Israeli believers such as Yosef Shulam and Lisa Loden protested that outsiders had no business taking such action in their country without seeking the cooperation of the local believers who are, after all, those who must face the consequences. The consequences were protest demonstrations against Jewish believers, book burnings outside the Israeli parliament, and the proposal of a new anti-evangelism law that would place Israeli Jewish believers in prison for up to one year for printing, distributing, importing or even possessing evangelistic literature aimed at promoting the Messiahship of Jesus.[10]

Morris Cerullo is not the only money preacher with whom the International Christian Embassy is associated. Its Scandinavian Leader Ulf Eckmann is an adherent of the 'name it and claim it' Hagin and Copeland school of heresy which, as we saw earlier, states that Satan, not Jesus, got the victory on the cross.[11]

When interviewed by a Jewish religious newspaper Mr Van der Hoven's wife stated that she did not believe Jews should become Christians but rather that Christians should become more Jewish. While it is true that Jews accepting Jesus do not cease to be Jews and Christians do need to rediscover the Hebrew root of their own faith (Romans chapter 11:18), Jews still need to be saved. The situation at the International Christian Embassy has reached such a low point that at one point a senior official was allegedly involved in an assault on an Israeli Jewish believer who had been distributing Hebrew New Testaments near a Christian Embassy function. The same individual has also made many pilgrimages to Toronto to bring the 'laughing experience' to Jerusalem. Since Jews are already very sceptical of anything to do with the gospel message, the damage such lunacy does to the Christian testimony in Israel is immeasurable. For its part the Christian Embassy has been plagued by a history of scandal which has seen many of its leaders—such as Dr. Michael Harry—resign in disgust and a number of its founders, including the late Colonel Orde Dobbie, the Singing Watsons of Canada, and others resigning to form alternative organisations. [*Bridges for Peace*, the *Ebenezer Fund* and *Wings of Eagles* all have similar policies on non-evangelism of Jews.]

I Will Require Their Blood At Your Hands

Some of these organisations repeatedly enter into agreements with the Israeli government and various other Jewish authorities, which require that they agree not to present the gospel to Jewish people, but rather to concentrate on loving Jewish people with some love other than the love of Christ. A love for the Jews which fails to give the Jews the Gospel, is not the love of Christ but a fleshly infatuation. The Jewish people are perishing without their Messiah. Nazis sent Jews to gas chambers, but Christian Zionists, by withholding the gospel from Jews, are in effect sending them to hell.

It is not my purpose to judge or condemn individuals, only to condemn the false doctrines of any organisation which is in rebellion against the Word of God—and leading others into that rebellion. The International Christian Embassy and other organisations like it have often courted good relations with right-wing Israeli politicians and rabbinic authorities who are responsible for anti-missionary laws in Israel. The International Christian Embassy has published a mission statement with a covering letter explaining its position on non-evangelization of Jews. It claims to fulfil Isaiah chapter 40 by comforting Israel, telling Israel that her iniquity is removed—without telling Israel the gospel message which is the only biblical way her iniquity can be removed. To say that the sin of Israel can be removed without the Blood of Jesus—the Jewish Messiah—is a blasphemous heresy known as 'dual covenant theology'.

Let Messianic Jews Speak For Themselves

The vast majority of leaders of Hebrew-speaking congregations in Israel, as well as the leadership of virtually every major Jewish evangelistic organisation in the world including *Jews for Jesus*, Dr Harold Sevener of *Chosen People Ministries*, Dr Arnold Fruchtenbaum of *Ariel*, Baruch Maoz of *Christian Witness to Israel*, the *Church's Ministry to the Jews*, Israel Harel of *Operation Mobilisation Israel*, The Lausanne Consultation on Jewish Evangelism, Yacov

Dhamkani of *The Trumpet of Salvation*, and many others have all stood firmly against the betrayal of the indigenous Body of Christ and Jewish believers in the name of the 'salvation of Israel' by the International Christian Embassy and other groups like it.

Action only followed after many pleas from the Jewish mission organisations that Christian Zionists stop rejecting the final command of Jesus and stop hurting the cause of Israel's salvation by siding with the opponents of the gospel in a land where the Church is persecuted.

A Christless Gospel Is No Gospel

The burning of Messianic fellowships and churches has become commonplace in Jerusalem, Tiberias, Beersheva, and Ashdod. The Israeli Supreme Court has tried to revoke the status of Jewish Christians as Jews, so enabling the rabbinic authorities to demand their deportation. Yet in its magazine the International Christian Embassy has quoted a politician who is one of the most notorious opponents of Jewish Christianity and Messianic Judaism in Israel, boasting of the Christian Embassy that: "They are the finest examples of Christian Zionism. Their only concept of mission is to convert Jews to Judaism and to gather Jews—not to Christianity, but in planes to Israel."[12]

Indeed, it is little wonder that a host of figures including Lance Lambert, Derek Prince, Orde Dobbie, Merril Watson, and a number of others formerly associated with the International Christian Embassy, will no longer have anything to do with it.

It is the local Hebrew and Arabic-speaking congregations and those Jewish mission organisations who preach Jesus which are His true embassies and ambassadors. It is they who deserve the prayers and support of Christians. Instead, large sums of money are diverted away from the true work of Christ among the Jews—their salvation—into the coffers and the social and political activities of an organisation which falsely claims to be the embassy of a Jesus it refuses to preach in His own land, to His own people; preferring rather to see them continue on a road to hell without Him who died for their sins.

Israel, We Love You—But Go To Hell!

The convoluted rationale for the above behaviour apparently holds the view that "If we do the things which Jesus said **are** our responsibility (preach the gospel to the Jews), the rabbis and Israeli authorities will not like us and will not allow us to do the things which Jesus said **are not** our responsibility." The analogy is comparable to that of a medical missionary in the slums of an impoverished country where babies and small children are dying of diphtheria. Since, as we know, small children dislike injections, the basic practice of medical missionaries in this kind of environment is to line up the children and inoculate them against the dreaded disease which kills them and then to give them a lollipop following the inoculation.

What would we think of a medical missionary who said simply: "I'm only going to give these children the lollipop and not the injection. I would rather watch them die than make them cry." Would you consider this a legitimate ministry? Would you support such a medical missionary who came to your church to ask for funds? Yet that is precisely what is happening today in the warped world of Christian Zionism.

Moreover, innocent Christians who are duped into funding such unbiblical and illogical ventures are often not told the truth about what is really going on. Instead of listening to the Jewish missions which are the real embassies, they listen to those who appoint themselves as spokesmen for what God is doing in Israel while going around the world sucking money and support away from where it really belongs—the local congregations and missions which preach Jesus to His own.

Many such errors are based on the idea that there is a blessing for the Jews outside a faith in Jesus, when in fact Jesus said there was nothing but a curse for the Jews outside His redemption. Some people associated with Christian Zionist organisations openly advocate a dual covenant theology or soteriology (a doctrine of salvation), saying that Jews can be saved by the old covenant. But as the writers of the New Testament said: "By the works of the law (which—as we have seen—unsaved Jews can't keep anyway without a temple or high priest), no man can be saved."

As I said previously, the Jews are heading for a Great Tribulation that will make the Holocaust seem minor by comparison. If there was ever a time when the Jews desperately needed their Messiah, that time is now.

An organisation less inimical to the cause of the salvation of the Jews than the International Christian Embassy, but equally misguided, is the Ebenezer Fund directed by Gustav Schiller. This organisation seeks to charter ships to bring Soviet and Ukrainian Jews to Israel. Mr Schiller himself is a gracious man with a sincere love for Israel and the Jews. I also affirm that the Jews of the former Soviet Union need to leave Eastern Europe as and when the Lord leads because of the acute danger of a violently anti-semitic right wing regime coming to power in partnership with the idolatrous Eastern Orthodox church. However, of what benefit is it for these Jews to come out of Russia only to go into eternal hell without Jesus? Mr Schiller had been part of a very dedicated group of Christians who had been active on behalf of Soviet Jews even before the Iron Curtain came down. In the early days, his associate Steve Lightle, himself a Messianic Jew, was telling people to prepare Russian New Testaments to give to the exodus of Soviet Jews who would be coming out in the following years. Sadly, this balanced approach which sought to see the Soviet Jews rescued from both the bondage of Communism and the bondage of sin gave way to a purely humanitarian endeavour which by deleting the ministry of the gospel from its ethos became a Christless endeavour. The Ebenezer Fund which was later established to charter the ships signed an agreement never to give the gospel to a Jewish person but to allow them to continue on their way to eternal damnation without their Messiah.

Other Christian organisations which bring Jews from Eastern Europe to Israel, such as the David and Jonathon Project, not only help Jews to come to Israel but, more importantly, help Jews to come to faith in the Messiah of Israel. There are also other issues of stewardship which projects of the International Christian Embassy and the Ebenezer Fund acting on behalf of Russian Jewry do not normally tell their supporters. For example, unless a Jew believes that Jesus is the Jewish Messiah, any Jew in Eastern Europe will receive free passage for their families and themselves from the Jewish Agency subsidised by the Israeli Government.

Jerusalem—A Magnet For Crackpots

A popular misconception regarding Christian Zionism is that due to its history of anti-Semitism, the Church has forfeited its right to give the gospel to Jewish people and should instead 'love them'. To put this another way: we should love them all the way to hell without the redemption of their Messiah.

Israel attracts Christians from all over the world who claim God has given them a special ministry. Inevitably, many of those 'ministries' are not Biblical. These poor deluded people may be recognised by the following tell-tale signs: they have been in Israel for a number of years but have never acquired the Hebrew language, and they eventually become part of some fellowship made up of other foreigners who are usually in the land on a temporary basis. It is acceptable for people in Israel temporarily to be members of an expatriate church but it is unbiblical for those who claim a ministry to the indigenous people not to become a part of them in language and culture.[13]

Sadly there have been many cases of mentally deranged Christians claiming to have 'the spirit of Elijah' whose only real claim to fame is that they have clinical papers written about them by the Psychiatric Faculty of Hebrew University at Hadassah Medical Centre.

The Feast of Tabernacles is an annual gathering for many of these people. Again, many sincere Christians, ignorant of the true nature of that event, are drawn to it. I recall a story from 1982 of a young Israeli soldier who was saved during the war in Lebanon. He was invited by some Americans to the Feast of Tabernacles where he began to weep and asked to leave. When asked why, he said that from birth he knew it meant something to be a Jew, but he never knew what it meant to be a Jew and an Israeli until he accepted Yeshua (Jesus) as his Messiah. That young soldier pointed out that in the Feast of Tabernacles there are over 100 banners lifting up the name 'Israel' but not one lifting up the Name of the King of Israel, her Messiah, Yeshua. It is perhaps not surprising that he asked to leave.

A Bible-based Response

At this point I again state my conviction that the rebirth of Israel as a nation is a prophetic sign to be recognized and that Christians need to affirm this. We must uphold Israel's right to exist, while, at the same time, not endorsing all the actions of the Israeli government which discriminates against Jewish Christians.[14]

What we can never accept, however, are expressions of that affirmation made at the expense of preaching the gospel of salvation. I repeat, so-called Christian ministries like the International Christian Embassy which not only refuse to give Jews the gospel but ask others who become associated with it to sign statements not to evangelize Jews either, are by biblical definition neither Christian nor ministries.

Israel—A Sign To Be Recognised, But A Gospel To Be Preached

It is true to say that the Jews need to see a recognition by real Christians of the prophetic significance of their nation and of God's ongoing love for them as a people. This must be done in order to mitigate the damage done by false Christians and the anti-Israel preaching currently expounded by so-called evangelicals, such as Rick Godwin, who preaches against the purposes of God concerning Israel and the Jewish people, teaching that "Israel is but wasted money".[15]

My wife's parents are Holocaust survivors and she is a former *refusnik* under the Communists. Her grandfather and many of her family were murdered in the Holocaust. Yet my very Jewish wife will be the first to tell you that while it was a terrible tragedy that false Christians murdered her grandfather in the name of Christianity, it is an even greater tragedy that when he died he entered into eternity without knowing Jesus as his Messiah.

The Word of God repeatedly makes it clear that if we do not warn the Jews and others to repent and accept Jesus, they will go to hell, but God will require their blood at our hands.[16]

Some day people like Mr Jan Willem Van der Hoven, leader of the International Christian Embassy, and Jay Rawlings (who it seems seldom appeals for the salvation of Jewish souls in his books or films about God's purpose for the Jews) will stand before the Judgement Seat of Christ watching Jewish souls from whom they withheld the gospel, being cast into hell. Among these will be the Israeli politicians whose friendship they courted at the expense of not speaking about Jesus.

Satan—The Real Author Of This Confusion

My anger is directed toward no one but Satan and is certainly not directed toward those sincere Christians who are being misled into thinking that this deception is of God, when the Word of God makes it clear that it has nothing to do with Him. Jesus said: "If you love me, keep my commandments."[17] He commanded that we give the Jews the gospel. It is not enough to tell the Jews we love them and that we recognise the prophetic place of their nation in God's plan but will tell them no more for fear of offending them. As Paul said: "I did not shrink from declaring to you the whole purpose of God."[18] Christian Zionists preach only one aspect of God's purpose and as a result turn it into a lie.

A Love That Does Not Give Christ Is Not The Love Of Christ

It is a valid statement to say that we cannot witness to someone unless we first of all witness to them in our lives. Certainly Jewish people who have been so alienated from the love of their own Messiah, in considerable measure due to the anti-Semitism of many false Christians, desperately need to see the genuine love of true Christians.

But genuine love is the love of Jesus. As Paul says: "My heart's desire for my people, the Jews, is that they may be saved"[19] and without someone to preach the gospel to them, how shall they hear it?[20] That is the true love of Christ for the Jews. Paul says if possible he would actually give his own salvation for the salvation of his people.[21]

That is what Paul, a Jew and an evangelist to the Jews, said two thousand years ago and that is precisely what the real Jewish mission organisations are saying today. We cannot believe both the teachings of the Word of God as expressed by Paul and Jesus and the gospel of Christian Zionism which says that we can love the Jews without giving them Jesus.

Where Do They Get This Christless Love?

We will now examine some of the passages of scripture from which Christian Zionism derives its unbiblical conclusions. Its devotees often argue that Christians must simply return the Jews to the Land and Christ will save them by direct revelation without any Christian witness.

While the text of Zechariah 12 indeed confirms this will happen, it will only happen at the end of the Great Tribulation once many Jews have already perished without Him. Others assert that there is a blessing and possibly even a redemption for the Jews, apart from Jesus. But the Word of God tells us there is no other name given under heaven by which men can be saved.

Satan, The Bible Twister

The argument that the Jews simply need to be returned to Israel by the Church and then they will believe comes from chopping out and distorting portions of Deuteronomy 30:1-3.

This is what we see happening in Israel today with the large numbers arriving in Israel from Russia, the Ukraine, Ethiopia, North America and the ends of the earth. This is exactly what the Word of God predicted would happen in Deuteronomy chapter 30; it is exactly what is happening today in precise fulfilment of that chapter. It is the exact opposite of the false teaching of Christian Zionism.

Comfort His People—But How?

The basic text drawn upon by Christian Zionism as a doctrinal basis for its Christless message of love to Israel and the Jews is Isaiah chapter 40 commencing with verse one containing God's exhortation to "Comfort ye my people."

Isaiah chapter 40 is a literary prologue to the four servant songs of Isaiah. As such it introduces the servant songs with a genre shift from the narrative in chapter 39 to the Hebrew poetry of chapter 40. The fourth and final of the Servant Songs—found in Isaiah chapter 52-53 is that of the Suffering Servant. Again we find the Messiah the Son of Joseph—or *Ben Ephraim*—in the Talmudic literature. Isaiah chapter 40 can best be understood in this context. It introduces the Servant Song series building up to the crucifixion of a Messiah who would die for the sins of Israel. To remove it from its context is to pervert it into something God never intended to say.

As we continue to study the chapter, we come to verse 9 where the text reads:

Get you up on a high mountain O Zion,
bearer of good news, lift up your voice
mightily O Jerusalem, bearer of good news;
lift it up and do not fear. Say to the
cities of Judah, 'Here is your God!'

The word translated 'good news' in this verse occurs twice. In Hebrew the word is *besor* and its Greek equivalent is *evangelion*. It means 'the Gospel'. So the way in which Isaiah chapter 40 commands us to comfort God's people is to give them the gospel.

The very fact that the phrase appears twice demonstrates God's desire that we obey Him in this command. Furthermore we are told not to fear, yet rather than being fearless, Christian Zionism fears offending the Jews so we do not comfort them with the comfort of the gospel that this passage actively commands.

No Removal Of Sin Except By The Blood Of The Lamb

Compounding the perversion of this text is the distortion Christian Zionism applies to verse two of Isaiah chapter 40.

Speak kindly to Jerusalem;
And call out to her, that her
warfare has ended, that she has
received of the Lord's hand double
for all her sins.

The text instructs us to tell the Jews that they have received double for their sins and their iniquity is removed. In the proper context of the chapter it is clear that this comes through the gospel when we say to them "here is your God"—that is, the Messiah Jesus. The lie of Satan propagated by Christian Zionism states that we can tell the Jews that their iniquity has been removed apart from the atoning blood of Jesus. I repeat, there is no way to remove iniquity except through the sacrifice of the Messiah. There is no removal of sin except by His blood.

When Christian Zionism draws upon this kind of perversion of the text it constitutes nothing less than a fundamental rejection of the cross of Jesus Christ as the only way of salvation. We cannot believe the teachings of the Word of God and the teachings of Christian Zionism. They are mutually exclusive.

In fact, from the viewpoint of literary criticism Isaiah chapter 40 is a literary prologue providing a preface to the servant songs climaxing with the final one of Isaiah chapters 52 and 53 where the theme of comforting the Jews with the gospel is again reiterated in Isaiah Chapter 52:7.

How lovely on the mountain are the
feet of Him who brings good news.

Once again we find the Hebrew word is *besor*, or gospel, the same as in Isaiah chapter 40. Paul quotes this verse in Romans chapter 10:15 and interprets it specifically as referring to Jewish evangelism and giving Jewish people the gospel of their Messiah. There is no reasonable—or exegetical way—to understand Isaiah chapter 40 in the preposterous manner which Christian Zionists twist it in their fundraising literature. The text and context will not allow these positions any theological or doctrinal credibility whatsoever. That is not what the text says in English, it is not what it says in the Greek Septuagint and above all it is not what it says in the original Hebrew.

Rabbinic Judaism—Neither Of Moses Or Christ

A further dilemma presented by Christian Zionism is the issue of Rabbinic Judaism which is often touted as an acceptable faith in the eyes of God. This view represents appalling ignorance of both Judaism and the Word of God.

The Judaism that God gave through Moses ceased to exist in accordance with the predictions of Daniel chapter 9 and Jeremiah chapter 2:13 in 70AD when the second temple was destroyed and the predictions of Jesus and Daniel were literally fulfilled. With no temple and no priesthood it was impossible to practise Mosaic Judaism.

It was at the Council of Yavne (Jamnia) near Tel Aviv that Rabbi Yochannon Ben Zakai, a classmate of St Paul from the Rabbinic School of Hillel and a fellow disciple of Rabbi Gamaliel, began the Jewish faith as it exists today. Rabbinic Judaism quickly planted a root based on the Talmudic traditions of men in place of the Levitical Judaism of Moses, which was based upon the Word of God.

The Origins Of Rabbinic Judaism

There were rival schools of Pharisaic Judaism during the second temple period. Chief among these were the School of Shammai and the School of Hillel. Rabbi Onkleos, an important figure in Judaism, who translated a *Targum* which bears his name; Rabbi Shaul of Tarsus—later known as Paul the Apostle; and Rabbi Yochannon Ben Zakai, were all concurrently enrolled in the same rabbinic academy.

Ben Zakai had been accused of being a Roman collaborator and also one who saved his own neck during the siege of Jerusalem by having himself smuggled out of the city before the Roman onslaught. At Yavne, Ben Zakai replaced the Temple with the synagogue and the levitical priest with the rabbi and so rabbinic Judaism was born. It developed further in the second century under the influence of Rabbi Akiva who falsely proclaimed Simon Bar Cochba to be the Messiah, and who excommunicated Jewish Christians when they failed to accept him as such—having already found their true Messiah in Jesus.

A Tale Of Two Rabbis

After the destruction of the temple, every Jew had a choice. They could either opt to follow Rabbi Shaul of Tarsus, that is St Paul the Apostle (who saw the Law and the Prophets fulfilled in Jesus so they no longer needed to worry about not having a temple and a high priest, as the Church was now their temple and Jesus was their High Priest). Or else they could follow Paul's classmate Rabbi Ben Zakai into a form of Judaism which was not biblical, but a man-made replacement to compensate for not having a Temple or a High Priest.

Changes were already underway. The early rabbinic literature tells us that for forty years before the temple was destroyed a scarlet thread which hung before the Holy of Holies in the temple on the Day of Atonement, and which turned white if the people's sins were forgiven, did not change colour.

In other words, from the time of Jesus' death, the sins of the Jewish people were no longer forgiven under the Law. Yet once Daniel's prophecies—repeated by Jesus—were fulfilled, once the Temple no longer stood, every Jew needed to make a choice whether to follow Messianic Judaism or Rabbinic Judaism.

A False Judaism And A Road To Hell

Upon his death bed Ben Zakai wept and his disciples came to him—as recorded in the Talmud—and asked him: "O mighty hammer why do you weep?" Ben Zakai replied: "I am about to meet *Ha Shem* (God) Blessed be His name; and there are two roads before me. One leads to Paradise, and the other to hell and I know not to which of the two He will sentence me." Ben Zakai confessed as he approached his death that rabbinic Judaism gave him no assurance of salvation. In contrast, his classmate, Rabbi Shaul of Tarsus, when facing death said: "Trouble me no further, I have run the good race, fought the good fight, and I now know that there is laid up for me a crown of righteousness from Jesus the Messiah, Our Lord."[22] So the scriptures show us that as Daniel and Jesus both predicted, Mosaic Judaism could no longer exist and has not done so since 70AD[23]—if not actually since about 30AD when Jesus died.

The question we must now ask is: "Which Judaism is valid?" Paul's or Ben Zakai's? As I have said above, I believe rabbinic Judaism is a false religion whose greatest achievement has been to lead untold millions of Jewish souls down the very road to the eternal judgement that Ben Zakai so clearly dreaded.

I certainly do not deny the scholarly value of early Talmudic literature in understanding the original Jewish background of the gospels and early Church. Nor do I discount the role which rabbinic Judaism has played in preserving the identity of Jewish people as a people according to God's plan.

However, without Joseph Stalin and Adolph Hitler, two of the most notorious murderers of Jews in history, the Zionist movement would never have managed to see the re-establishment of the modern state of Israel according to God's purposes. Simply because God uses someone, it certainly does not mean that they have any positive value. Stalin and Hitler put Jews in their graves. Rabbinic Judaism, by rejecting the gospel, and the Christian Zionists who refuse to preach it, put Jews into Hell.

Nothing New Under The Sun

It is true to say that the persecution of Jewish Christians by the synagogues precedes Christian anti-semitism by at least a century. The pagan government of Rome authorised the practise of Judaism by giving it the status of *Religio Licita* (a licensed religion). Christianity was initially seen as a Messianic sect within Judaism and therefore enjoyed a degree of protection under Roman law. After the excommunication of Jewish believers from the synagogue (as predicted by Jesus) Christianity was no longer protected, and Christians fell to the sword of Rome.

While Christian Zionism rightly makes much capital out of the anti-Semitism propagated in the name of Christianity over the centuries, it refuses to admit that Jewish rejection of the gospel and the persecution of Jewish Christians by non-believing Jews both preceded the advent of Christian anti-Semitism by more than a century.

At some point in the very early history of the church, rabbinic Judaism issued an amendment to the synagogue liturgy or *Sidur* called *Ha Birkhat Ha Minim*, adding it to the eighteen benedictions in the synagogue prayers. This addition is a curse upon Jewish Christians: praying to God that their names would be blotted out from the Book of Life. It remains a part of the liturgy of ultra-orthodox Jews to this day.

A Sense Of Betrayal

It so happens that my own children are Jewish Christians whom my wife and I raise to believe that Yeshua is their Messiah who died for their sins. We teach them that they are Messianic Jews who follow the King of the Jews: Jesus.

Messianic believers feel a sense of shock and horror when they see people who claim to be their brethren in Christ standing shoulder to shoulder with the same rabbinic Judaism which prays that they and their children be blotted out of the Book of Life. And then such groups claim that this is their ministry and ask for Christians to support them financially!

I repeat, Bible believing Christians who truly love Israel and the Jews with the love of Jesus will do everything they can to give Jesus to Israel and the Jews. They will pray for the salvation of the Jews, learn how to witness to Jews, and as the Lord leads, support Jewish evangelism. Above all, they will stand with the local Israeli Body of Christ, both the Messianic Jews and the Arab Christians. To their credit, *Prayer for Israel* and *Christian Friends of Israel* have always given platform to Israeli Messianic believers at their Jerusalem conferences. Christians who love Israel will of course stand against anti-semitism. They must also recognise that the Judaism of the Rabbis is a false religion which Jesus Himself condemned.

Biblical Judaism Is Fulfilled In Jesus

There are only two forms of Judaism which have ever been valid: One is the original Judaism that God gave through Moses and the other is the Messianic Judaism practised by Jewish Christians today. Jesus calls the false Judaism of the Rabbis, which rejects his Messiahship, corrupts the Torah with tradition, persecutes Jewish believers and leads Jewish souls into hell—a synagogue of Satan.[24] Yet Christian Zionism can often be seen applauding it!

The first epistle of Saint John chapter 2 describes 'antichrist' as "that which denies that Jesus is the Messiah and the Son of the Father."[25] Liberal Protestantism denies this and is thus a false Christianity and an antichrist religion. Islam denies this stating in the Koran that: "God has no Son" and is also therefore an antichrist religion. Rabbinic Judaism likewise denies the Messiahship of Jesus and the Father/Son relationship. So we see that Rabbinic Judaism too, by the definition of the Word of God, is an antichrist religion. [*Jews for Jesus* Founder, Moshe Rosen, in his 1991 address in Zeist, Holland, denounced Rabbinic Judaism as a false religion.]

Prediction Is Prediction And Command Is Command

A final error propagated by Christian Zionism is the confusion of prophecy with command. This way of thinking takes things predicted in the Bible and says that it is the priority of the church to cause these prophecies to be fulfilled. Along the way they will refer to many passages of scripture about the Jews returning to Zion with the help of Gentiles. In fact the League of Nations gave the British a mandate under the Balfour Declaration to return the Jews to Israel after World War 1.

The United Nations established Israel as a nation in 1948. Bearing in mind that the Hebrew word for nation and Gentile is the same word (*goy*; or *ethnon* in Greek); these prophecies were being fulfilled by the hand of God in history without any help from the Church—just as Jesus said they would in His final words in Acts chapter 1. Not so long ago Belgian airplanes chartered by the American government flew 'Falasha' Jews from Ethiopia to Israel without any help from Christians.

Christian Zionists refuse to acknowledge in their practice of confusing prophecy with command, that not only is it not blessed by God, but it also harms the indigenous Body of Christ in Israel. It also hurts Jewish evangelism financially when its high profile advertising drains millions away from the true work of God. They also refuse to recognise, in their confusion of prediction and command, that anti-semites mishandled scripture in precisely the same way.

Time and time again Christian anti-semites who murdered Jews sought refuge in the texts of Leviticus chapter 26 and Deuteronomy chapter 28. They claim that God said that He would give the Jews into the hands of their enemies after the rejection of their Messiah. So, like the Christian Zionists today, they decided that God wanted them to go out and fulfil these prophecies turning predictions into commands; constructing for themselves an artificial theology by distorting scripture in the same manner as Christian Zionists do today. All the while denying the fact that prophecy is prophecy and command is command.

Christian Zionism—Satan's Tool

At a time when the Holy Spirit wants to build unity in Christ between Jew and Arab as a testimony to both communities, Christian Zionism drives a wedge between Jews and Arabs in Christ. When an Arab turns from the lies of Islam and puts his faith in Jesus, and a Jew turns from the lies of Talmudic Judaism and puts his faith in Yeshua (Jesus), the reconciliation predicted in Isaiah chapter 19 that is to happen in the Millennium already begins to happen now within the Body of Christ in the biblical land of Israel.

Just as Jacob and his brother Esau were reconciled, so too one day Jew and Arab, these long estranged brothers, will also be reconciled (as even the Talmud affirms). This reconciliation should already be underway among Jewish and Arab believers through the power of the Gospel.

The plight of Arab believers in their own lands is perilous, and Christians need to remember that God has a special love, blessing, and promise for Arabs, because like Jews they are also Abraham's children.[26] The book of Genesis contains passages which clearly testify to God's eternal love for Abraham's other children who are prevented from coming into that blessing by the lie of Islam, just as unsaved Jews are impeded from receiving God's blessing by the lies of a false Judaism which rejects their Messiah.

Affirming God's purposes for the Jews does not mean automatically accepting anything done in the name of Zionism. God openly commands the Jews that in their return to their land they are to treat those who sojourn there as their own sons. While it is true that standards of living and freedom for Arabs living under Jewish rule are normally much greater than those of most who live under Moslem rule, there are—and have always been—very major problems. Things still remain far from God's ideal of justice as found in Ezekiel chapter 47.

Indeed some Jews try to apply this standard, only to discover that militant Islam prevents such a thing from being even of remote possibility. However no one can dismiss the fact that Arabs, even moderate Arabs, have often been the victims of injustice—certainly at the hands of their own kind, but also at the hands of the Israeli authorities.

As Christians the only means we have to address this problem is through our prayers and by bringing the gospel to both Jew and Arab. This, and not a political Gospel, is after all exactly what Jesus commanded.[27]

Conclusions

While it is a dangerous mistake not to affirm the prophetic purposes of God for the nation Israel, it is vital to realise that one purpose is that of the Great Tribulation from which the only rescue is acceptance of Jesus as the Messiah. The Jews are back in Israel for a coming hour which will be by far the darkest in their history.

Their only hope is faith in Jesus and the only hope that Christians can give them is Jesus. Those who argue with this argue with Christ! These were His last words to the Church before He left the earth. Those who wilfully reject His last words and lead others into rebellion will be called upon to give account. So, as we have seen previously, to ask Christians to love the Jews with a love that does not give them the only gospel that can save them from hell, is not a love from God but a deception from hell itself.

I cannot emphasise this sufficiently; each time a Christian supports an organisation which claims to have a ministry to the Jews but which does not include the gospel, they help pave the same road to hell upon which millions of Jews have already entered eternity.

I say again, the last thing Jesus said was: "Let God worry about the rebirth of Israel; you worry about the 'new birth' of Jewish souls."[28] What good is it if the Jews come out of Russia and go into hell without their Messiah?

As we have already seen, God is going to bless the Church through Jewish people before Jesus returns. He will continue to save Jews and He is going to achieve His prophetic purposes for the salvation of Israel, as detailed in His Word: not by use of Dual Covenant Theology, Christian Zionism or any other man-made endeavour.

You can be part of God's plan by bringing the good news of Yeshua the Messiah back home again to the Jewish people through whom God first gave it; by praying for the salvation of Israel and by supporting genuine Jewish missions and evangelism. As God has promised, He will bless those that bless Israel and curse those who curse Israel.[28] As I have attempted to demonstrate, the way appointed to bless Israel is with the gospel and the way you can curse Israel is by withholding it and by supporting these who withhold it. The choice is yours.

I repeat, the worst form of anti-Semitism a born again Christian can engage in is to refrain from giving Jewish people the good news of their Messiah who died for their sin, and whose atonement is the only way that will keep them and their children from hell.

If you are involved in this kind of Christian Zionism, and support an organisation which not only resolutely refuses to evangelise Jews but diverts support away from those who do, or which tries to bless Israel without giving Israel Jesus, then

THE DEVIL IS TAKING YOU FOR A RIDE.

Notes on ch.6

1. "We have seen that prosperity is a blessing of Abraham and that poverty is under the curse of the law, Jesus bore the curse of the law on our behalf. He beat Satan and took away his power. Consequently, there is no reason for you to live in poverty of any kind" (Kenneth Copeland, *The Laws of Prosperity*, Fort Worth, TX: Kenneth Copeland Publications, 1974:51). Hagin and Copeland like all faith teachers, reduce the the infinite value of Christ's sacrificial death by heretically claiming that Christ died in order that we may gratify ourselves with material indulgence and an easy life. "I believe that it is the plan of God our Father that no believer should ever be sick" (Kenneth Hagin, *Healing the Father's Provision*, Word of Faith, August 1977,9; quoted in D R McConnell, *A Different Gospel*, Hendrickson Publishers,1995:157,168, note 41).

   According to Hagin anyone who drives a Chevrolet instead of a luxury car isn't "being humble, that's being ignorant of God's law of prosperity" (Kenneth Hagin, *Authority*, p22.; quoted in Dave Hunt , *Beyond Seduction*, Harvest House Publishers, Eugene, Oregon, 1987:65).

2. Deuteronomy 27:26; Galatians 3:10-11; Romans 2:12, 3:19-20, 4:13 -15.

3. Psalm 19:8; 119; Romans 4:13-15.

4. Genesis 12:2-3;Romans 2:9, 3:2,19; Acts 7:38-42,51-3.

5. Exodus 1:8-11, 14, 3:7.

6. Esther 3:8-11.

7. Exodus 17:8,16; Deuteronomy 25:17-19.

8 The International Christian Embassy, based in Jerusalem told Gustaf Scheller from Operation Exodus (an organisation which provides ships to take Jews back to Israel), that if he was to bring Jews into Israel he was not to preach the gospel to them.

9 .Morris Cerullo's mailshots were exposed on the Andrew Neil programme 'This is your Life' in 1995.

10. Among the few Israelis who will endorse the International Christian Embassy are Ari Sorko Ram, a television actor, and his wife Shira. The Sorko Rams have always been controversial figures within Israel as Shira Sorko Ram underwent an *halakik* conversion from Christianity to rabbinic Judaism in what many local believers considered to be defiance of both 1 Corinthians chapter 7:17 and the book of Galatians. Others also felt that if she believed that Jesus were the Messiah, it was misleading to convert to a faith which denied Him without the rabbinate knowing that in fact she believes in Jesus.

    The Sorko Rams left Israel after their congregation *in Ramat Ha Sharon* collapsed amidst allegations of misconduct and impropriety. They agreed to abide by a decision of the local Body of Christ in Israel to withdraw for a time from the ministry in order to prevent a major scandal. They have since returned to Israel and, according to some reports, may be receiving financial backing from the International Christian Embassy although they neither lead a congregation in Israel, nor a Jewish mission organisation and are therefore in no way spokesmen for either the local Body of Christ in Israel or for Jewish missions. It is alleged that they approached Cerullo and asked to participate in his project by handling the follow up correspondence. The Sorko Rams were also responsible in large measure for importing John Arnott and the the Toronto experience' into Israel and at the same time, creating an outrageous spectacle during the funeral period of murdered prime minister Itzahk Rabin. It must be said that whatever Cerullo's intentions may have been, he certainly achieved little for the cause of Christ.

11. "Spiritual death means something more than separation from God. *Spiritual death also means having Satan's nature...*(i.e Jesus submitted to Satan's Lordship) Jesus tasted death—spiritual death—for every man."

For Hagin it was not on the Cross but in hell that redemption was secured: "...down in hell itself—Jesus satisfied the claims of Justice on the behalf of each one of us,...God in heaven said, 'It is enough.' Then he raised Him up. He brought His spirit and soul up out of hell—He raised His body up from the grave—and He said, 'Thou art my son, THIS DAY have I begotten thee' (Kenneth E Hagin, *The Name of Jesus*, Tulsa, OK: Kenneth Hagin Ministries, 1981, 31, emphasis original).

Hagin's follower Kenneth Copeland actually says that "Satan conquered Jesus on the Cross" (cited in H Hanegraaff, *Christianity in Crisis*, Nelson Word Limited, Milton Keynes, 1993:11).

12. Quoted in W. Riggans, *The Covenant with the Jews*, Monarch Publications, Tunbridge Wells, 1992:114.

13. 1 Corinthians 9:20-23.

14. The Israeli government also discriminates against Arabs in violation of Ezekiel 47:22-23. There have also been marked injustices against the Arab population, albeit not to the degree cited by Israel's critics.

15. "None of our (Spiritual) founding fathers ever believed in a national restoration of a nation of Israel on the earth during any millennium, or that the Jewish nation after the flesh would ever be a select, special people...Not one apostle, not one New Testament writer promises them any restoration of dirt land anywhere in the New Testament... It is hurting our witness to the Arab nations when we sanction anything Israel does. Political Israel is not Israel. They have no right...to be on that land" Rick Godwin, on his audiotape series 'The Shepherd-Sheep Relationship',1988, cited in M. L. Brown, *Our Hands are Stained with Blood—The Tragic Story of The Church and The Jewish People*, Destiny Image Publishers, 1992.

16. Ezekiel 3:18,19; Acts 18:6, 20:26.

17. John 14:15.
18. Acts 20:27.
19. Romans 10:1.
20. Romans 10:14.
21. Romans 9:3.
22. 2 Timothy 4:6-8.
23 Daniel 9:25-26; Matthew 24:1-3.
24. Revelation 2:9.
25. 1 John 2:22.
26. Arabs are descended from Abraham, Ishmael is their father, therefore the promises given to Ishmael and his descendants still apply to Arabs today. Genesis 25:17-18; 16:10-12; 17:20; 21:13,17-18.
27. Acts 1:6-8.
28. Genesis 12:3; 27:29.

Chapter 7

Lie 2: Restorationism

You Can't Restore What Never Existed

As we saw previously, in order to restore something, it must exist to begin with. Yet the modern 'Restoration Movement' with its particular brands of 'apostolic prophetic authority' and 'dominionist' and triumphalist 'kingdom authority' are fundamentally committed to the restoration of three things which never existed in Biblical Christianity in the first place: their style of apostles and prophets and 'the kingdom'. These things, however, derive from ancient errors that have always surfaced at critical moments in Church history.

A. Restoring Which Apostolic Authority?

The first is a version of apostolic authority which is alien to what is found in the true Apostolic Church. These ideas derive from the pyramid model of church leadership propounded by the early followers of Arthur Wallis. They place the apostle on the pinnacle of the pyramid with the prophets under them, followed by pastors, teachers etc, all ostensibly based upon the model for ministry and church government found in the book of Ephesians chapter 4:11.

The actual biblical view of apostolic authority however, follows a very different pattern. In the epistle to the Hebrews chapter 3:1, Jesus is called "The Apostle of our Confession". The word "apostle" here occurs with a definite article. It is He and He alone who is represented in Scripture as occupying the pinnacle place of Church leadership. All of the apostolic authority in the Church must derive from Him, be under His headship, and as we shall note, be exercised within the context of plurality and never as a one-man show.

The apostolic authority held by the original twelve Apostles and by Paul was chiefly doctrinal: either in writing the New Testament or in correcting error within the early church. It was not organisational.

Which Apostles—The New Testament's Or Restorationism's?

There is no evidence of the Apostles ever functioning as autocrats, and little evidence of them ever using their apostolic authority in matters of Church government that did not involve doctrine but were primarily organisational matters of ecclesiastical polity.

Biblical apostolic authority, contrary to the autocratic emphasis of most of restorationism and dominionism, was plural. Jesus sent the Apostles out in pairs.[1] In Acts chapter 13:2, the Holy Spirit said: "Set out for me, Barnabas and Saul."

Secondly, while it was essentially an authority that was exercised for doctrinal reasons, it had little to do with theocracy *per se* and we note the plural nature of its expression.

The leadership of the apostolic Church in Acts was, if anything, a reaction against the kind of theocratic institutionalism associated with the Sanhedrin in the gospels. And even this doctrinal authority was always manifested on the basis of plurality, not autocracy—as is evidenced in the council of Acts chapter 15. Autocracy later emerged in the post-apostolic Church with the teachings about mono-episcopacy by Ignatius of Antioch.[2]

Finally, we see that apostolic authority in the New Testament was an apostolic authority that was accountable. Paul and Barnabas regularly reported back to the church at Antioch which sent them out as missionaries. If we look closely we see a mutual submission among the Apostles recorded in Acts chapter 15.

None of the above feature in the models of apostolic authority associated with modern restorationism. Instead of plurality, such authority becomes autocratic and, not infrequently, dictatorial. Instead of being doctrinal, it is organisational, and to the degree it is doctrinal in its expression, the doctrines not infrequently disagree with the doctrines written by the original Apostles in the New Testament.

Spiritual Authority Or Heavy Shepherding?

It is no coincidence that the House Church Movement throughout Great Britain was continually plagued by what has come to be known as 'heavy shepherding'—as indeed have many restorationist churches throughout North America. This is what the prophet Ezekiel predicted:

> Those who are sickly you have not strengthened, the diseased you have not healed, the broken you have not bound up, the scattered you have not brought back, nor have you sought for the lost; but with force and severity, you have dominated them (Ezekiel 34:4).

There are numberless horror stories of Christians who have been spiritually and psychologically damaged by the practice of heavy shepherding in restoration churches. This has, in turn, left a sorry trail of backsliding, broken marriages, single parent families, and people who are now unable to have an assurance of salvation because they left a house church where they and their children endured all manner of spiritual and psychological abuse.

At the risk of repeating myself, the root of this can be traced directly to the the unbiblical model of apostolic authority which places an individual on a pinnacle with no accountability to any other authority.

In Great Britain particularly, most of the house church leaders were either men who were themselves unschooled in the Word of God or else people from strict Plymouth Brethren backgrounds who, after a Holy Spirit baptism experience, reacted against their Brethren upbringing. They moved from one extreme to the other—going from a non-charismatic Christian experience to a hyper-charismatic Christian experience where proper exegesis of the Word of God had little place.

It is a fact of life: when people have been hurt in one way, you will frequently see a pendulum swing to an opposite extreme.

The Cult Of Personality

Most of these churches that became institutions started as an alternative to denominational Christianity. Yet through their heavy shepherding and party spirit (both of which are firmly rooted in a wrong model of apostolic authority which they mistakenly construe to be biblical) they soon became ultra-denominational themselves.

Not infrequently, such groups become sects which are theologically churches but sociologically cults. Then in time as their 'apostles' depart further from the original doctrinal theology of the actual Apostles in the first century Church, who wrote the New Testament, they bend towards becoming heretical with the authority of scripture being replaced by the subjective revelation of the so-called 'apostle'. As we shall see, this is a form of Gnosticism which surfaced in the early Church and is again being resurrected throughout contemporary restorationism.

In early restorationist churches people would clap and cheer at meetings when someone left an established denominational church in order to 'get into the restoration' and follow an 'apostle' or 'prophet'. Right from its outset, much of this movement was more concerned with 'sheep stealing' than the salvation of the lost.

New Doctrine Equals False Doctrine

The doctrinal dimension of biblical apostolic authority began to be appropriated by some restorationist teachers and apostles when they began to have 'new doctrinal revelations'.

I do not say that apostolic authority does not still exist in the church: it indeed exists in at least three ways.

First, Christ was, and remains, The Apostle, with all other apostolic authority deriving from Him.

Second, apostolic authority as exercised by Peter, Paul, James and John still exists in the Church in the New Testament writings of those inspired men. Please note that these are the only writings which the Holy Spirit inspired as Canon and delivered to the Church through them. Any notion of 'new doctrinal revelation' must be rejected. Indeed, those so-called apostles and prophets who claim such 'revelations' are invariably restorationists or from the kindred spirit faith/prosperity group which has its roots, not in New Testament Christianity, but in early Gnosticism.

Finally, an apostle is by definition one who is sent to plant a church. The word finds its origins in the Hebrew word *Shaleach*, and the Greek term *Apostolos*. There are indeed church planting missionaries raised up by the Lord today. But, as in the New Testament models, they should ideally be sent out in teams to plant new churches and be accountable to the existing churches which send them. The non-accountable autocratic and dictatorial models of apostolic authority which restorationist leaders have often appropriated to themselves have absolutely no basis whatsoever in the Word of God .

In short, biblical apostolic authority is mainly doctrinal and concerned with the defence of truth from error. The alleged apostolic authority of restorationism has more to do with the unbiblical phenomena of heavy shepherding. As I have said already, the fruit of this practice is found in the devastation which this unscriptural version of apostolic authority has caused in the lives of many scarred Christians.

The New Testament is a doctrinally complete canon and there is no further basis for any other doctrinal revelation beyond what is found in the Bible which is ordained by God. The 'God has shown me' doctrinal innovations of restorationism may have indeed been shown to them by a god—but certainly not the God of the Bible.

Finally, biblical apostolic authority is accountable and has nothing whatsoever to do with the dictatorial decrees and often doctrinally absurd pronouncements of restorationist and dominionist leaders.

The models of so-called apostolic authority which restorationism is trying to put back into the Church, present the question: if these things are not found in scripture, where do they come from?

Any objective reading of church history would certainly show that such models have far more in common with the Papacy and the idea of a single leader as head of a *magisterium*, than they do with anything found in the book of Acts or the Epistles.

B. Restoring What Kind Of Prophets?

The second institution which restorationism wishes to restore to the church, but which has no basis in either Testament, is its concept of a 'New Testament prophet'. Indeed, we can detect certain differences between a New Testament prophet and an Old Testament prophet. In so far as the Old Testament prophets wrote the Old Testament, scripture and the New Testament was written by Apostles.

It can also be argued that Old Testament prophecy was chiefly concerned with predictions to nations—and to individuals in key positions of authority within nations—the ramifications of whose actions had an impact on the destiny of those nations. Most of this was, of course, focused on the nation of Israel, although the Old Testament does contain a considerable body of additional prophetic material concerning other nations.

New Testament prophets, however, as deduced from the examples in the book of Acts and references to that office in the epistles, appear to be chiefly concerned with bringing prophetic exhortation or warning to the church or to individuals and particularly leaders within the church whose actions help determine the destiny of the church and, possibly by extension, that of 'Christian' societies.

It would be difficult to derive any other differences between New and Old Testament prophets as seen in scripture. They fulfil essentially the same function, although it may be applied with a different emphasis accounted for by the differences between the two covenants.

What Is A False Prophet?

Deuteronomy chapter 18 and Jeremiah chapters 23 and 28 make it clear what a false prophet is. The New Testament warns repeatedly that, just as Israel had such false prophets, they would also come into the church, particularly in the last days. We are exhorted to both expect and beware of them.

I have been accosted by members of the late John Wimber's Vineyard Fellowship who have expressed dissatisfaction at my citation of prophetic predictions which originate from within the Vineyard and Kansas City fellowships that have failed to happen. However, Deuteronomy chapter 18:19-22 makes it clear that a false prophet is one who predicts things in the Name of the Lord that fail to happen, either by invoking another god (*Shed* or demon in Hebrew) or from the deception and futility of their own mind. These are false prophets and God commands that they be put to death (Deut 18:20).

Old Or New Testament, The Sin Is Serious

Although we no longer stone such false prophets under the new covenant, the sin is no less serious and it would represent wilful rebellion against the Word of God for the church to allow people who have 'prophesied' such things to remain in positions of leadership or prophetic ministry. Some individuals from the Vineyard Fellowship have responded by saying "This only refers to an Old Testament prophet". They also distort the text of 1 Corinthians chapter 13:9 which says "We prophesy in part", so New Testament prophets therefore, such as those from the Vineyard and from the Kansas City Fellowship, can be part right and part wrong in their predictions and still be regarded as New Testament prophets who cannot be criticised.[3]

In fact, before becoming a Christian, I knew a witch in New Jersey who read my tarot cards so accurately that she foresaw—through the cards—that I would become a Christian! She too was part right and part wrong in her predictions.

I would dare to say that, prediction for prediction, she was certainly more accurate than the Kansas City Prophet Paul Cain or Rick Joyner. In his book *The Harvest,* Joyner falsely predicted in the Name of the Lord that communism would become almost globally triumphant. He saw it taking over nearly the entire developing world and much of the developed world including parts of the United States—when in fact the complete opposite happened.[4]

Paul Cain of the Kansas City Prophets, joined by John Wimber of the Vineyard Fellowship and Mike Bickle of the Kansas City Fellowship, falsely predicted revival would come to Great Britain and spread to Germany in October of 1990. Cain told a large audience (during a message recorded on tape, video, and later published in a periodical called *Equipping The Saints*) that "I don't care what anybody says. You're going to see revival when you go out of here."[5]

Yet, in the ten years since the great revival predicted at the Docklands Arena in London, more mosques have been built in England than Churches.[6] Hard core drug addiction has nearly doubled.[7] Divorce, homosexuality, abortion and all manner of immorality, New Age religion and Islam have blossomed steadily, completely unhindered. Meanwhile the church and its influence has continued to decline.

Roger Forster and Graham Kendrick, who espouse dominionist and replacementist ideas within the Ichthus Fellowship, believe that annihilationism should be taught as a possible alternative to traditional views of eternal judgement. Annihilationism is the concept that after death the unsaved will become non-existent instead of suffering eternal hell, thus there is no place for eternal conscious torment as taught in scripture.

David Pytches, a Charismatic Anglican Bishop, wrote a book entitled *Some Said It Thundered*, which exhorted the charismatic movement within the Church of England (at such churches as Holy Trinity Brompton and St Andrew's Chorleywood) to follow Paul Cain and the Kansas City Prophets.

While it may be possible that Paul Cain and the Kansas City Prophets have sometimes been right, the witch who read my tarot cards was also often right and, again, probably had a better track record for accuracy than Paul Cain—except that she admittedly prophesies falsely by demonic power while Cain claims that his false prophecies come from God. I fail to see, given what we read in the book of Proverbs, why she should be considered a false prophet while Cain is not. As Proverbs states repeatedly: "A false balance and an unjust measure are abominations to the Lord".[8]

What About Promise Keepers?

The Promise Keepers movement also arose from within the Vineyard. It is led by Bill McCartney acting with the advice of his pastor James Ryle who teaches that the Beatles were 'anointed by God' but lost the anointing when they broke up in 1970.[9]

At a Promise Keepers rally held at a stadium in Colorado, 50,000 copies of the book *The Masculine Journey* by Robert Hicks were distributed among the audience. The book was apparently intended to be treated as a handbook. In fact much of its focus is centered on New Age male phallic symbolism and was based on the New Age teachings of one Robert Bly, author of *Iron John*. These teachings are of course, far removed from the teachings of Scripture. Scripture teaches male/female bonding where the Hebrew term *devek* (cling to) is used in Genesis chapter 2:24. The Bible teaches male fellowship but not male bonding. Male bonding is a homosexual concept and a New Age concept. There is no scriptural base to call it a Christian concept. The membership of Promise Keepers is full of men who are not born-again and who are not even being told they need to be.[10]

In *The Masculine Journey* Hicks writes: "I'm sure many would baulk at my thought of celebrating the experience of sin. I'm not sure how we could do it. But I do know we need to do it." He goes on to suggest that instead of condemning a young person's first experience with drugs or sex we could "look upon this as a teachable moment and a rite of passage. Is this putting a benediction on sin? Of course not, but perhaps at this point the true elders could come forward and confess their own adolescent sins and congratulate the next generation for being human."[11]

To turn the loss of virginity or an experience with illegal drugs into a religious rite of passage is sick and perverted. Add to this the fact that the "Seven Principles Of Promise Keepers" are not even all biblical, so that even Mormons, Roman Catholics, and non-evangelicals can adopt them.

Ed Coles author of the book *Maximised Manhood* has openly stated his approval of such heretics and money preachers as Oral Roberts, Kenneth Hagin and Jerry Saville.

Promise Keepers is not of God; it is a deception and a disgrace which in accord with standard Vineyard Gnosticism allegorises scriptures out of all reasonable context to make it seem to be something it is not, namely biblical.

Evil—Ripped From The Earth On June 9th, 1994?

It was predicted on the American Trinity Broadcasting Network by John Hinkle (in conversation with Paul Crouch) that evil would be taken from the earth on June 9th, 1994. Hinkle and Crouch asserted that John Wimber and Paul Cain had both received a similar message from heaven. On coast to coast television in front of millions of viewers, they said that there would be no more sick babies left in hospitals once evil was ripped from the earth on June 9th. These predictions were so absurd that even the most gullible must have wondered at their stupidity.

Yet still the avalanche of false prophets and false prophecies goes on unabated with the false prophets not being required to give account or take any responsibility for the damage and disillusionment that they have caused to the Body of Christ, nor for the destruction and havoc they have wrought upon the credibility of the Christian Church in the eyes of the unsaved. As Jeremiah points out in chapter 23:32:

> "Behold, I am against those who have prophesied false dreams," declares the Lord, "and related them, and led My people astray by their falsehoods and reckless boasting; yet I did not send them or command them, nor do they furnish this people the slightest benefit," declares the Lord.

Just as the false prophets of Jeremiah's day did the people no good by predicting the things of deception and futility of their own arrogant minds, neither do the prophecies of Paul Cain, Rick Joyner, John Hinkle, or Gerald Coates do God's people any good—similarly prophesying arrogantly from the deception and futility of their own minds.

You Made God's People Trust In A Lie And Counselled Rebellion Against Him

As Jeremiah told Hananiah:

> Then Jeremiah the prophet said to Hananiah the prophet, "Listen now, Hananiah, the Lord has not sent you and you have made this people trust in a lie.
> Therefore thus says the Lord, 'Behold, I am about to remove you from the face of the earth. This year you are going to die, because you have counselled rebellion against the Lord'" (Jeremiah 28:15-16).

Jeremiah told Hananiah "You have made God's people trust in a lie Hananiah, and counselled rebellion against the Lord". The same can be said of today's false prophets.

The lies may be different, but the liar remains the same. It is Satan who is the author of confusion, deception, and rebellion against the Lord. The false prophecies may be different, but the false prophets are the same and so is the Word of God that condemns them.

False Is False No Matter What Its Source

We must remember that to God it is irrelevant whether these people make their predictions in sincerity.

What is important is that they predict wrongly, misleading God's people, hurting the Church, defying the authority of Scripture, counselling rebellion against the Lord and undermining the credibility of the gospel in the eyes of the world which is perishing without it.

Let's again look at what Jeremiah says concerning such men:

> Thus says the Lord of hosts, "Do not listen to the words of the prophets who are prophesying to you. They are leading you into futility; they speak a vision of their own imagination, not from the mouth of the Lord.
> "They keep saying to those who despise Me, 'The Lord has said, "You will have peace'; and as for every one who walks in the stubbornness of his own heart, they say, 'Calamity will not come upon you.'
> "But who has stood in the council of the Lord, that he should see and hear His word? Who has given heed to His word and listened?
> "Behold, the storm of the Lord has gone forth in wrath, even a whirling tempest; it will swirl down on the head of the wicked.
> "The anger of the Lord will not turn back until He has performed and carried out the purposes of His heart; in the last days you will clearly understand it.
> "I did not send these prophets, but they ran. I did not speak to them, but they prophesied.
> "But if they had stood in My council, then they would have announced My words to My people, and would have turned them back from their evil way and from the evil of their deeds"

> (Jeremiah 23:16-22).

Today the same God says, "Do not listen to these who are speaking visions from their own imagination, preaching Dominionism and saying, 'Destruction will not come upon us but we will be the Church Triumphant.'" If they had indeed been sent by the Lord, their prophecies would have proved true and that is how we know God did not send them. Those who continue to follow them join in their rebellion today just as they did in the days of Jeremiah. God's instruction is clear: "Do not listen to them."

As It Was, So It Is

The book of Jeremiah is vital in understanding this issue. In New Testament eschatology the last days of Judah before the Babylonian captivity are taken and represented as a type of what will happen to the church in the last days.

As we saw earlier in our examination of Midrash, the Old Testament prophets, particularly Ezekiel, Daniel and Jeremiah, prophesied for three time-frames, sometimes all at the same time, and sometimes even all in the same sentence. They prophesied for their own time, for the first coming of Christ, and for matters pertaining to His return—often one fulfilment being the type of another.

The New Testament takes the themes from the prophets about the Babylonian captivity and what led up to it and presents them anew as a message for what the Church is to expect in the last days. In other words, what happened in the last days of Judah teaches about what will happen in the last days of the Church.

This is why, for instance, the book of Revelation uses the phrase, "Fallen, fallen, is Babylon the Great" from Isaiah and Jeremiah before the Babylonian captivity. It is also why, in the Olivet discourse in Matthew chapter 24, Jesus presents afresh the themes of Daniel (a captivity prophet) concerning predictions about the Temple being defiled, and those of Jeremiah about the Temple being destroyed in the last days before the Babylonian captivity. He also repeatedly warns of false prophets and false teachers coming to deceive the elect in the last days of the Church, as had happened in Jeremiah's day.

To Understand The Present, Look To The Past

In warning about the last days in Matthew chapter 24 and Luke chapter 21, Jesus alludes to the situation with the false prophets and false teachers in the days of Jeremiah. They were telling the people a Triumphalist and Dominionist lie, when in fact divine judgement was coming. But the people chose to believe false prophets rather than true ones. Jeremiah himself says that the situation in his own day will be replayed in the last days once again.

> "The anger of the Lord will not turn back against these false prophets until He has performed and carried out the purposes of His heart: in the last days you will clearly understand it" (Jeremiah 23:20).

In the last days of Judah the Jews were sacrificing their babies to demons.[12] Yet, today, if we were to take all of the clinical reasons for the total sum of abortions performed in the western Christianised democracies such as the U.S., Canada, Great Britain, Australia, New Zealand, Germany, Holland, etc, and put them together (including ectopic pregnancy, vaginal cancer, and accidental radiation-induced mutanogenesis during gestation), these would account for less than one per cent of total abortions performed.

In other words, more than 99 per cent of abortions are non-therapeutic; they are not performed for any medical reason whatsoever but for socio-economic reasons, or what Jesus called "The worship of Mammon."[13]

There is no doubt that non-therapeutic abortion is theologically and spiritually a contemporary expression of demon worship. If God did not spare the natural branches (that is Israel) for such wicked atrocities neither will His judgement be spared from the so-called Christian nations.[14] Yet, just as in the days of Jeremiah, the false prophets are saying, "We shall be victorious and judgement shall not come."[15]

What Do You Say Now, Paul Crouch?

I ask you, Paul Crouch, if evil was ripped from the earth on June 9th, 1994, as your television programme claimed, how is it that you seem to be the only one who knows about it?

Again, this is precisely, "What will we do in the end?"[16] If Lamentations shows what happened to Israel as a result of this kind of unrepentant behaviour, it applies no less to what will happen, and is to a degree already happening, in the Church.

And My People Love It So

Today, nothing has changed. Many Christians prefer to listen to men who are, by biblical definition, proven false prophets, and also to proven false teachers like Benny Hinn[17] and Rick Godwin and David Chilton (who teach that Matthew chapter 24 is not about the last days) rather than listen to real prophets and real teachers who are telling them the truth such as Hank Hanegraaff, David Hunt, Basilea Schlink and David Wilkerson.

This is what happened in Jeremiah's day. This is what the Word of God says would happen in the last days and this is exactly what is happening today. While judgement approaches, the false prophets say there will be peace. The Hebrew concept of peace, however, is not merely the absence of war but rather a fullness of blessing. So these men try to build people up but it is all illusion setting them up for disillusion:

> "For from the least of them even to the greatest of them,
> every one is greedy for gain, and from the prophet even to
> the priest, every one deals falsely.
> And they have healed the wound of My people slightly,
> saying, 'Peace, peace', but there is no peace"
> (Jeremiah 6:13-14).

I repeat, that is what the false prophets of Judah told the people with their false victory message in the days of Jeremiah, and that is exactly what the false prophets of restorationism with their false triumphalist message are saying to the Church today. They are doing exactly what the Word of God warns such people would do in the last days. They prophesy falsely, rule by their own authority—and once again, God's people love it so.

Gimmick To Gimmick, Fad To Fad

When predictions fail, people tend to gravitate towards the next fad to keep the movement alive. It is no secret that the same kinds of churches which followed Paul Cain and John Wimber on this road to nowhere (such as St Andrew's Chorleywood, with David Pytches, and Holy Trinity Brompton, with Sandy Millar, in the U.K.), are the same churches who grasped on to the 'laughing in the spirit' fad which was imported into Great Britain, Australia, and New Zealand. Ironically the phenomena was much smaller in scope where it originated in South Africa and Canada, and even then it did not take off in the U.S. until it arrived at Pensacola.

The laughing phenomena and its adjuncts, while simply the re-appearance of the excesses that took place with the Montanists, the Munster Anabaptists and the Shakers, are misinterpreted by those ignorant of Church history as something new. Those like Guy Chevreau who know these things are not new have ignored the fact that they were always proven to be ungodly when they occurred in the past.

The fact that the laughter resounds, in the opinion of many, with the flavour of the demonic is not a judgement which we must either affirm or reject; what is important is to realise that the phenomena are a result of taking certain Bible verses out of context. In one sense things like Toronto/Pensacola are from God in that they are the judgement He said He would bring on those in the last days who neither love Him nor love a knowledge of the truth.[18]

Emotions are good servants but dangerous masters. Emotion is the function of the soul and as the New Testament teaches, it is the Word of God that divides soul from spirit and shows us what is flesh and what is spirit.

So, as expected, emotion reigns in churches where the Word of God is not expounded, but effectively replaced by supposed 'pictures' and visions, which are not biblical, and by predictions that don't happen.

Watchman Nee spoke of this 'laughing in the spirit' phenomenon in the 19th century as a 'soulish outburst' disguised as being spiritual which captivated immature Christians who were untaught in the Word of God.[19]

We Call It Grace—God Calls It Rebellion!

Scripture tells us plainly that people will continue to follow men who are proven false prophets by the standards of the Word of God and this a matter of sin and wilful rebellion against the Lord.

God's grace is designed to bring us to repentance and to restore us once we do repent. If there is no repentance, do not expect any grace. He is a God of grace, but He is not mocked!

Those christians and churches who continue to follow men like Coates, Cain, Hinkle, and others, are in direct rebellion against the Word of God. Sadly, pastors of churches which continue to recognise the validity of the ministries of these men will one day give account to the Lord for the state of the sheep whose welfare they are betraying into the hands of false prophets and false teachers. As the New Testament teaches, the shepherds will one day give account to the Chief Shepherd for how they took care of the sheep.[20]

Cognitive Dissonance—The Psychology Of Losers

Now it stands revealed: the core of the problem is sin. Rebellion, lack of discernment, ignorance of the Word of God, and finally, an all but complete rejection of Him. These spiritual reasons underlie psychological and socio-psychological factors which naturally propel people to behave this way. Festinger, the sociologist who was interested in the social psychology of religion, extensively researched the phenomenon he called 'Cognitive Dissonance'.

Cognitive dissonance is what allows people to make an irreversible decision to commit themselves to a group identity, which has in turn committed itself to some prediction. This commitment continues even when the prediction fails to happen. Rather than leaving the group, people will tend to be more committed to it.

Even at the present time, the Jehovah's Witnesses continue in increasing loyalty to a cult whose leaders have repeatedly made false predictions about the end of the world, instead of coming to grips with the truth that their leaders have predicted things falsely in the Name of the Lord.

The late Rabbi Menachim Schneerson, leader of the Lubovitch Hassidic sect of ultra-orthodox Jews, prophesied falsely in the Name of the Lord that the Messianic redemption would come by the Jewish New Year (*Rosh Ha Shanna*) of 1991. He said that the end of the cold war was the beginning of the fulfilment of Isaiah's prophecies of spears being beaten into pruning hooks and that the Messianic redemption would come in September of that year, the month in which the Jewish New Year occurred.

Yet his followers remained as dedicated as ever—in fact, some would argue, they became more enthralled in spite of the fact that he plainly violated the Torah and got it wrong. Most of his followers actually claimed he was the Messiah and upon his death at the age of 91 some believed that he would rise from the dead.

To Be Better We Must Be Different—But Are We?

This same phenomena can be found among restorationist christians and others who take on their baggage. Once the prophecies fail to happen, instead of obeying the Word of God, and demanding that those who prophesied falsely repent and be removed from ministry, they continue with a renewed sense of dedication, grasping for the next prediction.

In a sense false prophets represent only one aspect of a broader problem among pentecostal and charismatic Christians today. Having turned from a proper emphasis on the Word of God, and therefore abandoned the spirit of the Bereans we read of in Acts chapter 17 (where they diligently searched the Scriptures to see if certain teachings, prophecies, and practises, were in agreement with the Word of God) such churches have no other course left open to them but to take that of progressive self-deception.

Instead of emphasising repentance, and admitting they got it wrong, the leaders tend to invent or invite new forms of trendy hype to cover up the reality of their failure and to keep the artificial momentum going. Once again, if there is no repentance, there is no grace, only self-deception and religious claptrap.

Give Me A Word—Or Give Me *The* Word?

Jeremiah has much to teach us in relation to this problem. We live in a world where Christians rely increasingly on people to come in and give them pictures, visions, and words, supposedly from the Lord by so-called 'prophets' who are for the most part deficient in their knowledge and understanding of Scripture, and who rely upon invented doctrines which please themselves and tickle their listeners' ears.[21]

These words, pictures and visions become replacements for the guidance and direction the Holy Spirit gives through Scripture and the 'prophets' become man's substitutes for the true prophets of God who are always, first and foremost, men and women of the Word.

God will only entrust prophetic ministry, prophetic gifts and prophetic revelation to people whose first basis is scripture and the authority of scripture. As there is no new doctrinal revelation, any new revelation that God gives will have to be in agreement with the teaching of the infallible revealed Word of God. It is no coincidence then that those who have established a record for giving false prophecies, such as Gerald Coates and Paul Cain, are people who are first and foremost in severe doctrinal error. We read once again in Jeremiah chapter 23 verse 28:

"The prophet who has a dream may relate his dream, but let him who has My word speak My word in truth. What does straw have in common with grain?" declares the Lord.

Jeremiah tells us that these dreams and predictions are 'straw' and have no nutritional value whatsoever. The Word of God, however, is 'grain'. Like wheat and tares, straw and grain look very much alike until you get up close to them. Then you can distinguish between them and see which is worthless. It is only ever someone with a strong doctrinal basis in the Word of God whom God will raise up to a genuine prophetic office.

Have We Been Eating Grain Or Straw?

It is unfashionable but true: all of the doctrinal guidance and ninety percent of the personal direction God has for us is already in the scripture, and that is where we should go for guidance and direction—not to someone who bounces around from church to church giving people 'words' and 'prophecies'. Truly there is nothing new under the sun.

When we see Christians continually going to meetings in order to receive 'a word', that is a sure sign that they themselves are not the students of **the** Word that God has called them to be. Worse still, it is usually a matter of the "blind leading the blind" because the people who put themselves forward as the so-called prophets, wander around from church to church, giving people many words, instead of emphasising right doctrine. And how can it be otherwise, since they are not students of the Word themselves?

This is not to say God will not give people 'words' and that He will not use people with prophetic giftings to do it. It is to say that our main source of direction and leading from the Lord will be what is already in the Bible and those whom God may use to give words to other people in this manner will, once again, be people whose top priority is always what is written in the Bible in terms of right doctrine.

Unless we have a firm grounding in the written Word of God (the *logos* as it has been called), we will not know if a spoken 'word from the Lord' (sometimes called a *rhema*) is true instead of being a silly invention of someone's imagination—or worse, a direct lie from the enemy.

False Doctrine Is Leaven And Leaven Puffs Up

The best way to understand what a false prophet is is to look at a true one. Daniel foresaw the future of global events right up until our present time in his vision found in chapter 9 of his book. In verse 2 of that chapter, we see that Daniel was diligently studying the Word of God, specifically the prophet Jeremiah. At the same time as he fasted and prayed, he was asking God to give him deeper understanding of biblical prophesy. Daniel was a true prophet. God did indeed reveal tremendous visions of future events to Daniel because he was a man of the Word, and a man of deep prayer. Above all, he was the kind of person whom God could trust with such deep revelations.

True Prophets And False Ones

You will always find the following to be true. True prophets are men who subscribe to true teaching. Jesus said, "The eye is the lamp of the body. If the eye is sound the body will be sound also."[22] The eye is the lamp of the body but God's Word is the lamp unto our feet (Psalm 119:105). We must grasp the principle of the church as a body with different members. We are told in Isaiah chapter 52: "How lovely on the mountains are the feet of him who brings good news", and in Ephesians chapter 6 we are instructed to have "our feet shod with the shoes of the gospel of peace". In the body of Christ the feet are therefore its evangelists!

This is why the New Testament exhorts Christians twice as much about right doctrine as it does about right conduct. If we do not have right doctrine, we will not know what right conduct is.

The charismatic movement, however, has been characterised from its earliest days by experiential theology where doctrines are either invented or seen as divisive and unimportant (as we shall see when dealing with the problem of ecumenism). Thus without right doctrine, charismatics and the current generation of pentecostals often have little idea of what right conduct is. We have charismatic born-again Catholics, praying in tongues to Mary and the dead, which the Word of God calls an abomination, and Christians being instructed by their leaders to follow teachers who teach error and make predictions which never happen.

One person I have known to prophesy accurately is David Wilkerson. In 1987 he prophesied the crash of the stock market that occurred in October of that year. He also accurately foretold the war in the Gulf nearly four years before it happened. How can this be? Answer: he is a student of the Word and the emphasis in his church in New York is always on the Word.

God Does Nothing Without Revealing It To His Servants The Prophets

Another figure I knew to prophesy accurately was Steve Lightle who wrote a book entitled *Exodus II*. He flew to Israel from Moscow (more than five years before the collapse of the Soviet Empire and the fall of the Iron Curtain) in early 1985. He arrived at a fellowship that I was co-leading in Galilee in Northern Israel and informed a sizeable group of us that he had stood before the Kremlin in Red Square and prophesied that because the Soviet Union was persecuting the Church, not allowing the gospel to be preached and not allowing the Jews to return to Israel, in fulfilment of the prophecies of Jeremiah that they would return from the lands of the North, God would do to the Soviet Empire what He did to ancient Egypt in the days of the Exodus. He then made prophetic announcements to let the gospel be preached and to let God's people (the Jews) go.

Lightle's first prediction was that there would be a blight on the Soviet's land. Almost immediately after that, the Chernobyl disaster happened. His second prediction was that the Soviet war machine would collapse. Not long after, the Soviets withdrew from Afghanistan and the Warsaw Pact fell to pieces. His third prediction was that God would destroy the cult spirit of Lenin worship throughout the USSR. There were literally dozens of factories and warehouses that did nothing but produce and distribute statues and icons of Lenin whose veneration, both Richard Wurmbrandt and Alexander Solzenytsin tried to explain to the West, was, in fact, a kind of religion. Lenin's corpse was continually re-embalmed and kept on continual display in Red Square.

Today, just as Lightle prophesied, every one of those warehouses and factories has closed down and statues of Lenin all over the former Soviet Empire have been pulled down or have had their heads sliced off.

Lightle's final prediction was that God would destroy the Soviet Union. It would have been unthinkable to predict the downfall of the Soviet Union in 1985 when all the talk was of Star Wars—a new arms race—and the Cold War was at its peak. Yet, God said He would do nothing without revealing it to His servants the prophets.

It is in people like Steve Lightle and churches that obey the Bible where we find authentic prophetic ministry—and not in the likes of the Kansas City Fellowship or the Vineyard. Brethren in fellowships like these, which teach things fundamentally contrary to the Word of God, and practice things the Word of God warns against, are brethren who are in trouble. Because they are our brethren, we must love them enough to tell them they are in trouble—as God told Ezekiel to do. [23]

But as God also told Ezekiel, "expect the House of Israel not to listen to you when you tell them the truth from my Word because they are stubborn and obstinate." If they will not listen to the Word of God, most of these people will not listen to the truth when they hear it anyway.[24] I say again, this is what happened in the last days of Judah—and it is what will happen in the last days of the church!

While I have seen true prophets like David Wilkerson and Steve Lightle predict incredible things with devastating accuracy, I have also seen the likes of Paul Cain, John Hinkle, and Gerald Coates make failed predictions which are never questioned by their followers.

If these men repented, admitted they had been carried away in the futility and deceptions of their own minds, being misled and misleading others; if they had the integrity and courage to lay their ministries down, and apologised for the damage they have done to the Body of Christ, God would forgive them (and so would I).

Let me make it abundantly clear: I do not hate them, but I hate what they do. I love them in Christ, so for His sake and theirs, I hope they repent and step down. Yet, as Ezekiel was warned, I certainly don't expect it.[25]

False Prophets Within Or Without?

Lightle, Wilkerson, and Basilea Schlink, are all people whom I believe fulfil the Bible's criteria of true prophets just as those previously mentioned fulfil the Bible's criteria of false ones who come to deceive the church in the last days.

This is of the utmost importance. Most Christians wrongly assume that the false prophets of whom Jesus warned in the Olivet discourse, are the Jehovah's Witnesses, Mormons, Hare Krishnas, and other groups which are clearly Satanic cults. However, the context in which Jesus and Paul spoke in Matthew chapter 7:15, and in Acts chapter 20:29 respectively, was that the false prophets whom the Word of God really warns us about are those who would come into the Church deceiving, if possible, even the elect.

Jehovah's Witnesses and Mormons mainly deceive unsaved people. Restorationists and dominionists deceive Christians. A Gerald Coates or a Paul Cain are much more lethal to the people of Christ than any Mormon or Jehovah's Witness will ever be.

The principle is again that just as true teachers and true prophets go together[26] so too false teachers and false prophets go together.[27] The apostle Peter uses the two terms virtually synonymously. Men who prophesy falsely will inevitably teach falsely. Their prophecies are wrong because their doctrines are wrong.

Teaching And Prophecy—True Or False ?

In the same way that true prophets will hold true doctrines, false Prophets will proclaim false ones. As we shall see in a later section the Apostle Peter in his general epistle uses the Greek term *Parasouxousin* meaning to "lay next to". Peter tells us that false prophets secretly introduce destructive heresies by laying truth next to error—just as Satan did in his temptation of Jesus, when he tried to misuse Scripture to achieve his ends.

The way in which modern false prophets and false teachers mishandle the Word of God, using eisegetical and Gnostic methods of interpretation, appears to be in complete harmony with the style exhibited by Satan in his handling of the Scriptures as found in the temptation narratives and in the seduction of Eve in Genesis. A subtle distortion of biblical truth is laid next to things which are actually true. Indeed, today, Jehovah's Witnesses do the same thing.

In other words, to understand why Gerald Coates' prophecies about New Zealand were false, we must look at his doctrines. Coates teaches that the rapture of the church must be relegated to the area of fantasy and myth. The Word of God teaches that the Lord Himself shall descend, the trumpet shall sound and the dead in Christ shall rise and we shall meet them in the air (1 Thessalonians chapter 4:16-17). Yet this pivotal and foundational truth, which has been the hope and inspiration of Christians for centuries, and which Paul tells us by the inspiration of the Holy Spirit so that we might comfort each other with it, is denied by Gerald Coates as 'fantasy' and a 'myth'. [27]

Coates' own prophecies are sometimes wrong because his doctrines are wrong. His predictions are sometimes false and not of God because his teachings are false and not of God.

A similar tendency to false prophecy can be found in all these people and those who follow them. So just as Paul Cain has been hopelessly wrong in his prophecies, he is hopelessly wrong in his doctrines.

Paul Cain calls William Branham, "the greatest prophet that ever lived in any of my generations or any of the generations of revival I've lived through."[28] Yet Branham was a man who identified himself as the angel of Revelation chapter 3:14 and began to baptise people in his own name. This is Paul Cain's role model and mentor!

Bedlam In Britain—Well, Where Is Revival?

Paul Cain, along with Mike Bickle, was brought to England from America by the late John Wimber. As we shall see when we examine the subject later, John Wimber was, by theological definition, a Gnostic whose ideas came, not from the New Testament, but from the heretics of the third and fourth century. This fact helps to account for his habit of perverting the Word of God into saying things which its text and context can never justify.

In his presentation at the Docklands Arena in London, Bickle wrongly taught that Elijah was a man who asked God to destroy Israel because of Baal worship, when in fact the only thing the text that he referred to says is that Elijah thought that he was alone—not realising that there was a faithful remnant of 7,000 who would not worship Baal either.

Bickle then went on to say that Elijah was taken to heaven in a chariot as a judgement from God as a result of his alleged sin! Bickle also taught that we should be like the prodigal's father instead of his brother and accept other Christians and other churches even when we know them to be in error.

However, the text of the prodigal son shows that the fault of the prodigal's brother was not that he would not accept his brother unconditionally, but that he refused to accept his brother after he repented and returned to his father which is something totally different from what Bickle claimed the story meant in his nonsensical interpretation of the text.

Arguably, Bickle's contortion act with the Word of God is perhaps the most ludicrous I have ever come across.

I repeat, Wimber, Bickle, and the Kansas City Prophets' prophecies are wrong because their doctrines are wrong. Their prophecies do not come true because their teaching is not true. Their false predictions come directly from their false doctrines and unbiblical pre-suppositions.

As The Shepherds, So The Sheep

I once asked a prominent evangelical Anglican theologian in Britain how an Anglican Bishop like David Pytches, or a charismatic Anglican pastor like Sandy Millar, could have their churches follow a man like Paul Cain whose mishandling of Scripture is heretical and whose predictions are almost as ludicrous as they are unscriptural.

The Anglican theologian told me it is because the charismatic movement has never had any Bible teaching but was all based on emotions, experience and any kind of doctrine that someone chose to invent. This is because in the last several decades, the Church of England in the U.K. has not taught its clergy the Word of God in its Theological colleges. Instead they learn Higher Criticism. Hence, men like Pytches and Millar will call the baseless ramblings of someone like Paul Cain the Word of God, because they themselves do not know any better.

The leaders of the charismatic movement in the Church of England are by and large doctrinally ignorant men, who are uneducated in their knowledge and understanding of the scriptures God gave us to protect us from deception, and to equip us for His work. Their leaders cannot give their flock what they themselves do not have.

Restoring The Zwickau Prophets And The Montanists Of Phrygia

Just as the Restoration Movement is trying to restore a particular version of apostolic authority which is not biblical, never existing in the New Testament to begin with, so too they are attempting to restore a version of prophetic ministry which is not biblical and never existed in the New Testament either.

Neither the prophets of Israel nor the prophets of the early church ever behaved in this way: divorcing passages of Scripture from their context, inventing absurd doctrines, giving people words and visions from the futility of their own minds and calling them prophecies, and making false predictions in the Name of the Lord for which they accept no responsibility even after they fail to come to pass.

What is actually being restored by restorationism is not the prophetic office of the Bible but the false prophetic office of other dangerous periods in Church history.

For example, in the early Church Montanist prophets made these kinds of erratic predictions, using an over-realised eschatology as their theological base. In the sixteenth century the prophets of Zwickau[29] behaved in precisely the same way that the Kansas City prophets are doing today, making wild predictions on the back of an over-realised eschatology, and believing in a triumphalist kingdom that had already come. Like Cain and Wimber, these two 'schools' amplified the importance of signs and wonders which became a highway that people were drawn to after the dis-illusionment which followed their failed predictions.

The Zwickau false prophets predicted great things which never happened for Munster in Germany, while the Montanist false prophets falsely predicted events for Pepuza in Phrygia. The Kansas City false prophets predicted great events which never happened for London in England. In each case, their doctrines were essentially the same, their eschatology was certainly much the same, their extreme emphasis on signs and wonders was the same—and so were the lies they persuaded God's people to trust in.[30]

The Old Lie Comes Back To Haunt Us

The third item which the Restoration Movement is trying to restore which is not biblical, is its over-realised eschatology known generally as dominionism or triumphalism. As we have noted in an earlier section this error, while having no roots in New Testament doctrine, has clear roots in the Judaization of the Church and the reconstructionism that created such chaos in the Middle Ages and last, but by no means least, in the failure of Protestantism to restore full biblical Christianity.

This doctrine has surfaced many times in Church history,

always rearing its head at turning points in periods of social transition which affect the Church ecclesiologically. Decades ago, it surfaced as the old 'Manchild and Manifest Sons of God' heresies (propagated by such figures as Rushdooney), though rejected by most pentecostal denominations at that time as heterodox.[31] The Neo-Reconstructionist version of this error has had as its apologist Garry Noth, who has attempted to identify Christian Dominionism with American capitalism.

Nothing New Under The Sun

As we have already noted, the same types of error that Satan raised up in the early Church in order to seduce it make a comeback in the last days. In the early Church those with a low Christology, who denied the deity of Jesus, were called Arians. Today they are known as Jehovah's Witnesses. The book of Galatians shows the Sabbatarian and dietary legalists and *nomianists* who came to be called Judaizers. Today we call them Seventh Day Adventists.

The early Church called the 'oneness' teaching that the Father was Jesus, Jesus was Jesus, and the Holy Spirit was Jesus, Sabellianism or Patripassionism. Today it is called Jesus Only United Pentecostalism.

In the early Church, hyper-Dispensationalists who hacked the Bible up along extreme dispensational lines were called Marcionites. Today the Exclusive Brethren sects who adhere to the errors of John Nelson Darby, also treat the scriptures along radically dispensational lines. They deny that the epistle of James is for the Church and teach in effect that the Sermon on the Mount is part of the Old Testament intended for the Jews alone.

In the early church the two greatest and most damaging errors were Gnosticism (whose epicentre was in Alexandria) and Montanism another form of gnosticism which held to an over-realised eschatology. The Bible teaches what we may call an *'inaugural eschatology'* (one of whose proponents was George Eldon Ladd whom many restorationists erroneously claim to follow).

The Vineyard Movement attempts to draw on the eschatology of theologian George Eldon Ladd to construct its own version of the 'now but not yet' concept. According to this view the Kingdom—while not yet fully established—will be fully established **prior** to the return of Christ and not **with** his return. To try to attribute this to Ladd is to take his position to extremes. It is worth considering here that the Icthus Movement similarly takes the ideas of T. Austin Sparks to similar extremes that cannot be correctly attributed to him in their efforts to propound their Manchild/Manifest Sons of God teaching.

The Zombie Of Montanism

Inaugural eschatology teaches that the kingdom is now—but not yet. The kingdom of God arrived with the death and resurrection of Jesus but will be fully realised upon His return, as we read in Daniel chapter 7:22:

> **"Until the Ancient of Days came, and judgement was passed in favour of the saints of the Highest One, and the time arrived when the saints took possession of the kingdom."**

The dominion and the kingdom would be given to saints upon the return of Christ. Dominionism says that this was a reference to the first coming of Christ and not the second and that Satan is now bound, so taking a post-millennial view. From this, they make 'kingdom declarations' that the Kingdom is 'advancing violently'!

This resurrects the errors of Montanism in the early Church. Just as Tertullian became absorbed into it through an over-emphasis on signs and wonders, only to leave himself partially discredited and severely disillusioned, so too many people today are drawn into this error for the same kinds of reasons found in the early Church.

The Church father, Irenaeus, in his epic work *Against All Heresies*, defended the place of signs, wonders, and charismatic gifts, but blasted the lies of Gnosticism and the Gnostic errors of Montanism which said that the Kingdom has fully come in the church in some sense, independent of the return of Christ. Yonggi Cho, the Kansas City Prophets and the proponents of the Toronto Experience, the Montanists were notorious for making false predictions in the Name of the Lord concerning events to take place on specific dates and at specific locations (such as the city Pepuza). They also permitted women to run wild in defiance of Paul's teaching on the role of women. What we have today is nothing more than Montanism and the charismania which Paul wrote against to the Church at Corinth and which have now come to us masquerading as contemporary charismatic Christianity.

The Grand Delusion

The worst example of this is without doubt March for Jesus processions organised by singer Graham Kendrick and Gerald Coates who follow the dominionist view that we will now conquer the whole world for Christ before He comes. They also propagate 'speaking into the heavenlies' the 'things which are not' and bringing in the kingdom. Once again, this 'kingdom proclamation' philosophy (with music as an instrument in spiritual warfare), becomes a major, if not the major, emphasis instead of traditional evangelism. In these 'kingdom pronouncements', they declare to the spiritual world that they are taking dominion and claim to possess a kingdom authority which they claim is currently 'advancing violently'.

As anyone who looks at the crime, divorce, and substance abuse statistics can easily see, there is indeed a kingdom which is advancing violently: New Age and Eastern religions overtake formerly Christian societies in what can only be described as an onslaught. But it is certainly not the kingdom of God.

I again make the point that the organisers of the March for Jesus, Graham Kendrick and Roger Forster of the Ichthus Fellowship, propagate not only a dominionist and replacementist eschatology, but lean towards an annihilationist view of judgement, so that in the gospel according to Kendrick and Forster it is not necessary to repent to keep from going to everlasting hell. Rather one should repent because if you don't you will be annihilated in God's final judgement. This, of course, means that after you die you will simply cease to exist. Coupled to the rise of ecumenical unity with Rome, which is itself in pursuit of ever closer unity with non-Christian religions, and the suggestion that people can escape hell as the punishment for rejecting Christ what we see is an insidious combination which is slowly but surely undermining the Great Commission.

Naturally this does not compare well with the preaching of John Wesley, George Whitfield, D.L. Moody, and the other true preachers of the gospel who were not afraid to confront a fallen world with the reality of an eternal Hell for those who fail to repent and reject the love and forgiveness of Jesus.

Indeed, the same Greek term *Aionion ton aiones*, whose Hebrew equivalent is **Olam Olamim** meaning "forever and ever" is not only used for the torment of those who reject Jesus but is also used for the glory of God, the High Priesthood of Christ, and our salvation. If Hell is not forever and ever, neither can we be sure that Heaven is either.

The March For Jesus

The March for Jesus is right in that it can provide a focus for evangelism, but its theology is wrong and as a result the march is useless in throwing back the powers of evil.

While we all agree on the need for Bible-believing Christians, of all backgrounds, to stand together to preach the gospel, this is clearly not the main theological emphasis of the leaders of the March for Jesus.

Unfortunately, most Christians and evidently most Christian leaders who become involved in these marches, think of them as a uniting of Christians to lift up the Name of Jesus. They do not understand the underlying unbiblical theology of its leaders and organisers. Indeed, given Graham Kendrick's natural talent as a musician, it is probable that many people are drawn into this movement through the music, not understanding the absurd theology which underlies it.

Yes, we can speak into the heavenlies that which the Holy Spirit specifically leads us to, but to say that we are taking dominion over kingdoms and principalities because God has given us a blank cheque to do so is simply ridiculous.

I must stress here that I have no opposition to the concept of Christians marching to proclaim Jesus. On the contrary, I think it a very good thing in itself. What I do take exception to is the unbiblical philosophy of 'spiritual warfare' promoted by its organizers.

I also have no doubt about the sincerity of Roger Forster and Graham Kendrick as brothers in Christ, nor do I question their integrity or intentions. As I was first born again through a cult called The Children of God, I have no doubt that people are saved through Ichthus. At issue are their dangerous and—of this I am absolutely sure—unbiblical beliefs.

The New Age movement introduces the Eastern religions' Mother Earth mentality into western theism. Compare this to Faith Forster's book, *Femininity of God* and you may readily understand my concerns.

During the 1995/96 March For Jesus in Dublin, Southern Ireland, ex-Roman Catholics who had become born again evangelical christians complained about the ecumenical nature of the march. Their complaints centred around the fact that charismatic Catholics were part of the procession carrying banners of the virgin Mary and were condemning their ex-Catholic brothers and sisters for having left Roman Catholicism. Interestingly, similar complaints were voiced in New Zealand when the Mormons participated in a March For Jesus while holding firmly to their belief that Jesus is the half brother of Satan!

Why Didn't The Apostles Do It?

The Greco-Roman world of the Apostles was charged with demonic forces which permeated the cultural, religious, political, and social fabric on almost every level—yet we never see the Apostles trying to exercise 'kingdom dominion' or throw back the powers of darkness using the formula invented by Graham Kendrick or Roger Forster. Why? Because it is useless!

When Paul preached in Athens, we are told plainly that the demons being worshipped there vexed him.[32] Paul's weapon, in addition to prayer, and unlike what we see today in dominionism, was the preaching of the gospel to the unconverted as the way of proclaiming the kingdom and not 'speaking things into the heavenlies'.

A natural companion for this triumphalism is the unbiblical practice of 'binding and loosing' in terms of 'taking cities for Christ'.[33] These things come from a misunderstanding of Matthew chapter 12:29, whose context deals with the meaning of the word *ekbalo*—the casting out of demons, not taking spiritual dominion over a city. Here and in Matthew chapter 16:19, which similarly deals not with taking spiritual dominion over a city, but with Apostolic authority being given to the disciples.

Acts chapter 15 contains a clear example of New Testament 'binding and loosing' where apostolic authority was used to define Christian doctrine. Gentile christians were bound to four commandments based on the Noahic covenant, but loosed from obligation to keep the Mosaic covenant.

The unbiblical man-made strategies practised by dominionism today, seem to actively promote misunderstanding of 'binding and loosing', the hollow proclamations of kingdom authority which is not Biblical, and the use of loud music to 'speak into the heavenly places' were never used by Paul or the Apostles. The Apostles never taught these things and never practised them. Furthermore God never put them in His word for us.

In their encounter with evil today, triumphalists resemble most of all the priests of Baal on Mount Carmel with their big talk, big noise, and big expectations—all of which come to nothing. They bear no resemblance to God's prophet Elijah.

We see the dominionists march and we see that they also control the programme at the Spring Harvest Holiday Camps, and continue as the loudest voice within the Evangelical Alliance. Yet crime, adultery, divorce, substance abuse, homosexuality, the occult, New Age, eastern religions, child abuse and the breakdown of society get progressively worse year on year.

Meanwhile the evangelical church steadily declines in its power to do much about anything, except have another meaningless march or rally run by people whose only gospel, by their own admission, is to tell unsaved people caught up in the maelstrom of wickedness that if they don't repent and accept Jesus, they will be annihilated after death and will not exist anymore; which is precisely what these poor, lost people believe anyway.

Warfare Is Not Child's Play

The principles of warfare in the Old Testament demonstrate principles of spiritual warfare in various respects. It is no coincidence that God would not allow the Hebrews to go to war until they were twenty years of age (Num 1:3).

It is surely a matter of the spiritual maturity of the individual when they are prepared for God's service in the full sense. But even when God called people in their youth, such as Timothy and Jeremiah, they were young men and not children.

All Christians can certainly witness, but scripture teaches that there were demons so powerful that the Apostles could not cast them out. But as Charismania spreads into pentecostalism we see the dangerous and unbiblical practice (adopted by certain elements within the 'King's Kids' organisation and Christian Outreach Centre pentecostal churches) to have children laying hands on drunks and casting demons out of street people.

As usual, the driving force behind this reckless and irresponsible lunacy is the late John Wimber's Vineyard Fellowships, where children are being urged to lay hands on adults.

Verses such as "a child shall lead them"[34] in their context have nothing to do with what is going on today. God used the boy David in order to shame the men of his time because of their terror of Goliath. Things haven't changed much, except that whereas God prepared David to meet Goliath, our children have not been prepared—instead they are being given Saul's armour to wear.[35]

That children have a simple childlike faith is true, that their flesh has not yet been as corrupted by the world as the rest of us is also true—by and large. But to send children into spiritual warfare for which they have not been prepared by God is not only an expression of spiritual cowardice but also recklessness which might well endanger the children.

In full-blown encounters with the demonic realm (bearing in mind much of what Vineyard people call demonic is not) those performing the ministry can themselves become vulnerable to spiritual attack and demonic oppression. Ephesians chapter 6 describes the kinds of armour needed for spiritual warfare. It is enough for children to resist the lures and snares of Satan in their own walk with Jesus, and for this reason God has placed them under the protective covering of their parents. For Christian parents to expose their children to encounters of this kind is to open them to the possibility of the kinds of spiritual and psychological problems that produce 'basket-case' Christians.

There is no New Testament basis for such actions, and they represent a trick of the devil to endanger our children which he is only able to perpetrate because of our ignorance of the Word of God. God warns us that His people can perish for lack of knowledge,[36] and this includes children. Those engaging in such practices may be doing nothing more than putting a millstone around their own children's necks. Once again it is these proven teachers of error who, unwittingly, become the agents of the enemy in bringing this trap into the camp of the Lord solely in order to harm our children.

Restore The Kingdom To Whom?

In His final words Jesus is asked about the restoration of the kingdom to Israel, something He does not deny is to happen at some future date. Yet it is here, and here alone, that the phrase "restoring the kingdom" occurs in scripture. It is found nowhere else and occurs with reference to the restoration of Israel—not to some triumphal Church. It is, therefore, no coincidence that most restoration teaching is not simply replacementist but anti-Israel and anti-Semitic.

I Will Bless Them That Bless Thee

We must remember God's wonderful promise to Abraham that He would bless those who blessed Abraham and curse those who cursed Him. We must also note that this same promise was repeated to Abraham's descendants. After the Spanish Inquisition tortured Jews, the Great Armada of Spain was destroyed by the British and from that point Britannia, not Spain, ruled the waves.

During World War Two the Germans built walls around the Jewish ghettos of Europe and any Jew climbing over the wall to escape was machine gunned to death. Within a few years a wall was built around Berlin, the once glorious German capital, and any German climbing over it was machine-gunned to death. The Berlin Wall remained standing until the last leader of the generation of Germans responsible for the Holocaust and the Third Reich was dead. It was immediately after the death of Rudolf Hess in Spandau Prison that the Berlin Wall came down.

Of all the great empires of the ancient world Rome, Greece, Egypt, Persia and Babylon have largely disappeared from history, but despite centuries of persecution and genocide perpetrated against them the Jews survive in their ancient land in defiance of the odds of history, solely because God keeps His promises.

It is unquestionably the case that given the levels of immorality in the United States, Denmark and Holland (three nations with a strong Christian heritage but which have backslidden into all manner of immorality and idolatry) part of the reason that the judgement of God has not already fallen on them is because they, perhaps above all other nations, have most blessed the Jews.

What About Britain?

When Great Britain abrogated the Balfour Declaration, causing Jews to go to concentration camps instead of to the land

God (and the British Government) had promised them, much of London was levelled in the blitz. If Jews would burn, so would Britons. Then, in trying to block the re-establishment of Israel in order to appease the Arab/Moslem world, Britain invoked divine retribution upon itself. No sooner had Churchill said, "The sun never sets upon the British Empire" than the sun began setting every twenty four hours on a rapidly evaporating empire!

Most people in Britain were shocked when Winston Churchill—having lead Britain through the war, was humiliated by a landslide election defeat as his reward from the British people once the war was over. It is no coincidence that one week earlier Churchill said: "I want nothing more to do with the subject of the Jews returning to Palestine." Within days, the British people whom he had encouraged to a costly victory wanted nothing more to do with him.

Regrettably, Great Britain is no longer great, and Britannia no longer rules the waves, or anything else for that matter. Britain has become little more than an offshore strategic outpost of their American cousins, who chose to bless the Jews after the war. Of late the United Kingdom has become an offshore economic and political colony of continental Europe ruled increasingly, not by its once proud Parliament, but rather by Eurocrats in Brussels and central bankers in its historical enemy Germany.

After Queen Victoria was converted to evangelical Christianity through the ministry of American evangelist D.L. Moody, she supported the cause of Zionism because she knew if Britain blessed Israel, God would bless Britain. Today, a century later, the British Royal Family is the subject of public ridicule and scandal, no longer a bulwark of Christian values, but rather those of the New Age and Freemasonry.[37]

I believe this might not have happened to this once Christian nation had it remained truly Christian and had it continued to bless the Jews instead of cursing them (for a current example: the anti-Israel teaching of evangelical Anglican clergyman, Canon Colin Chapman). Britain's decline has roots in the decline of England's Church.

As a consequence, with even its so-called 'evangelical wing' following such unbiblical teachings, it is no wonder that Islam and Hinduism are growing in Britain while the Church of England—justifiably, but nonetheless tragically—withers on the vine.

In a public debate with an Arab evangelist over the divinity of Christ in London's Albert Hall, the Moslem scholar Ahmed Deedat stated: "Anglicans are better and more honest than other Christians because their bishops admit that Jesus was not God. If your own bishops whom you call your leaders don't even believe that Jesus is God, why should we Moslems believe it?"

While a supposedly evangelical Archbishop of Canterbury sits in Lambeth Palace, the former Secretary of the Evangelical Council of the Church of England, Bishop Gladwin, addressed a special celebration for homosexuals and lesbians in an Anglican service in London's Southwark Cathedral. This same Archbishop addressed an Episcopal congregation consisting of hundreds of sodomites and lesbians in California.

Archbishop George Carey also participated in pagan religious festivals in inter-faith ceremonies. Clearly "I am the Lord thy God, you shall have no other gods before me" no longer means anything to the hierarchy of the Church of England or its supposed 'evangelical' leader. In his book *The Meeting of Waters* George Carey pushes for union with Roman Catholicism despite its many erroneous doctrines.

Rome has as much a different gospel today than it did when the evangelical founders of the Church of England broke with its doctrines after Henry VIII broke with the papacy. Rome still prays to the dead, practises such idolatry as transubstantiation and icon veneration and preaches another gospel which believes that salvation comes through priest-craft and sacraments instead of the completed work of Christ. It also teaches that corrupt popes have been infallible when they spoke *ex cathedra*, and that Mary had no sin and co-redeemed us.

It does not seem to trouble the current evangelical

Archbishop of Canterbury (nor other ecumenical evangelical Anglicans such as Sandy Millar) that Thomas Cranmer—the first evangelical Archbishop of Canterbury, William Tyndale, Bishop John Hooper, Nicholas Ridley, and Hugh Latimer and the other founders of the evangelical branch of the Church of England chose to be burned alive rather than compromise with these same Roman doctrines that no longer seem to cause George Carey any serious problem.

Naïve evangelicals at Holy Trinity Brompton were enraptured when George Carey became Archbishop instead of a liberal. When Satan has evangelicals like George Carey unwittingly in his service he needs no liberals.

Like Nation Like Church

What is happening to the Protestant countries today mirrors what is happening to their churches: Jesus calls Christians to be salt and light. The decline of the Protestant democracies culturally, morally, politically and economically simply reflects the decline of the Christian influence that gave them their success.

As these countries turn from Christ, they turn from the Biblical principles upon which their concepts of government, culture and economy were built. The mammon worship in secular society has as its parallel the mammon worship of a materialistic Church. The decline of the west will not stop unless the decline of the Church in the west is halted. However, instead of following the Biblical agenda of repentance and returning to our first love,[35] we prefer to follow hype, unbiblical doctrines, and the delusion of triumphalism in a doomed attempt to try to pretend that decline is not really happening. Ironically in fact the kinds of things we are doing to supposedly stem the decline only accelerate it.

The Decline Of Western Pentecostalism

The old time fire has burned out in America, Britain and Australia. What happened in the early days of pentecostalism is now a phenomenon of the Third World and not of the West.

My own denomination, the Assemblies of God, was intended to be doctrinally united in theological terms while congregations remained autonomous and self governing. Today the opposite is the reality.

The Assemblies of God is now becoming theologically fragmented but organisationally centralised and hierarchical. Decisions are made behind closed doors and decreed by executives with little, if any, say from the congregations. Meanwhile the traditional pentecostal doctrinal convictions that once cemented the denomination together are being abandoned. Pre-millennialism is being replaced by Post-millennialism, Holiness is being replaced by worldliness and Holy Spirit power is being replaced by expensive hype.

The American Scene

The biggest religious scandals to have rocked American evangelicalism (Jim Bakker and Jimmy Swaggart) involved Assemblies of God ministers. These scandals saw the term 'born again' become a household joke and the gospel seen as a confidence trick in the eyes of a general public who are perishing without it. False teacher Benny Hinn was sued in America after laying his hands on someone in order that the individual might be 'slain in the Spirit'. This unbiblical phenomena bears no resemblance to what is actually written in Revelation when John was in the Spirit and "fell as if slain".[38]

The apostle was terrified—not laughing in hysterics—the same as the experience of the prophet Daniel. In the Bible, when such things happened the proof of what happened was not that they went down on their knees but what happened after they got up. This was clearly seen in the case of the young man from whom Jesus cast out the demons who had previously been throwing himself into the fire. When he was 'slain in the Spirit' the people thought he was dead but Jesus said he was not. Compare this to Benny Hinn's lawsuit (which he settled out of court by payment of an undisclosed sum) where one of the persons supposedly 'slain in the Spirit' fell on top of an old lady and killed her.[39]

Whenever this phenomena happened in Church history (as in the ministries of George Whitfield and John Wesley), it was unsaved people who fell under the power of God and repented, not undiscerning Christians being manipulated by hypnotic induction and behaving like clowns.

Moreover, the only place in the New Testament where those 'slain in the Spirit' fell backwards was when the soldiers came to arrest Jesus—and they were under judgment. It is noteworthy that those who experience God's blessings always seem to fall forward in an attitude of worship and humility.

Presumably as some sort of damage limitation exercise, Benny Hinn proclaimed that he had repented of his materialism and his prosperity teaching. However, subsequent evidence on video shows clearly that in terms of his lifestyle since his 'repentance', the only thing Benny Hinn has repented of is his repentance.[40]

The sad fact is that crisis and division has overtaken most of the major pentecostal denominations of the developed world. Some of the most genuinely respected pentecostal ministers—men such as David Wilkerson—have effectively pulled out of the Assemblies of God. The trend towards fragmentation continues and is becoming a global phenomena. Some leave in discouragement over the failure of the denominational leadership to stand for righteousness. Others have become so drunk on their own pride after becoming involved in triumphalism that instead of seeking to build the kingdom of God, they resort to building their own empires.

The leadership of the Assemblies of God had neither the courage nor the determination to stand up to men like Bakker before it was too late. They were more impressed by the hollow success of 'television christianity' than they were by the demands of a holy God to preserve the standards He set out in His Word. They did nothing until it was too late and now they cannot stop the denomination's disintegration .

Had they acted as they should when they should, the gospel would not have been discredited, the Assemblies of God would not have been seen as a hotbed of scandal and corruption in the eyes of the public, and perhaps the ministries and marriages of men like Bakker, who probably began as true brothers in faith, could have been spared.

The British Scene

The decline of western pentecostalism is nowhere more tragically shown than in Great Britain. Centralisation has become so acute that the executive has embarked on a plan to double the number of Assemblies of God churches in Britain despite the fact that its finances, magazine circulation and conference attendance are at an all time low.

In the final months of the Second World War it was Hitler who halved the size of German divisions in order to have twice as many German flags on the battle map. The Allies sliced through them as if they were nothing. In an apparent imitation of this strategy, the Executive of the British Assemblies of God is doubling the number of churches they have without the new church planting being reflected in numerical, spiritual or financial growth.

Such gimmickry has characterized most of the efforts of British pentecostalism to reverse the downward trend. The biggest evangelistic enterprise ever attempted by British pentecostalism was called the JIM Challenge (Jesus In Me) of 1994. Its aim was to imitate the practices of pentecostal churches in other areas of the world where revival was happening with the view that such a programme would see the same kinds of results in Britain. The goal was for British pentecostalism to grow by a quarter of a million during the Jesus In Me outreach. While we should praise God for every soul saved, the real growth figure after JIM was just a few percent of the initial target figure.[41]

If British pentecostalism was truly dynamic and alive in Christ to grow by a quarter of a million people in a month, (the way pentecostalism is growing in Africa, Latin America and Asia) it wouldn't need a special programme to do it—it would happen anyway as a consequence of its vitality in Christ.

A similar scheme was initiated by Reinhard Bonnke, who thought that by an expensive direct mail evangelistic campaign he would break up the fallow British ground: virtually nothing happened.[42]

Yet still the executives of British pentecostalism gravitate from one scheme to another in a desperate search for a quick-fix solution. They try everything except repentance and returning to the doctrines and dynamism of their own pentecostal roots. The most excessive of these gimmicks by far has been the 'Toronto Laughing Experience' (see Lie 6) heralded by the leadership of the Assemblies of God and the Elim denomination in Great Britain as a powerful move of God. In an article in *Joy* magazine promoting the laughing phenomena, American restorationist Rick Godwin said that 1995 was to be the best year ever for the Assemblies of God in Britain.[43]

The denomination was already in serious financial decline when its mission board, comprised of Ray Belfield, Ray Westcott and John Wildrienne, found themselves liable for the bankruptcy of a hotel complex in Germany. This plunged the Assemblies of God missions programme into a financial crisis with major liabilities. Rather than "the best year ever" as Godwin predicted, the second interim auditors' report declared fourteen out of sixteen executive departments of the UK Assemblies of God financially insolvent. The biggest single loser was their publishing and book selling operation under the direction of Colin Carson—a Rick Godwin protégè—which was forced into insolvency.

Restorationists such as Gerald Coates and Terry Virgo as well as charismatic Anglican leaders such as Sandy Millar of Holy Trinity Brompton and Bishop David Pytches and his successor, Mark Stibbe, all promoted the 'Toronto Experience'. But an even bigger promotion of the Toronto phenomena came from the Elim pentecostal denomination: its leaders Wynne Lewis (now retiring), Gordon Hills, Ian Bilby, and Colin Dye remain involved in the advertising and promotion of Morris Cerullo who, indulging in the sin of simony, was actually selling "Your part of the present Move of God" for a £60 registration fee.

Elim minister David Blake published an article in the movement's magazine in defence of Christians imitating animals. The amount of press that Elim gave the 'Toronto Blessing' and the amount of advertising of Morris Cerullo in its literature is almost unbelievable. There seemed to be a certainty that the laughing phenomena was a harbinger of a revival that would reverse the spiritual and moral landslide that has overtaken Great Britain.

It is of major importance that we note how, when the real power of God falls, large numbers of people are truly saved and the powers of darkness thrown back—as in the book of Acts or any true revival. Since the 'Toronto Blessing' phenomenon first arrived in Britain several years ago, however, let us consider what has happened.

✦ In August 1996 3,300 IVF implantable fertilised human embryos were systematically exterminated under UK law. During this time large meetings were held at Kensington Temple (KT) and other Elim churches. What happened at these meetings? Were the people urged by their leaders to get down on the floor and beg God to stop this genocide? Were they urged to get down on the floor and pray that the scientists about to carry out this slaughter would repent and be saved? Were they urged to get down and beg God to withhold his judgment from a nation that would do such a thing? No! Elim people were urged by their leaders to get down on the floor and laugh in hysterics and bark like dogs because God was doing a great thing. God may have been doing a great thing but please tell us, Colin Dye and Wynne Lewis, which god?

✦ The New Age Nine O'clock Service[44] in Sheffield with its public sex scandals discredited the Church, and was seen on national television news.

✦ A sodomite and lesbian service in Southwark Cathedral was addressed by an evangelical bishop John Gladwin. I know what we have to weep about, but I fail to see what we have to laugh about.

✦ The European Court ruled that the British Government cannot legally block continental pornography being broadcast into Britain.

✦ The revelation almost weekly in the press and on TV of an stream of so-called Christian clergy (mainly paedophile Roman Catholic priests) sexually abusing small children.

✦ The adoption of children by homosexuals and lesbians was legally established and recently taken up by the Church of England Children's Society. The only thing I can think of more sick and perverted than this is the belief that banging on dust-bins lids and imitating ancient pagans is going to stop it.[45] Even the secular press, Mormons, Moslems, and cults realise we are rapidly losing the moral battle for Britain. All this since the advent of the 'Toronto Blessing'.
So, tell me—why were Elim people laughing, Gordon Hills?[46]

✦ The exposure on TV of Morris Cerullo, and all his paraphernalia which consists of everything from his £24 'miracle handkerchiefs' which remove debt, to the death of various people, including an 8 year old child, after Cerullo pronounced them healed (some stopped medical treatment), again discredits the Church.[47]

✦ The publication of the blasphemous New Inclusive Bible.

✦ The draft ratification by the UK Conference of Christians & Jews, headed by a supposedly evangelical archbishop, of a document which condemns missions and evangelism aimed at converting people from other faiths.

✦ Elim's Ian Bilby who led the Toronto Experience in New

Zealand was ousted from the ministry for adultery. Elim's John Foster, who led the rush into TB on the Isle of Man was sent to prison for Paedophilia.

✦ The setting of a national schools curriculum by the Government to teach our children that, while family values are the cornerstone of a moral society, marriage is not essential to those family values.

✦ The Prince of Wales—the future monarch and 'Defender of the Faith'—proclaimed that Britain should look to Islam,[48] a religion which beheads people for becoming Christians, and under whose shariah law, the prince himself would have been decapitated for adultery.

✦ The arrests of Christians for preaching the gospel in Yorkshire. A part of the alleged impetus for this is a political fear of offending the Islamic and homosexual community with the gospel.

✦ The Yorkshire newspaper carried a report that a woman diagnosed as having psychiatric illness went to Ken Gott's 'Toronto experience' church in Sunderland for some months. After obtaining 'the blessing' she went home and murdered her seven-month old baby infant—stabbing it 70 times.

✦ The Anglican Bishop of Jarrow, Rt Rev Alan Smithson proudly proclaimed to the National media that he was giving up reading the Bible for Lent in order to read the Koran in his quest to find 'deeper spiritual truth''.

✦ In order to motivate British pentecostals, the Elim denomination of Britain under the leadership of Wynne Lewis embarked on a campaign to roll out the red carpet for the kinds of prosperity preachers who have already given the gospel a reputation for financial deception in the United States.

Again, American television 'evangelist' Morris Cerullo has engaged in such practices as telling people that if they would mail him faith offerings of £25 ($41), he would send them a handkerchief anointed with oil from Jerusalem, having the power to remove debt.

Poor and uneducated Christians who were already in debt responded to this manipulative fund raising, but needless to say, many complained their debts did not disappear.

Audrey Reynolds went to Cerullo's Mission London in 1992, certain she had been healed of an ankle injury. She felt well and therefore stopped taking all medication including her anti-epilepsy drugs. Six days later she had a fit and drowned in her bath. The Southwark Coroner, Sir Montague Levine, concluded: "It is a tragedy that she went to this meeting and thought she had been cured of everything. Sadly it led to her death." Yet it was Morris Cerullo whom Wynne Lewis and Pastor Colin Dye of Kensington Temple, London, insisted on featuring as the keynote speaker at the 1994 Elim Conference.

Let us now further examine those of Morris Cerullo's activities which have had such serious consequences in Great Britain. We begin with his £25 'Holy Ghost Miracle Handkerchief' to remove debt; his Simony. Then move into a long list of bogus healings debunked by the Christian medical profession and which became a national spectacle. Among these so-called 'miracles' was a four year old child falsely pronounced healed by Cerullo in a large London arena before an audience of thousands. The child died shortly afterward.

Dr. Peter May, a respected evangelical physician and member of the Christian Medical Fellowship and Church of England General Synod, asked for a list of six of Cerullo's best medically documented miracles. When these were eventually forthcoming not one proved to have been a genuine cure. The tragedy of these kinds of deaths is that they were covered by the media, undermining Christian witness to the general public.[49] Dr. May and other physicians went on to warn of the very serious dangers associated with the claimed healing ministry of Morris Cerullo.

The above is not to dispute the authentic biblical gifts of healing[50] or to deny that Jesus can and does still supernaturally heal people today. It is to say that the media and medical professions have been able to convincingly substantiate that Morris Cerullo is a charlatan. The same is also true of Benny Hinn.

Morris Cerullo was found guilty of all four charges brought against him by the UK Advertising Standards Council in relation to improper fundraising. He finally resigned from the Evangelical Alliance in Great Britain.[51] In defence and support of Cerullo, Kensington Temple the flagship church of the Elim denomination led by Colin Dye, also resigned from the Evangelical Alliance—as did more than thirty satellite Elim churches. Colin Dye remained on Cerullo's council. At the time of writing the Serious Fraud Office has launched an investigation into Cerullo's British organisation.

The public can only perceive Elim's ongoing endorsement of Cerullo as an affirmation of what they see as corruption, manipulation and a potentially lethal form of charlatanism. In view of some of Cerullo's teachings (e.g. "You're not looking at Morris Cerullo; you're looking at God. You're looking at Jesus")[52] it is difficult to see Elim as sanctioning anything other than blasphemy and heresy for the foreseeable future.

The Australian Scene

The invitation to Australia by the Assemblies of God of Benny Hinn brought considerable media attention. Hinn has made much publicised statements of repentance of his apostate teaching. Among his doctrines was the bizarre revelation that there were no fewer than nine persons in the Trinity. He also 'revealed' that women gave birth through their ribcages before the fall of man. And ignoring what the bible calls necromancy or communing with the dead, he has visited the graves of Katherine Kuhlman and Aimee Semple McPherson in order to receive some 'anointing' from their remains. Hinn was involved in the abomination of necromancy, claiming visits from the ghost of Katherine Kuhlman.[53]

If someone who believed such outrageous things had indeed repented, one would surely expect him to set aside his ministry for having misled people.

Also, if a leader does not display the biblical requirements for Christian leadership in the terms set out in 1 Timothy are we not entitled to question the individual concerned on his failure to withdraw his books which propagate the selfsame errors and deceptions—if his change of heart is real? Moreover, why has Hinn continued to add more heretical statements to those of which he claims to have supposedly repented?[54]

The Assemblies of God in Italy banned Benny Hinn yet under the leadership of Andrew Evans, the Assemblies of God in Australia imported him (as they did Marilyn Hickey). Eye witness accounts of people coming out of her meetings held at Paradise Assemblies of God in Adelaide include women "uncontrollably drunk in the Spirit" and "vomiting in the Spirit".[55]

The pentecostal leadership in Australia embraced the ministry of Rodney Howard-Browne to a degree not even seen in Great Britain. Browne teaches that he would "rather see Satan manifesting than nothing happening". In his booklet *The Coming Revival* he openly states that if Satan or the flesh manifests, just praise God for it because "at least something is happening". Rodney Howard-Browne, who received his 'Laughing Spirit' from Kenneth Copeland, teaches that it is wrong to suppress the flesh because someone may also suppress the Holy Spirit.[56] The Word of God, however, commands Christians to crucify the flesh so that what is truly of the Spirit can blossom.

In an outlandish display with Kenneth Copeland, Howard-Browne and Mike Evans prophesied that the 'Laughing Revival' was in fact the great end times revival. Later it was picked up by Randy Clark and John Arnott[57] and became known as the 'Toronto Experience'.

In his book *Catch the Fire* Guy Chevreau[58] claims the 'Laughing Experience' is a common link with the great British revivals. He maintains that the 'Laughing Phenomenon' was a feature of these revivals. However in Daniel Roland's book[59] we see that George Roland and George Whitfield **stopped** the hysterics (just as did John Wesley), believing them 'devilish' (demonic) and disrupting of the real move of God.

Andrew Evans, who had been General Superintendent of the Australian Assemblies of God, was quick to import the teachings of Rodney Howard-Browne into Australia after a visit to Holy Trinity Brompton in London. The 'laughing phenomenon' was also propagated by Australian pentecostals such as Kevin Connor and Phil Pringle. The executive of the Australian Assemblies of God actively opposed anyone who did not accept the phenomenon as an authentic move of God. Among those who opposed it were: Philip Powell, the former General Secretary of the Assemblies of God, Aeron Morgan, former President of Commonwealth Bible College; and Dr. Barry Chant, the pentecostal academic and Principal of Mount Tabor College.

The tragedy of the situation is that the level of biblical knowledge among most of the Australian pentecostal leadership is possibly below that of Great Britain.

Executive member Alun Davies, who presides over a Bible College in Melbourne teaches that 'legion' was the name of the demoniac and not of the demons who possessed him as we read in Mark chapter 5. Davies also lectured students on New Age shamanistic practices—such as visualisation—thus influencing the next generation of pentecostal ministers with eastern mysticism.

After David Yonggi Cho 'prophesied' in the Name of the Lord that the flagship Assemblies of God Church in Australia known as 'Paradise' in Adelaide would grow to over 10,000 members[60] there seemed to be a great need to sweep this false prophecy under the carpet and find an alternative to put their hope in. When the 'Toronto Blessing' failed to deliver the promised revival, Andrew Evans publicly admitted that it didn't last. However, he offered no apologies to the Sure Hope anti-cult ministry, which had been derided for warning that TB would not bring revival. Then, after Toronto had blown itself out, the next gimmick to sway people's attention away from the failed 'phenomenon' arrived in the form of Benny Hinn's 1997 campaign.

Frankly, the degree of scandal, heresy, and hypocrisy in the Australian Assemblies of God is frightening. The shameful spectacle of the executive leadership suing other Christians in court—at the expense of honest believers who paid their tithes and offerings—was widely reported in the secular media to the public detriment of the reputation of pentecostalism and its Christian testimony. It is a great pity that the executive insisted on such a course of action instead of resolving their differences scripturally.

Predictably, the conference was both badly attended and a financial disaster. However this has not stopped the organisers from attempting to feature Benny Hinn at Elim conferences even after the revelations documented above. Hinn asserted that those who challenge him would see their children destroyed.[61]

Real Growth Or Transfer Growth?

What the leaders of British pentecostalism—who are apparently intent on importing such trickery into their congregations—refuse to come to terms with, is that in the United States, where most prosperity preachers originate, it is not they or their churches which see the most people saved.

In America, it is the traditional pentecostalism of David Wilkerson, Nicky Cruz, and Sonny Arguinzoni that sees the most drug addicts, alcoholics, homosexuals, prostitutes and street people saved. It is these who have the most impact on sin. The reason that prosperity preachers seem to have large churches is because they suck people from other churches who wish to have their ears tickled with 'name it and claim it' doctrines.

If You Can't Beat Them, Join Them?

In the meantime British pentecostalism has resorted to restorationism to prop up its ailing fortunes. The Assemblies of God alone lost thousands of members ten years ago to the restorationist house church movement. Now the same Kingdom Now theology and hierarchical systems of Church government which were the hallmarks of the house churches are being rapidly integrated into British pentecostalism.

The Elim denomination in Britain has abandoned its pre-millennial statement of faith in deference to the growth of dominionist influence within Elim, and in New Zealand it was Elim (as we shall see later)—which helped to import house church leader Gerald Coates and did the most to publicly amplify his false prophecies of an earthquake that never happened. When Coates told local leaders such as Hudson, Salisbury and Elim's Ian Bilby that he believed the Lord spoke to him powerfully about a coming devastating earthquake for a specific April date, Salisbury was sceptical but Bilby believed it as a direct revelation. Being on the Pacific rim of the earthquake belt seismologists report minor tremors in New Zealand on a regular basis and there was no scientific evidence to suggest an imminent earthquake. Not surprisingly, nothing happened. Nonetheless under Bilby's leadership New Zealand saw Elim churches taking survival courses and trying to warn the country of a non-existent disaster. The public fall-out which resulted could have been headlined as 'Born-Again earthquake hoax'.[62]

Saddest of all is that due to the decline in biblical knowledge among most of the younger generation of pentecostal ministers and the very low biblical and academic standards of most pentecostal Bible colleges, even in America, but more so in Australia, South Africa and Great Britain, there is little awareness that Kingdom Now theology is simply about the repackaging of the old 'Manchild' Manifest Sons of God heresy associated with Rushdooney, and which pentecostalism unanimously rejected as heresy a generation ago.[63]

The Decline Of American Black Pentecostalism

Church growth, particularly among pentecostals in America it is mostly among Roman Catholics, Jews, Asians, Hispanics and others. Traditional Protestant pentecostalism long ago began to fizzle out, as has traditional pentecostalism, and the unique pentecostal/Baptist traditions. The crime rate, single parent families and drug abuse found in black America are witness that the gains made by the Civil Rights Movement in the 1950s and 1960s amount to very little in reversing the plight of black America.

It is a sobering thought that in America, thirty years after the civil rights movement won its first major victories, the average black American is no better off than he was then and is in many ways worse off. Beneath the socio-economic explanations for this state of affairs are spiritual factors which stem not only from the racism of white America, but also from the falling away of many young black Americans from the faith of their fathers. The same faith which underlined their fathers' victory in the fight for freedom from slavery and won legislation against anti-black discrimination.

The abolitionist movement that saw the end of slavery in England and America grew directly from the influences of evangelical Christianity: John Wesley, William Wilberforce and John Newton in Britain and the north American revivalists in pre-civil war America.

The civil rights movements of twentieth century America and the non-violent expressions of the anti-apartheid movement in South Africa both rose from the influences of Christianity in the black communities of those nations.

Black America must return to the gospel. The Lord Jesus favours the poor and the oppressed and by turning to Jesus black people found the sense of moral righteousness and self worth that came from knowing a Saviour who found them so important that He died for their sins.

The fact that so much of black America has turned from Christ to 'crack' accounts for more of the black dilemma than all the other causes of that predicament put together. Even if all white Americans repented of their racism, it would not alter the self-destructive tendencies that black America perpetrates against itself by the single act of having turned from the gospel, the same gospel that their grandparents and great grandparents held so precious as the centre of their lives. It is only Jesus who has ever done black people any good and it is only Jesus who ever will do black people any good now. No programme, no social policy, no economic plan, will ever change the plight of black America if black America does not return to Jesus.

Heretical black money preachers such as Creflo Dollar, Miles Munroe and Fredrick Price have done as much damage as their white counterparts. The moral vacuum in black society is being filled by militant Islam. The Nation of Islam (whose founder Elijah B. Muhammed taught that his mentor Wallis Farad was a divine being) is regarded as being as racist as the Ku Klux Klan.

The Nation of Islam's message sees Christianity as a white man's religion which has been used to enslave blacks. Their message conveniently omits the fact that the first countries to abolish slavery were Christian but the last ones to retain it are Moslem. Eldridge Cleaver claimed to have seen black slaves in Algeria and the slavery of blacks is still practised in violation of international human rights agreements in such Moslem nations as Sudan.

The civil and human rights abuses that have been perpetrated against blacks by non-white governments in black African countries are far worse than even the darkest days of apartheid. While I make no defence of any racist or socially unjust practice anywhere, poor blacks in the housing projects of America and Britain are much better off than those in the slums and villages of Angola, Zaire and the Ivory Coast. Standards of living and human rights abuses in the Central African Republic, Burundi, Rwanda, Ethiopia and Nigeria make the plight of western blacks appear relatively mild. The moral outrages and atrocities in post colonial Africa have been unspeakable. Yet in areas of strong evangelical growth like Ghana and Kenya there is, at least in relative terms, a positive impact from the Christian influence in terms of both standards of living and human rights.

Islamic Africa has offered the black man more of the same old oppression. Christianity has been the faith of black progress and Islam the faith of black regression.

Just as dangerous as the Nation of Islam is Rastafarianism.

According to the ideas of their late teacher, Markus Garvey, it is claimed that blacks in America and Europe are in the Babylonian captivity and that Haile Selassie (the late Ethiopian autocrat) was Jesus Christ. They believe this despite the fact that he made no such claim about himself and that his family maintain that he found Rastifarianism to be incompatible with his own beliefs in the Ethiopian Orthodox church (a version of African Coptic Christianity).

Most Rastafarians who 'came home' to Ethiopia as their promised land later returned to the housing estates of New York, the council estates of London and the slums of Kingston, Jamaica, preferring life in the "captivity of Babylon" to the delusion of life in what Rastifarianism taught was their homeland. Put bluntly, life was simply better in the injustice of the white man's world than in the far worse injustice of the black man's world.

I do not mean this in any racist sense, but I again assert that common sense shows that faith in Jesus has always been the only way forward for the black man—as for every human being.

As Protestant Christianity declines in America and Europe, Christianity is emerging as an explosive force across the sub-Sahara and into central and southern Africa. Very soon the white man will be the pagan and the black man the missionary whose task it will be to bring the Gospel to him—as was illustrated by the Lambeth conference of bishops in 1998 over the issue of homosexuality.

We Can't Import Revival

We should thank God for the large Hispanic, Asian and West Indian churches of the United States. However, America cannot rely on what God is doing in other countries to have sufficient overspill effect to reverse the downward spiral of American evangelical Christianity.

Much capital is made in Great Britain of the country's largest church—Kensington Temple. The problem with Kensington Temple is that it is not even English. It is an Afro-Caribbean church made up of immigrants and foreign students and their families who have come to Britain from poorer countries in the British Commonwealth where God *is* working and where revivals *are* happening. Virtually the only white people in Kensington Temple are those on the platform.

The fact remains that, try as we may, we cannot import revival. Hype is not anointing, prosperity preaching does not save souls, and Kingdom Now theology will not bring the kingdom now. It will only bring disillusionment and failure.

Touch Not My Anointed?

The confidence trick perpetrated by the prosperity and Kingdom Now preachers happens because they are mavericks, accountable to no one but themselves. They are neither attached to the body, nor under the head. Yet they call themselves 'anointed' and say that we, the true body, must not criticise them, even when they teach that which which flagrantly contradict the revealed Word of God. This is also their cry even when they engage in immoral practices—although the Word of God says that those who do such things will never see God.

It is indeed true that King David would not touch Saul,[64] because Saul was God's anointed. However, this never prevented David and Samuel from telling the truth about Saul. They spoke of how corrupt he had become, how backslidden was his regime and how treacherous were his deeds.[65]

"Touch not God's anointed" does not mean that the Church should remain silent in the face of the corruption of God's Word.

If the prophets of Israel had misinterpreted "touch not my anointed" the way the followers of Benny Hinn, Rick Godwin and the late John Wimber do today, there would have been no Israel. And if the apostles had misinterpreted it in this way there would be no Church.

The term 'Christ' comes from the Hebrew *Ha Moshioch* meaning *"the* anointed one". It is Jesus alone who is God's anointed. As we read in Acts chapter 2:33-36, it is Jesus who has the Holy Spirit poured out on Him. Note how the text draws on the imagery of Psalm 133.

> Behold, how good and how pleasant it is
> For brothers to dwell together in unity!
> It is like the precious oil upon the head
> Coming down upon the beard,
> Even Aaron's beard,
> Coming down upon the edge of his robes.
> It is like the dew of Hermon,
> Coming down upon the mountains of Zion;
> For there the Lord commanded the blessing—life forever.

This text describes anointing by first talking about unity. The picture is that of Aaron the high priest, whom the epistle of Hebrews tells us is a type of Jesus. The oil is poured out upon Aaron's head and then from his head it runs down over the rest of his body.

So on the day of Pentecost, the Holy Spirit was poured out on Jesus. It is He who is the anointed High Priest. We are the members of His body, some of us arms, some eyes, others feet.[66] In order to be anointed we must be united to the rest of His body and under His headship, for there is none anointed but Him. This is what Messiah—the Christ—means. It is He therefore and only He whom we are not to touch.[67]

A Kingdom Of Power?

We live in a world obsessed by the quest for power. Whether it be more power in a car engine or more computer power, the quest for power is ongoing. That quest has now also come into the Church, but we seem to have a different definition of power to the one in scripture.

It is entirely biblical to associate power with anointing. But what kind of power? The apostle Paul demonstrated tremendous power in miracles, signs, wonders and healings, but never said the **proof** of his anointing was his power. Rather he said the proof of his anointing was that he bore the marks of Christ on his body.[68]

That is to say, it was his crucified life that proved his anointing, not his power to do signs and wonders.

Paul saw himself as "an imitator of Jesus"[69] and Jesus was anointed for burial before he was anointed for power and dominion.[70] While much is spoken of the anointing and power claimed by prosperity preachers and dominionists today—the two are natural bedfellows—the one thing we do **not** see when we look at them or their ministries are the signs of crucified lives.

That is why, despite all their talk of power, there simply isn't any. Yes, it is possible that God may use them for His own glory and for the good of others in certain situations but again, as Jesus said, this proves nothing about the minister or the ministry; it only proves something about Jesus.[71]

We hear the 'power ministries' talking about power, but again it is the traditional churches displaying old time pentecostal power (such as the robust ministries of David Wilkerson and Chuck Smith in the United States) where there is real power and—as we saw earlier—phenomenal growth among even the most sin-ridden in society.

Not only do the so called 'power ministries' commonly associated with dominionism and, frequently, prosperity preaching prove themselves unable to bring very large numbers to salvation, but their money preaching has the opposite effect, driving the unsaved away. Most of their growth is transfer growth of people being lured from other churches with hype that titillates the ears and showmanship that pleases the eyes, but has no power to see sin thrown back.

Similarly, triumphalists sing that they are "building a kingdom of power not of words". Yet those countries in which these choruses are sung most are the very ones where the Church is failing most. They sing, proclaiming that they have power to take dominion, and claim the kingdom is being taken by them forcefully while the statistics say otherwise. In Britain it is only the minority communities who are responding to the gospel; again the 'overspill' effect from the developing world. The indigenous Church falters as the population wanders further and further from its Christian heritage.

Restorationism and triumphalism are not new in Britain. They go back to the very beginning of the charismatic movement. The house church movement that first embraced them is well over a quarter of a century old. However right up to this present time, we have heard their words but have not seen their power.

Despite the empty and mainly unscriptural rhetoric of the marches and the music, and the assertive tone of dominionist claims to have power—we see that they do not have any power. Real power is the *Dunamis* that Jesus promised in His final words. It is first of all actual power and not hype, and it is the result of anointing and not the proof of it. It is the power of the Holy Spirit and therefore will agree with the words the Holy Spirit inspired to be written in scripture. It will not be contrary to them. It is the Bible-based power which Wesley and Spurgeon demonstrated, and not the unbiblical hype we call 'power' today.

Words are useless unless they are the result of power. The Docklands fiasco in 1990 to which Roger Forster and Graham Kendrick were party, had words from John Wimber, Paul Cain and Mike Bickle, but no power. Their promised revival never materialized because it was only words. Talk is cheap. Where is the power? Until we go back to the final words of Jesus we will never find it.

Decline Of The Anglican Charismatic Movement

There is no better example of how the charismatic renewal has affected western Christianity than that shown today by the Church of England. Today the Church of England is generally regarded as something of a joke, even by many Anglicans. It is little more than a spiritually, morally, and theologically fragmented institution held together by buildings, property and lame tradition that most people no longer care about.

Even its own Archbishop of Canterbury called it "nothing but a toothless old woman muttering in the corner"[72] (despite the fact that it is he and others like him who help to keep it that way), while others perceive it as an intoxicated 'has been' too detached from reality to realize that it is like a drunkard choking to death on his own vomit.

Given its spiritual and doctrinal fragmentation, and since about the only thing holding English Anglicanism together today is money, it is no coincidence that this church is under severe financial judgement of God. If it is money that holds the Church of England together instead of the truth of God's Word, it is no wonder that it is in the area of money that the Church of England is plainly experiencing the effect of God's judgement.

This follows not only its refusal to repent, but the cowardice and compromise of so many of its evangelical members. They do not stand up and fight the way that Latimer, Hooper, Ridley, Wilberforce, Shaftsbury, and Ryle did when the Church of England still had something worth fighting for.

I do not believe God will intervene to prevent the continued collapse of the Church of England unless there is true repentance. Neither do I believe there will be such a repentance, unless there is first repentance by the present Archbishop of Canterbury for his betrayal of the cause of Jewish evangelism, followed by a purge of the anti-Zionism adopted by its liberal wing, and also many who call themselves evangelicals. We must, of course, remember that in Anglican terms, evangelical does not necessarily mean 'born-again', but simply means 'not Catholic' and 'not liberal'.

Can Evangelicals Save The Church Of England?

There is a growing view among evangelicals in the west that Anglicanism can be 'turned around for Christ' because evangelicals are in the ascendancy while Anglo-Catholic and liberal influences are supposedly in decline. A majority of candidates for the Anglican ministry would claim to be charismatic/evangelicals while attendance in non-evangelical Anglican Churches is at an all-time low. Is this view valid?

What About The Alpha Courses?

Alpha courses originate from Holy Trinity Brompton and are under the direction of Sandy Millar's curate Nicky Gumbel. The Alpha courses are fundamentally unscriptural in that they are Pneumo-centric as opposed to Christo-centric.[73] In other words they are focused on the supposed ministry of the Holy Spirit. In John chapters 14-16. Jesus makes clear that the work and ministry of the Holy Spirit is always to lead people to Jesus and that the Holy Spirit never points people to Himself. Conversely the Baal worship of the Old Testament teaches us that when the true God is worshipped in the wrong way, then an alien spirit coming in His Name will counterfeit Him making His people forget His name.

In exactly the same way the Name of Jesus is forgotten in the 'Holy Spirit' centered worship we see today. Note that Baal is the Hebrew term for husband and Master. Jehovah was to be Israel's Baal and was to be worshipped on one high place which was specified as "Mount Zion on the sides of the North". Baal worship of the Canaanite's demon—which claimed to be the Baal of Heaven—did not **begin** with idolatry but by worshipping the true God in the wrong way in a manner not in accordance with scripture. They began worshipping the true God on high places not ordained by scripture and ended worshipping a false god whom they confused with the true God. This is the demonic aspect which underlies much of what we see in Toronto and Pensacola. Our faith is based on no one other than Jesus to whom the Holy Spirit points exclusively.

Unlike at Holy Trinity Brompton or in Benny Hinn's book *Good Morning Holy Spirit*, the Holy Spirit is never prayed to in the Bible except when he is worshipped in the context of the Tri-unity of the Godhead. Such choruses as 'Come Holy Spirit, let your fire fall' have absolutely no biblical basis and are in fact totally alien to biblical Christianity. Moreover Toronto/Pensacola phenomena actually go the way of the Jehovah Witness cult in reducing the Holy Spirit to an inanimate 'it'. So when we hear people saying "my Pastor went to Pensacola to get 'it' and bring 'it' back", they are treading on dangerous ground because the Holy Spirit is not an it, He is "He". This is of course why we pray to the Father in the Name of the Son through the Spirit. He is a distinct person in His own right.

Alpha's director, Nicky Gumbel, admits that Alpha is but a door into the Toronto Experience.[74] A study carried out in England of approximately 200 persons who supposedly came to faith through the Alpha course revealed that very few, if any, could explain the basics of the gospel in terms of repentance, justification and atonement.[75] This is entirely understandable when we realise that Alpha comes from Holy Trinity Brompton, the Bedlam of British Charismania, which embraced the false prophetic predictions of revival given by John Wimber and the so called Kansas City Prophets. It has also embraced every other trend that has come down the road. The only thing that 'Toronto Fire' has done for the Church of England is to leave it in a worse state than it was in before the 'fire' fell. With homosexuals and lesbians meeting in cathedrals, a bishop giving up reading the Bible for Lent in order to read the Koran, and the Prince of Wales—the future Defender of the Faith—saying that Christian Britain should look to Islam (a religion which executes people for becoming Christians) it is not surprising that charismatic Anglicans can roll on the floor and laugh all they want while their nation and its Christian heritage is plunged deeper into the cesspit of post Christian immorality. Not only will Alpha not solve the problem—it will help deepen it.

True evangelism cannot be separated from discipleship. Jesus never commanded that we make converts, rather He told us to make disciples. Alpha courses can never make disciples according to any biblical model because Alpha courses are not biblical.

The North-South Divide

As Anglicanism declines in Great Britain and most of the western world, it is growing in Roman Catholic countries, in Africa and in Asia. With the notable exception of Desmond Tutu, nearly every African bishop is an evangelical. While the charismatic leadership of Anglicanism in Britain is ecumenical in its orientation, large numbers of ex-Roman Catholics who have become Anglicans in Iberia and in South America reject Roman Catholicism, seeing it as something out of which they were saved.

While Anglican clergy in Britain will argue for New Age and interfaith beliefs being integrated into Anglicanism, Anglicans face persecution in Nigeria at the hands of Moslems and also from the Roman Catholic church. The dynamic leadership and courageous faith seen in 17th and 18th century Anglicanism is alive and well in the developing world—while compromise and even cowardice are the order of the day in the West.

Victory By Default?

High church Anglo-Catholicism is dying under the weight of its own rituals, and has no place to go except back to 'Mother Rome'. It is also true that liberal Anglicanism is dying under the weight of its irrelevance. Its chief expositor, Don Cupitt, admits that there is no longer a choice except between what he calls 'fundamentalism' and 'post modernism' (the belief that there can be no absolute meaning given to anything). Ancient documents such as the Dead Sea Scrolls demonstrate the fallacy of the 'higher critical' pre-supposition that the Bible texts 'evolved'. The rise of evangelical critical scholarship pioneered by F.F.Bruce demonstrated convincingly that the writers of the New Testament had a familiarity with first century Jewish Palestine, and could not have been the products of second or third century redactors interpolating texts at a later point.[76] Even Bishop J.A. Robinson, said that John's Gospel had to be written much earlier than he originally believed and was not an invention or embellishment of the Church at a much later time in Christian history. He further demonstrated the likelihood that the whole New Testament had been completed before the fall of Jerusalem in AD70.[77]

The traditional Darwinian evolutionary hypothesis on whose philosophy much so-called critical scholarship was based has long since passed away. Hence, their philosophical base is outdated.

Thus, higher criticism is dead because its philosophical base is dead. Its philosophical basis is dead because its scientific base is dead (except in the minds of non-scientists).

St. Paul predicted the emergence of liberal theology as holding "a form of religion but denying the power therein."[78] Being devoid of any actual spiritual content, liberal churches leave a vacuum in the hearts of those who attend them which they are unable to fill with social and political gospels. Man is a created being made in the image of God and will naturally tend to seek Him, thus such people will either come into evangelical expressions of christianity, or gravitate towards the influences of the New Age movement. This is clearly seen in much of Anglicanism, with St James Piccadilly in London acknowledged as the flagship of the New Age church of England, and sadly, more recently the Rev Tony Higton erstwhile rector of Hawkwell in Essex and now president of CMJ.

As a result, liberal churches have no product to 'market' and so fare very badly among the wide variety of choices of spiritual meaning and direction in the western world today.

But the question is: "as the liberal and Anglo-Catholic branches of Anglicanism commit suicide, will the evangelicals and charismatics automatically prevail as a result?"

History Gives The Answer

During the Protestant Reformation, Lutheran and Reformed churches could claim to have been founded by men such as Luther, Calvin, and Zwingli, who for all their faults were primarily motivated by a desire to reform the church along biblical lines. The Church of England can make no such claim. By its own admission, it was born out of the whoring of a corrupt king who murdered over 70,000 of his own subjects. He opposed the Reformation, and received the title Defender of the Faith from the Pope for his services. Thus, Anglicans can claim no integrity in the **institutional** origins of their church. It was the result of the political considerations of a womanising monarch. Their church sprang essentially from the womb of political corruption.

None the less the first time evangelicals began their ascent as a majority influence within the Church of England was during the Reformation. On one side they faced nominal Protestants who only converted in order to acquiesce to the demands of King Henry the Eighth so that they might safeguard their own livelihoods. While on the opposite side were those whose true loyalties remained with the Papacy.

During the reign of Bloody Mary, the nominal Protestants returned to Rome and joined the Catholics who had, at least in spirit, never left it. The evangelicals within the Church of England who genuinely tried to reform it along the lines of continental Protestantism were either forced into exile or were martyred, as was the case with Ridley, Latimer, Cranmer, and Hooper. So the Catholics became more Catholic, the nominal Protestants became more nominal and the evangelicals were forced out.

In the aftermath of the exile, the Puritans became the evangelical movement within Anglicanism and were soon in the ascendant. Historically the outcome of the struggle was bound up with the English Civil War. The Puritans were faced on the one hand by nominal Protestants known as Latitudinarians who had become liberal in their theology and on the other by Anglo-Catholics. Once again, the evangelicals were forced out.

Early Methodism began as a charismatic renewal led from within the Church of England by the Wesleys and George Whitfield. The Methodists were faced by 'anti-enthusiast' nominal Protestants on one side and on the other by Anglo-Catholics who asserted episcopacy and Catholic-style hierarchy against them. Once again, in the 18th century as in the 17th and 16th centuries, the evangelicals were on the rise but were ultimately forced out.

The 19th century saw the Evangelical Movement of William Wilberforce and the Earl of Shaftsbury. For the fourth time evangelicals were in the process of becoming the clear majority within the Church of England. And so once again the Catholics became more Catholic—with the rise of the Oxford and Tractarian movements led by John Henry Newman and Dr. Pusey—while German rationalism made its first inroads into theology at Oxford and Cambridge. Once again, the liberals became more liberal. As a result, the Plymouth Brethren made an exodus as yet again the evangelicals were forced out.

Thus the present trend in Anglicanism is not the first time that evangelicals have been in the ascendancy in England and looking as if they might take over as the major influence within the church. Our overview of Anglican history reveals that it is something that happens once every century or so. At the present time, the liberals are again becoming more liberal (with the resurrection and virgin birth being openly denied by bishops), while Anglo-Catholics grow more Catholic, as we hear all too clearly in the calls of Archbishops Runcie and Carey that Anglicanism should do all in its power to go back to Rome.

Charismatic evangelicals within the Church of England deceive themselves when they think that what is happening now is in any way unique in Anglican history or that its results will be any different. The time will come when, like the Puritans, the Methodists and the Brethren, they will face the choice of coming out or compromising. The present evidence gives every suggestion that the trend towards compromise will win the day. Perhaps nothing exemplifies this more than the behaviour of George Carey as an evangelical Archbishop of Canterbury: withdrawal of his patronage of Jewish evangelism; his refusal to stop the worship of demons in Anglican Churches in the form of 'interfaith worship'; and his wish to pander to the Papacy.[79]

The Real Question

Anglican history has not been all bad! There have been mighty men and women of God in it as there have been in other churches and denominations. And there have been sincere Christians who tried to be both loyal to the Church of England and to Christ and the teachings of His Word.

But we must ask a question. If men such as William Tyndale, John Hooper, the Puritan Fathers, John Wesley, George Whitfield, the Earl of Shaftsbury, William Wilberforce and J.C. Ryle were unable to change the Church of England from within—and were unable to despite the fact that they stood firmly on the Word of God—why should charismatics in today's Church of England think that they will be able to change it from within, when both they and their leaders do not appear to have even the most elementary knowledge of the Word of God when compared to their forefathers?

What Makes This Time Different?

There are some ways in which this particular time does appear to be different to the many other times when evangelicals appeared to be on the ascendancy in the Church of England and to have some prospect of 'winning it back for Christ'.

The first difference is that the contemporary church's spiritual and moral condition is one of growing depravity. In the past there has not been the atheism, the homosexuality amongst lay and clergy, the same sex marriages, and the interfaith worship of foreign gods that exists today. Neither has there ever been the flagrant denial of fundamental Christian truths, such as the resurrection and virgin birth, let alone such widespread defence of those who advocate these heretical positions by the majority of bishops and leaders.[80] The Puritans, the Wesleys, and the Brethren were up against all manner of heresy and wickedness within the Church of England but nothing even remotely approaching the wholesale apostasy which exists today.

The second difference is that in times past, the evangelical movements within the Church of England were Bible-based. Today, in stark contrast, the charismatic movement within the Church of England is largely experience-based. Few of its followers, or for that matter, even its leaders, have any more than a superficial grasp of the doctrinal truths of scripture. They prefer emotion, false prophecies (which never happen), and unbiblical fads to the authority of the Word of God. Modern charismatic Anglicans do not have the grounding in scripture that the evangelical movements within the Church of England have had in the past. Neither do they have the conviction or the power. All they have is rhetoric and hype.

In past centuries, the leaders of the evangelical movements within the Church of England were Bible-based men of uncompromising courage who stood against Rome, liberalism, and corruption, even at the expense of their own lives. Today's charismatic leaders are men whose practices are clearly not Bible-based, and the essence of whose ecumenical philosophy is compromise—at the expense of the true evangelical faith itself.

They Pay The Piper, But Don't Call The Tune

Because charismatic and evangelical churches are larger than liberal and Anglo-Catholic ones, and because born again Christians contribute more generously to the church, evangelical and charismatic Anglicans find themselves in a dilemma.

Through the diocesan system, larger churches with higher revenues make proportionally larger payments into a central fund through their diocesan offices. This money is then used to subsidise the smaller, mainly liberal and Anglo-Catholic Churches and to help pay the salaries of liberal, Anglo-Catholic and homosexual clergy.

Hence with what they assume to be their tithes and offerings given to God, ordinary Anglicans are financing the propagation and preservation of sacramentalism, homosexuality and unbelief in their church. So, far from fighting unbelief, homosexuality, and New Age religion in the Church of England, the born again Christians of Anglicanism are picking up the bill for it.

While certain individuals such as Tony Higton in the past and possibly David Samuels have had the guts to face up to this outrageous reality, most charismatic and evangelical Anglicans either don't know, don't care, or lack the courage of their convictions to do anything about it.

So instead, at Holy Trinity Brompton, and St Andrew's Chorleywood, they sing their triumphalist choruses, laugh hysterically during their meetings, stake their hopes on prophecies that do not come true, wink the eye at heresy, choose man made doctrines over the Word of God, and then financially underwrite the cost of the wholesale spiritual, theological and moral destruction of their church and nation.

Slave Of Tradition Or Slave Of Christ?

In Anglicanism today evangelicals and charismatics come under the leadership of bishops who are—in the West at least—more frequently than not, liberals or Anglo-Catholics.

In binding themselves to a system of Church government whose legal head is a monarch, (and the future monarch Prince Charles, a New Ager)[81], and whose episcopal model of leadership follows the Ignatian mono-episcopacy of Roman Catholicism and Eastern Orthodoxy rather than New Testament models of plural leadership, evangelicals and charismatics in the Church of England cannot possibly change it from within any more than the Puritans or the Wesleys were able to.

Evangelicals and charismatics find themselves under the authority of unbelieving bishops. Yet even believing bishops routinely compromise with the system, pledging loyalty to the monarch as the head of matters temporal and spiritual in their enthronements as bishops. With the odd exception they would not usually dare to stand up against the liberalism and unbelief in the diocese over which they preside.

Moreover, although the Thirty Nine Articles of The Church of England are mainly Bible-based, most Anglicans do not believe them. Additionally, even evangelicals cannot easily refuse to baptise babies bearing in mind that the old Book of Common Prayer, still used in much of Anglicanism today, heretically pronounces sprinkled babies as 'born again'. They must also invent ways to give meaning to the ritualistic practices of confirmation which Anglicanism took from Roman Catholicism.

This rite has two origins. One is to confirm the faith that was ineffectually 'accepted' by proxy in infant baptism, and the other to confer baptism of the Holy Spirit. Yet most Anglicans confirmed are never born again to begin with and are certainly not baptised in the Holy Spirit at their confirmation. There is usually no real meaning, only dead ritual and tradition orchestrated by a bishop dressed in the robes of Babylonian priestcraft borrowed from the wardrobe of Rome.

Few evangelical Anglicans, Lutherans, or others who have had the charismatic renewal would dare to refuse to baptise a baby—even those who will admit that it is unscriptural. Few would also refuse to confirm the faith of those who actually don't have any. A confirmation ceremony was broadcast on television in England where a bishop was laying hands on practising homosexuals in the sacramental rite of confirmation. A week later that same bishop laid hands on born again Anglicans in an evangelical parish and performed the same ceremony.

Here lies the heart of the problem: since the Elizabethan Settlement centuries ago, Anglicanism has been a futile exercise in holding together a tottering house of cards with true believers and nominal Christians under the same roof with a leadership who falsely claim to share the same faith. As we noted earlier the roots of this are in the Judaisation of the church, Erastianism, and the failure of the Reformers to fully reform. The Greek definition of Church (*Ecclesia*) means an assembly of those who are called **out of the world**, not a fellowship of those called together with those whose world it is.

If there is one lesson an objective analysis of Anglican history teaches, it is that even the most gullible of evangelical or charismatic Anglicans would have to concede, if they are to be honest, that "you cannot put new wine in old wineskins." If there is a hope for the Church of England, it is not to be found in England, but thousands of miles away in the developing world, provided they have the good sense to go their own way in accordance with scripture, and refuse to inherit the defective genes of their congenitally ill English mother.

The Word of the Lord to charismatic and evangelical Anglicans could not be more clear, yet few will hear it, because few want to hear it. Nonetheless that word remains the same: "Stand on

God's Word alone—**Get Up And Fight, Or Get Up And Leave**—but don't stay and pretend it's all right when it isn't, or pretend that it will get better—when it will not."

Unless God's people in the Church of England return to the Word of God, get themselves leaders in the same mould as Hooper, Latimer, Ridley, and Ryle—instead of the compromising theocratic politicians they have today—stop compromising, and stop following those whom the Word of God declares to be false prophets, they have no hope, no chance and no future.

I Shall Curse Them That Curse Thee

It is no coincidence that the Church of England Commissioners recorded the staggering loss of many hundreds of millions of pounds right after George Carey withdrew his patronage from Jewish evangelism and attacked it on the airwaves.[82] These massive financial losses have pushed the Church of England to the point of insolvency where it may eventually be unable to continue supporting its clergy. However, as I said before, unless there is repentance their future holds only further judgement and inevitable collapse. Of this Anglicans may be absolutely confident.

Heresy, ecumenism, homosexual clergy, compromise with demonic religions and the refusal of most of the 'born again' Christians among the Anglicans to either stand up and fight or stand up and leave, have all combined to bring God's judgement upon Anglicanism.

The last straw was when their leaders dared to touch the apple of God's eye.[83] Once anyone sets their face against the Jews, He will stand no more. And that is exactly what the Church of England has done.

I say again—the way to bless the Jews is to give them the gospel. The way to curse the Jews is to oppose giving Israel the gospel. Under the leadership of men like Colin Chapman[84] with his anti-Zionism and pro-Islamic bias and Archbishop George Carey with his stand against Jewish evangelism—the Church of England has most certainly cursed the Jews.

Restorationism—Christian Anti-semitism?

As scripture makes clear, God still blesses those who bless the Jews and curses those who curse them, not for the sake of the Jews alone, but for the sake of His own Name, and for the sake of His promise to Abraham and the Patriarchs. Just as Christian preachers in the Post-Nicean church, along with Roman Catholic and Eastern Orthodox theologians in the Middle Ages, and later Luther during the Reformation, perpetrated an anti-Semitic doctrinal theology within Christendom, so today a new version of Replacement Theology—which is not simply anti-Israel, but also anti-Jewish—is on the rise within evangelical Christianity, hard on the heels of Restorationism and Kingdom Now theology.

At this point I must introduce you to a very dangerous false teacher from the United States, Rick Godwin (who also has a money orientation in much of his preaching) who teaches Christians that Matthew chapter 24 and other New Testament scriptures are not about the last days despite the fact that Jesus taught it so that the Church would be prepared for the last days. In fact Godwin simply borrows his doctrines from David Chilton, another Restorationist, and packages it in American tele-evangelist styled hype. Godwin teaches that the Jews get nothing from God, that Israel is nothing but wasted money, and if Christians say that Israel fulfils prophecy, it only makes Arabs (Moslems) hate them.[85]

Bryn Jones, a British restorationist, published in his magazine *Restoration* cover stories in effect demanding that the Church raise up a prophetic voice **against** Israel. A few months following his refusal to retract, Jones' magazine and business enterprise *Harvest Time* went bankrupt.[86] If nothing else this demonstrates that when God says "I will bless them that bless thee, and curse them that curse thee."[87] He really means it.

I accept that Christians may be incorporated into this promise of blessing those who bless and cursing those who curse through the ingrafting principle demonstrated in Romans chapter 11, but never to the replacement of the original promise to the Jews.

The most frightening element of Godwin's teaching comes with the bizarre statement "that those seeing a purpose and a plan of God for Israel are trying to resurrect the ashes of a red heifer."[88] His partner, English restorationist Andrew Shearman was reported as having said that God was not interested in that piece of sand on the other side of the Mediterranean. It is worthy of note that as in centuries past, this sort of anti-Jewish preaching always rises at a time of growing international anti-Semitism. It is not difficult to find examples of Neo-Nazi and Neo-Fascist movements in Italy, Spain, France, Germany, Russia and Britain at the same time as figures like Godwin, Shearman and Jones come to prominence in the church.

An Ancient Error Reborn

Because restoration theology succumbs to the ancient error that the Church will conquer the entire world and set up the Kingdom of God before Christ comes, restorationism usually allows no prophetic purpose for Israel and the Jews because it believes the return of Christ depends not upon the prophetic purposes of God for Israel, but on a form of *Neo-Reconstructionism* which says they must conquer the whole world and set up the theocratic rule **before** He comes.

Others involved in restorationism and dominionism might see some kind of prophetic significance to events in the Middle East but would take a heterodox (not orthodox) view of them. One example is the Kansas City prophet Paul Cain, who was closely associated with the late John Wimber. Paul Cain apologised to Saddam Hussein for what the Americans and British did to him following Hussein's genocidal massacre of his own people, his rape of Kuwait and his missile attacks upon Tel Aviv and Haifa.[89]

To understand such twisted thinking we need to understand the nature and origin of restorationism and its Kingdom Now and triumphalist pre-suppositions; also dominionist and hyper-charismatic rhetoric.

Are We Bereans?

Those who argue for such practices can only do so on the basis of feelings. Feelings, however, are emotion. They are good servants but lethal masters. It is the Word of God that cuts flesh from spirit and those choosing to follow such things, instead of examining them in the light of the Word of God, are not simply blind, but wilfully blind. They choose deception; that is to say, they choose rebellion.

The spirit of the Bereans that we see in Acts chapter 17 is gone from most of the Church. The Bereans wisely examined all doctrine in light of scripture to see if it was true and if they found no basis for it, they would not accept it. Those in mainstream pentecostal and charismatic churches today evaluate things, not on the basis of God's Word, as the Bereans did, but on the basis of what it is they want to hear and what they believe to be true in their hearts.

We must remember that it is exactly this line of thinking that Mormonism uses as its proof of what is true and what is not. The standard Mormon testimony today is that they have "the feeling in their heart—and the burning in their bosom" which confirms to them that the teachings of the Mormon cult are true.

Objectively, there is not a lot of difference today between the criteria for evaluating what is right and what is wrong by most charismatics, pentecostals and Mormons. Instead of the standard of God's Word being the measure of what is true and what is false, the litmus paper becomes emotional whim, personal preference, and what we mistake to be "the witness in our hearts", when what is in our hearts often does not agree with what is in the Word of God. As Jeremiah wrote: "The heart is deceitful above all things, and desperately wicked: who can know it?"[90]

These unbiblical practices seem absolutely correct to those who are caught up in the hollow atmosphere of churches that propound them, but as God says:

There is a way which seems right unto man,
but the end of which is death and destruction.   **Prov 14:12**

No Bunker Mentality

My rejection of triumphalism is not to suggest that the New Testament teaches a 'bunker' mentality. It does teach that there will be a faithful remnant as in the days of Noah, but it does not teach a gospel of retreat. While Jesus did say to the church in Thyatira that they could only strengthen the things which remain, the Bible does teach that a time would come at the close of the age, before the return of Christ, when night would come in which no man could work, much the same as when God closed the door of Noah's Ark and no more could be saved. So we see that there is no biblical basis for a bunker mentality.

Jesus said that when we see world events lining up with prophecy about the end of the age (prophecies which dominionism denies are about the end of the age), the Gospel of the Kingdom should be preached. Again, He never requires Christians to adopt a bunker mentality, but rather to proclaim the gospel with our minds set on the offensive against the sinfulness of this fallen world.

Noah's Family—A Ragged Remnant?

Triumphalists like Mike Bickle, however, falsely insist that Christians who do not accept their position advocate a bunker mentality in preaching what he derogatorily calls the "doctrine of the Ragged Remnant". By Bickle's definition, Noah and his family were a ragged remnant, yet Jesus says Noah's family is a type of the church in the last days.[91]

If there was ever a time for Christians to get out of the bunker and fight, that time is now. Yet, until God has an army of Christians prepared to fight for the truth instead of unbiblical illusion and deception, there are only battles to be lost and none to be won.

As I stated earlier, we must remember the purge of leaven. God is always much more concerned .with the sin among His own people than He is with sin amongst the lost. Until He gets us—His own people—right, He can never use us to get the unsaved right with Himself. As long as we persist in following false teachers and false prophets, who the Word of God says are in open rebellion against Him—unless they are willing to repent and step down—we will never truly be following Jesus. Unless we get rid of hype, we will never have a true anointing or true revival.

What Is Revival?

Revival is not a lot of people getting saved. A lot of people getting saved is the result of revival. After all, you can't revive people who were never alive to begin with.

Revival is the Church repenting of its sin, its false doctrine, and its lukewarmness, and returning to its first love. This accounts for much of the reason why programmes, Church growth models, and evangelistic crusades in the western world, achieve relatively little in either stemming the tide of evil or reversing the decline of the Church. In Britain, for instance, there will never be a revival until the Church has the courage and integrity to call to account those false prophets who have predicted that revival was just around the corner.

True revival is earth-shaking and society-transforming because in it we see the power of the living God at work. It has nothing whatsoever to do with charismania, transfer growth of people leaving one Church for another to have their ears tickled with prosperity doctrines, Hollywood-styled hype on 'Christian' television, prophetic predictions that fail to happen or Kingdom Now rhetoric.

Revival is what happened in the book of Acts and what happened under Moody, Wesley, and Spurgeon. It can and will happen again, when we again have leaders like Moody, Wesley, and Spurgeon, instead of the impotent assortment of hype-artists, false prophets, false teachers, heretical confidence tricksters and 'theocratic politicians' who all too often pass as substitutes for real leaders today.

Conclusions

The Restoration Movement is dedicated to the restoration of things from the Apostolic Church that were never in the Apostolic Church—things that have no Biblical basis. What it actually tries to restore are Gnosticism and Montanism, errors that, but for the grace of God and the courage of Bible-based theologians, nearly demolished the post-Apostolic church.

These wild beliefs have always shown their head at crucial times in Church history, the present time being no exception. They have always involved warped mishandlings of scripture, misuse of spiritual gifts and signs and wonders (charismania); false predictions and crazy expectations pronounced by prophets who are no prophets at all; personality cults, heavy shepherding, replacement-ism, reconstructionism, and above all, the arrogance of false shepherds and false prophets driven by an insatiable lust for power, position, and self-importance.

They have always come to nothing, but in the process have always damaged the church and those in it, particularly those seduced into following their lies. It is an old lie of the old liar and because doctrinal knowledge of the Word of God is at an all-time low, it is an appropriate time for him to raise up those who will feed God's people such lies. Jesus warned of this and said it would come.[92]

No matter what Chilton and Godwin try to tell you, Matthew chapter 24 **is** about the last days; Israel **does** fulfil prophecy; Jesus **is** coming again for a faithful remnant. As Jesus said: "As it was in the days of Noah, so it shall be when the Son of Man comes."[93] It is not a time to hide in the bunker, but to herald the return of Christ to the lost and to build an ark for the saved. If we believe the Word of God instead of the ancient errors being trumpeted today by deluded men, we can have a place on that ark. As Jesus also said:

> **"When you see these things happening, lift up your head for your redemption draws near."**

If you are a dominionist, if you are following triumphalist rhetoric, if you believe Kingdom Now theology—I say in all seriousness:
THE DEVIL IS TAKING YOU FOR A RIDE!

Notes on Chapter 7

1. Luke 10:1; Mark 6:7.
2. The epistles of Ignatius to the churches in Asia: *Early Christian Writings* (Penguin classics)
3. Vineyard prophet David Ravenhill says : "I believe the test of a prophet is not whether his word comes to pass, it's his lifestyle. It's the character of the individual. That is how you test a prophet...It's not a matter of whether the word comes to pass or not, it's the nature of that person's life." David Ravenhill, "Understanding Prophecy and Its Fulfilment, Introduction to the Prophetic Tape 90917, "17 September 1998, audiotape. Cited in Hank Hanegraaff, *Counterfeit Revival*, Word Publishing, Dallas. 1997:75.
4. Rick Joyner, *The Harvest*, Pineville, NC: Morning star Publications, Inc., 1990.
5. The meetings held at the Docklands Arena are documented on a video series called 'Equipping the Saints'.
6. According to claims ot the Islamic Council for Great Britain.
7. According to the Home Office Statistical Bulletin, Issue 23/97, from 1990 to 1997 inclusive violent crime rose 53%. According to the Home Office Statistical Bulletin, Issue 22/97, from 1990 to 1996 inclusive the number of notified drug addicts rose 255%.
8. Proverbs 11:1.
9. J. Gardner, *Promise Keepers?*, St Matthew Publishing, Cambridge, 1996:17.
10. Robert Hicks, *The Masculine Journey: Understanding the Six Stages of Manhood*, NavPress, 1993:177.
11. "Their passion for unity at the expense of doctrine means they welcome as members, without question, both Roman Catholics and Mormons. With a commitment not to violate the theologies of members and to 'no evangelism' as an unwritten promise, PK now embraces an ecumenism not experienced since the Reformation." J.Gardner, *Promise Keepers?*, St Matthew Publishing, Cambridge, 1996:8-9.
"Men reached through PK are unlikely to be steered into churches concerned for sound Biblical teaching or grounded in the Truth." Ibid., 11.
12. Jeremiah 7:30-31; 19:5-7; 32:35.
13. Matthew 6:24; Luke 16:13.
14. Romans 11:21.

15. Jeremiah 5:12-13, 30-31; 6:13-15; 8:8-12; 14:13-16; 23:16-17; 28:15-17; 29:8-9.
16. Jeremiah 5:31
17. See footnote 60.
18. 2 Thessalonians 2:11.
19. "They could not contain themselves and kept on laughing. What is this? Can this possibly be the fullness of the Holy Spirit? No, this is plainly one of the works of the soul". Watchman Nee, *The Latent Power of the Soul*, Christian Fellowship Publishers, New York, 1972:71.
20. 1 Peter 5:2-4; Hebrews 13:17-21; Ezekiel 34; Jeremiah 23:1-4.
21. 2 Timothy 4:3-4.
22. Matthew 6:22.
23. Ezekiel 3:20.
24. Ezekiel 3:7.
25. Ezekiel 13:8-23; 33:6; 34:10.
26. I Corinthians 12:28, 2 Peter 2:1.
27. *What on Earth is the Kingdom* Gerald Coates, Kingsway 1983
28. Bob Jones and Paul Cain, "Selections from the Kansas City Prophets, " audiotape (tape 155C).
29. Mgr R.Knox, *Enthusiasm*
30. Jeremiah 28:15.
31. See footnote 62.
32. Acts 17:16.
33. Such misguided notions have been advanced by John Dannen and Floyd McLung of YWAM.
34. Isaiah 11:6; Mark 9:36; 10:11-15; Luke 9:47-48.
35. I Samuel 17:37-47.
36. Hosea 4:6.
37. "Prince Charles is just one among the Royal Family who has endorsed Alternative Medicine as a whole but Royal involvement with the paranormal runs much deeper." Roy Livesey, More Understanding the New Age, New Wine Press, Chichester, 1990:98.
"...in Freemasonry the Duke of Kent is seen to be the man at the top..." Ibid., 106.
Further reading: John Dale, *The Prince and the Paranormal*, Bury House Christian Books, Clows Top, Kidderminster, Worcs.
38. Revelation 1:17.
39. Ella Peppard died from complications she suffered after someone was slain in the spirit on top of her at a Benny Hinn meeting in Oklahoma city. G. Richard Fisher, Stephen F. Cannon, and M. Kurt Goedelman, "Benny Hinn's Anointing: Heaven sent or Borrowed?" The Quarterly Journal, Personal Freedom Outreach 12, no.3. July—September 1992:12.
40. Hinn was quoted in October 1991 by Christianity Today as saying that he

"no longer believe(s) the faith message, ". Yet, he was soon back with the prosperity gospel on the "Praise the Lord" programme on TBN on the 26 December 1991 and the 16 and 17 of April 1992. How far Hinn has returned into the Faith camp is debatable, though his favourable allusions to both Oral Roberts and Kenneth Hagin (in the programmes mentioned) would indicate that it is further than he is prepared to admit.

41. The evangelistic agencies involved with the 1994 Jim campaign reported 269 converts from 46 events, according to an Evangelical Alliance survey. Statistics cited in: Roland Howard, Charismania—When Christian Fundamentalism Goes Wrong, Mowbray, London 1997:128.

42. In 1994 the German Charismatic evangelist Reinhart Bonnke distributed a booklet called 'Minus to Plus' to the majority of houses in Britain, and his publicity referred to millions of converts. However, a survey undertaken by the Evangelical Alliance reported that the campaign led to less than one convert per participating church. Ibid.,

43. Joy Magazine.

44. Further reading; Roland Howard, *The Rise and Fall of the Nine O'Clock Service*, Mowbray, London, 1996.

45. The next fad after the Toronto Blessing is a renewal of celtic spirituality which encourages pagan practices and diverts from the gospel message. Further reading; Paul Fahy, *Modern Celtic Spirituality*, St Matthew Publishing, Cambridge, 1996.

46. Gordan Hills is Field Superintendent for Elim.

47. For details of Cerullo's money scams see: Rowland Howard, *Charismania—When Fundamentalism Goes Wrong*, Mowbray, London, 1997:41-43. Concerning, the deaths of people that Cerullo has pronounced healed, see footnote [118]. Natielia Barnes aged 4 died as the result of Morris Cerullo pronouncing her healed.

48. Prince Charles said this on his visit to Saudi Arabia in Spring 1997.

49. In an ITN Interview, Dr Peter May, pubicly challenged Cerullo's miracle claims. Cerullo's 1993 advertising stated that 2250 were healed in the 1992 mission. Yet, even a survey conducted by Morris Cerullo World Evangelism cited only 476 people claiming to be healed. The religious documentary programme *Heart of the Matter* followed this up by asking Cerullo to produce the three best miracles from his last mission, for medical scrutiny. After some time Cerullo came up with nine 'miracles', although only six permitted access to medical notes. Heart of the Matter and several national newspapers squashed the medical evidence (basically, there was no verifiable, evidence of the supposed illnesses in the first place), and were condemning in their conclusions, inferring that the idea of miracles was fanciful and that MCWE's presentation of the facts was at times misleading.

For a comprehensive medical evaluation of the miracles submitted by Cerullo see: Roland Howard, *Charismania—When Christian Fundamentalism Goes*

Wrong, Mowbray, London, 1997:61-69.

50. 1 Corinthians 12:9, 28.

51. Cerullo was under constant review from the Evangelical Alliance because of his prosperity teaching and fundraising letters. Many Charismatics complained to the Evangelical Alliance about Cerullo's offensive and immoral mailshots. Of particular concern was his 'Confidential Messiah Project', in which he sent an envelope with a Jew's name on it needing the donor's sponsorship to receive the Christian message. Eventually, in October 1996 the Evangelical Alliance unanimously voted to expel Cerullo. Almost immediately Cerullo voluntarily stood down.

52. "Did you know that from the beginning of time the whole purpose of God was to reproduce Himself? ...Who are you? Come on, who are you? Come on say it: "Sons of God!" Come on, say it!...And when we stand up here, brother, you're not looking at Morris Cerullo; you're looking at God. You're looking at Jesus." Morris Cerullo, *The Endtime Manifestation of the Sons of God* (San Diego: Morris Cerullo World Evangelism, Inc.,n.d.), audiotape 1, sides 1 and 2. Cited in: H. Hanegraaff, *Christianity in Crisis*, Nelson Word 1993:358.

53. Benny Hinn, "Double Portion Anointing, Part #3" (Orlando Christian Center, n,d.),audiotape #A031791-3, sides 1 and 2. This sermon was also aired on TBN (7 April 1991).
    Earl Paulk endorses his son-in-law Steve's communication with his dead mother. Earl Paulk, Held in the Heavens Until... God's Strategy for Planet Earth (Atlanta: K Dimension, 1985), 21-23.

54. 1 Timothy 3:1-13.
    "God the Father is a person, God the Son is a person, God the Holy Ghost is a person. But each one of them is a triune being by Himself. If I can shock you and maybe I should—there's nine of them." Benny Hinn "Benny Hinn" program on TBN (3 October 1990).

55. The author and others were eyewitnesses to this at Paradise Church, Adelaide, Australia in June 1996.

56. Rodney Howard-Browne, *The Coming Revival*, RHBEA Publications, Louiseville. 1991.
    Kenneth Copeland reduces Jesus to a mere man and divests Christ of every shred of deity. He asserts that Christians are as much incarnations of God as was Jesus. Indeed, Copeland goes as far as to say that he is so much like Christ that if he had the knowledge of the Word of God that Jesus did, he himself could have redeemed mankind.
    Kenneth Copeland, "Substitution and Identification" (Fort Worth, TX: Kenneth Copeland Ministries, n.d.), audiotape #00-0202. Cited and examined in Hank Hanegraaff, *Christianity in Crisis*, Word Publishing, Milton Keynes, 1995.
    Copeland teaches that Jesus "went into the pit of hell as a mortal man made sin" (What happened for the Cross to the Throne? side 2.). Copeland also says

that "It is important for us to realize that a born-again man defeated Satan" (Copeland, "Jesus:Our Lord fo Glory, " Believer's Voice of Victory (April 1982). Quoted in Michael G. Moriarty, *The New Charismatics*, Zondervan Publishing House, Grand Rapid, 1992:375.

57. Randy Clark is a leader in Vineyard. John Arnott is the Founder and Senior Pastor of the Toronto Airport Church Fellowship—formerly Toronto Airport Vineyard Church.

58. Guy Chevreau, *Catch the Fire—The Toronto Blessing*, Marshall Pickering, London, 1994:209+.

59. *Daniel Rowland and the Great Evangelical Awakening in Wales*, Eifon Evans, Banner of Truth Trust, Edinburgh, 1985:158+.

60. 12.1.86 on a tape "The Holy Spirit":
"...by His (Holy Spirit's) instruction God had enabled me to build the largest church in the world, now God wants me to have one million active members by 1990, and this is not my project, it's the project of the Holy Spirit, and the same Holy Spirit spoke to me very clearly when I was sitting on this platform 'son, this church will grow to the number of 10,000 in less than three years.' because my ears are very finely tuned to the Holy Spirit and I could hear His voice now, hear, the Holy Spirit is your senior partner and Dr Andrew and you, you are his junior partner, you've got to listen to Him, work together with Him....."

61. "Now I'm pointing my finger with the mighty power of God on me ... You hear this. There are men and women attacking me. I will tell you something under the anointing now, you'll reap it in your children. You'll never win...And your children will suffer...you'll pay, and your children will. Hear this from the lips of God's servant. You are in danger. Repent, or God Almighty will move his hand..." Benny Hinn, quoted in Christianity Today, 15 October 1992, following an address to an audience at Melodyland Christian Center, Southern California. Cited in Martyn Percy, *Words, Wonders and Power, Understanding Christian Fundamentalism and Revivalism*, SPCK, London. 1996:157.
"Now let me say something else, and I really don't care if you like this or not, you have attacked me your children will pay for it." "If you care for your kids, stop attacking Benny Hinn." H. Hanegraaff, *Christianity in Crisis*, Tape 1, Side 1.

62. See Beware the New Prophets by Bill Randles (SMP 1999) page 117ff

63. Rousas J. Rushdoony is heralded as the 'father of reconstructionism'. He was a Reformed Calvinist, who believed the elect's task was to take dominion over every part of this earth's social structure by applying biblical law to it. Similarly, the 'Manchild' Manifest Sons of God sought to set up the Kingdom on earth now. This phenomena came out of the Latter Rain movement in the early 1950's under the headship of John Robert Stevens. He and the other modern apostles he set up, often claimed to receive new revelation from God.

The Manifest Sons of God claimed that their group was the only arena in which salvation was available and that they were the only body of believers that God was restoring to the New Testament structure. These were rigid authoritarian structures where members gave mindless allegiance to a leader's teaching. The fundamentalist Manifest Sons considered themselves to be 'little Christs' continuing the incarnation on earth.

Further reading: Michael G. Moriarty, *The New Charismatics*, Zondervan Publishing House, Grand Rapids, 1992.

64. 1 Samuel 24:6-7.

65. 1 Samuel 13:13-14; 15:22-28; 19:18.

66. 1 Corinthians 12:12-27.

67. 1 Chronicles 16:22.

68. Galatians 6:17; 2Corinthians 4:10, 11:23; Philippians 3:10.

69. 1 Corinthians 11:1.

70. Matthew 26:12; Ephesians 1:20-23; Revelation1:6.

71. Matthew 7:22-23.

72. George Carey said this on BBC Radio at the announcement of his appointment as Archbishop.

73. For further reading see: E. McDonald, *Alpha—New Life or New Lifestyle? A biblical assessment of the Alpha Course*, St Matthew Publishing, Cambridge, 1996.

74. See *Alpha—New life or New Lifestyle?*

75. David Richardson, 'Alpha—the Omega in Evangelism?'. *Prophecy Today*, September/October 1997:6-8.

76. E.P. Sanders and a new crop of Jewish scholars who study New Testament documents from a Judaic viewpoint such as Rabbis, Jacob Nuesner, Pinchas Lapide, David Flusser, Gezer Vermes of the Dead Sea Scrolls Commission, all confirm the validity of Gospel narratives as second temple period Jewish literature in their literary character and historical and cultural flavour.

77. *Redating the New Testament*, J.A.T.Robinson SCM ISBN 1 85931 007 9

78. 2 Timothy 3:5.

79. George Carey withdrew his patronage of Jewish evangelism immediately after he was appointed Archbishop. In 1997 he marched in processions to Mary and other religions' Holy Sites and endured the consecration of Hindu gods. He said, "What gifts the Holy Sites give us according to whatever beliefs you have." Whatever happened to "I am the Lord your God, you shall serve no other gods but me"?

80. When the Bishop of Durham , David Jenkins denied the resurrection two thirds of the Church of England's Bishops defended him.

81. See footnote 37.

82. This was took place when George Carey appeared on the radio with the Chief Rabbi Jonathan Sacks, shortly after his appointment as Archbishop.

83. Zechariah 2:8.

84. Cannon Colin Chapman is the former principle of Trinity College Bristol where the evangelical branch of the Church of England trains its clergy in the West of Britain.

85. "It is hurting our witness to the Arab nations when we sanction anything Israel does. Political Israel, is not Israel. They have no right... to be on that land." Rick Godwin, on his audiotape series 'The Shepherd-Sheep Relationship' 1988. Cited in M. L. Brown, *Our Hands are Stained with Blood—The Tragic Story of The Church and The Jewish People*, Destiny Image Publishers, 1992.

86. Bryn Jones's Harvestime Enterprise collapsed after he cursed Israel in 'Restoration Magazine' May/June 1991.

87. Genesis 12:3

88. See footnote 85 'The Shepherd-Sheep relationship' Tape.

89. On a tape recorded from a live statement by Paul Cain introduced by Rick Godwin at Morning Star HQ.

90. Jeremiah 17:19

91. Matthew 24:37-38 & Luke 17:26-27.

92. Matthew 24:24

93. Matthew 24:37-38.

Chapter 8

Lie 3: Faith-Prosperity Gospel

Nothing undermines the Body of Christ, nor the credibility of the Christian Church in its mission to evangelise the world more than the advent of faith—prosperity theology, with its accompanying over emphasis on signs and wonders to the virtual exclusion of repentance and the authority of scripture.

This is in no way to deny biblical truths concerning prosperity when they are understood and applied biblically and not experientially. Neither is it to deny the validity of signs, wonders and gifts of the Spirit when understood and applied biblically. I affirm the place of gifts of the Spirit including healings, prophecy, and the miraculous—when practiced in accordance with the teachings of the Bible, and I reject the cesssationist doctrines as being an unbiblical error.

The Origins Of Biblical Prosperity

The basis of the biblical understanding of prosperity is found most clearly in Deuteronomy 8: 3-5 and 16-20.

And He humbled you and let you be hungry,
and fed you with manna which you did not
know, nor did your fathers know, that He
might make you understand that man does
not live by bread alone, but man lives
by everything that proceeds out of the
mouth of the Lord. Your clothing did not
wear out on you, nor did your foot swell
these forty years. Thus you are to know
in your heart that the Lord your God was

disciplining you just as a man disciplines
his son.
In the wilderness He fed you manna which
your fathers did not know, that He might
humble you and that He might test you,
to do good for you in the end. Otherwise,
you may say in your heart, "My power and
the strength of my hand made me this
wealth."
But you shall remember the Lord
your God, for it is He who is giving you
power to make wealth, that He may confirm
His covenant which He swore to your fathers
as it is this day.
And it shall come about
if you ever forget the Lord your God, and turn to
other gods and serve them and worship them,
I testify against you today
that you shall surely perish. Like the
nations that the Lord makes to perish
before you, so you shall perish; because
you would not listen to the voice of the
Lord your God.

In God's model we notice three features that are commonly omitted by those who preach a prosperity message. The first of these is that God allowed His people to be hungry in the wilderness that He might humble them and test them before He blessed them. The emphasis today, however, is on not suffering because they claim Jesus suffered for us.

The Bible's teaching is not simply that Jesus died for us but that He calls us to pick up our own cross and die with Him. A gospel that does not preach the Cross in its full sense is not the gospel of Jesus. Times of blessing and prosperity in God's economy, both for individuals and for corporate groups, are preceded by times of breaking, testing and moulding. Because of our old nature, unless we are first broken and remoulded, these blessings become grounds for pride, self sufficiency and at best trying to serve God in our own strength.

Yet there is practically no talk of this crucial biblical truth in the manipulative preaching of faith-prosperity ministers. They emphasise, not the blessings of the Cross, but rather a quest for blessings without it. They do this to extract money from people in a manner no different to the way the moneychangers of Jesus' day profiteered from the blood of the lamb and hawked their wares in the Temple (as we noted in our exposition of the Jewish background of Palm Sunday).

Secondly, the message of Moses must be seen in the context of the Deuteronomic legislation and the covenant with the Jews. To appropriate these things from the Jews and apply them to the Church is a manifestation of the errors of Replacementism. Even those prosperity preachers who see a prophetic place for Israel still adhere to a Replacement Theology.

These blessings for Israel were wholly dependent on Israel's faithfulness. So, churches and ministries which do not encourage people to carry their crosses, and live a crucified life, are certainly not being faithful and therefore the covenant promises could not apply to them in any biblical sense.

What most of replacementism does is to say that the promised blessings of the covenant are for the Church, but the curses are for the Jews. As we have seen this is neither plausible nor scriptural.

What we can say is that the principles of blessing and cursing found in the Mosaic law can apply to the Church, but the covenant itself cannot. We are told in Hebrews[1] that we have a new and better covenant. It is on this basis that some prosperity preachers argue: "Since our covenant is better, should it not also include prosperity?" They go on to argue: "How can it be better if the Jews were promised prosperity in this world, but we are not?"

First of all, we note that the Law could not give salvation, only the New Covenant of grace could do that. Secondly, Israel had a Theocratic society the Church does not (despite the ramblings of reconstructionists and dominionists). Furthermore note that even the promises of prosperity in the Old Testament were not set out along the lines that the prosperity preachers would have us believe.

This brings us to the third difference: the blessings and prosperity set out in Mosaic Law were never for an individual, but for a nation. The blessings would come if the nation was faithful, but they are not guaranteed for individuals (as so much of Ecclesiastes, Proverbs, Job and Psalms make clear).

What we can argue for is an application of the principles; but there is no formula to be found anywhere in the Word of God along the lines that the prosperity preachers deceive people into believing.

We can have some sympathy for reconstructionists and restorationists as individuals (although not as leaders) on the basis that their motives may not be wrong, although their doctrines certainly are. But this cannot be generally said for faith-prosperity preachers. While many of them may have begun as honest servants of the Lord, it is now difficult to see them as anything less than a ring of swindlers, heretics and confidence tricksters out to pervert the Word of God in order to put money into their own pockets. That is how the world sees them, and this is how Christians ought to see them also.

Not only do they preach another gospel, but most of them are doing it for their own aggrandizement as is evident from their self indulgent, opulent lifestyles.

The Principle Applies—Not A Formula

We can easily argue from the application of principle that the higher standards of living enjoyed in the Protestant democracies spring from the biblical influences on those societies; affecting their moral fibre, their cultures, economies and structures of government.

Conversely, the poverty that we see in Hindu, most Islamic and most Roman Catholic countries results from the lack of biblical influence in those nations. It is sobering to realise that idolatry brings poverty.

In Europe for instance, the countries which have rejected Roman Catholicism such as Britain, Scandinavia, Germany, Holland, and Switzerland are the wealthy countries. Even those nations where Roman Catholicism is not practised such as Belgium, France and, increasingly, northern Italy are wealthy countries. The staunchly Roman Catholic and Eastern Orthodox nations such as Ireland, Southern Italy, Spain, Portugal, Greece, Poland and Russia are the poor relations of Europe. There would appear to be a direct connection between false religion, idolatry and superstition and a nation being cursed. It is only to the degree to which biblical principles permeate the social, economic and political fabric that a nation will tend to prosper.

What needs to be rejected, however, is the transfer of principles which affect nations to individuals. Jesus said "the Son of Man had no place to lay His head" and "a servant is not above his Master". The Apostle Paul's life often became so difficult that he despaired of it. Yet these prosperity preachers present a different message to that of the Lord Jesus and the apostle Paul.

Job was one example of a faithful man who suffered despite his faithfulness and, in fact, because of it. Yet Benny Hinn calls Job "a carnal man".[2] Either God's Word is wrong, or Benny Hinn is wrong. The Word of God calls Job a righteous man. The best that can be said is that Benny Hinn is a foolish babbler who should be silenced and called to repentance. If he did then he would lay down his 'ministry', submit to the authority of the Church and go and learn the Word of God before he tries to teach people things that he obviously does not know himself. Recently, in a theological examination of one of his books, Bible students at a pentecostal college in Australia found eleven major doctrinal errors and heresies in only three pages!

Hinn's attack on Job was in fact no different from Roman Catholic Cardinal Rau's attack on St Paul during the Renaissance, when he urged Florentine Christians to read the Greek and Roman classics rather than Paul's writings in the New Testament because they were, in his view, decadent and disgusting.

Rau said this, of course, because Paul's philosophy of the Christian life was contrary to the materialistic concept of the 'Christian life' of the Roman Catholic Church during the Renaissance period. And just as the Church of Rome murdered Savanarola for standing against the abominations of Renaissance Roman Catholicism in Florence, so too the prosperity preachers would probably love to see an end of their critics today—for precisely the same reasons. As Benny Hinn has preached "I just want to find one verse in the Bible that says, 'if you don't like'em, kill'em.'" [3]

The CNN exposures of Benny Hinn, which were broadcast during 1997, have been even more troubling. Despite public promises to do so he steadfastly refuses to reveal his salary. He also refuses to join the Evangelical Council for Financial Accountability.

Given the revelation that Hinn and his entourage spent some $33,000 on flights aboard Concorde which was paid for by donations from among the poor, the sick, and the unemployed—after he promised to trim his lavish lifestyle—it is perhaps unsurprising that non-christian broadcasters expressed astonishment that one man could deceive so many gullible people.

By the end of 1997 a number of major lawsuits were pending against Hinn, following the allegedly illegal detention of protesters outside one of his meetings.

Later the same year Hinn was revealed as a self-confessed necromancer—that is one who communes with the dead—since he apparently seeks advice at the grave of Katherine Kuhlman.

Most tragic of all are the deaths of some of Hinn's followers who he himself had declared healed of serious illnesses. These tragedies were made public on CNN.

Because the biblical principles of wealth and blessing can only be applied nationally, and since God's blessings depend on national faithfulness to Him, there is no basis for the idea that God gives prosperity to the backslidden Protestant democracies just because these false doctrines are preached.

The English-speaking democracies in particular have broken the New Covenant as nations and societies, every bit as badly as Israel has violated the Old Covenant. If the blessings can only come corporately on nations, they cannot come on a backslidden nation. It is rather the curses of Leviticus chapter 26 and Deuteronomy chapter 28 that follow on from rebellion.

I believe that the economic decline of America, Britain, and most of the other Western democracies, which once enjoyed biblical foundations in their national heritage, is a clear and direct result of backsliding. So if we are to argue for an application of the blessings and curses of the Mosaic law, our message should be one of judgement not one of prosperity as Oral Roberts, Kenneth Copeland and Kenneth Hagin would have us believe.

The Real Origins Of The Faith-prosperity Error

As we have observed in our treatment of the Palm Sunday narrative, the Jewish community of Jesus' day had three cardinal errors in their eschatology and Messianic expectation. These were, a Kingdom Now gospel, a prosperity gospel, and a signs and wonders gospel. These same three mistakes today render the Church no more ready for Jesus' return than most of the Jews were ready for His first coming.

In their confusion of the son of Joseph with the son of David and their further confusion of Zechariah chapters 9 and 12, they did not see, or want to see, a Messiah who came not only to die on a cross for their sin, but to beckon them to die with Him.

He told us not to trust in this world, but in a coming kingdom which He would inaugurate at His first coming but establish on His return.

Without the Cross there is no real significance to Jesus' life. Those who adhere to the ideas of E.W.Kenyon have a crossless Christ who is no Christ at all. Kenyon taught that Jesus did not win the victory on the Cross (even though He said "it is finished") but rather won the victory when He became a Satanic being in hell and of one nature with Satan. Since the central and pivotal importance of His death on the Cross is thus nullified, it follows that our "dying with Him" on the Cross is similarly dismissed as irrelevant.

Instead of taking up our cross and following Him in the hope of His return when His true and lasting reward will be with Him, the message of the prosperity preachers becomes one of over-realised eschatology built on Gnostic pre-suppositions. Put simply this is: "We don't have to suffer, so name it and claim it, because the reward is now."

For the true Christian, whatever blessings God may bestow on us now, be they those of family, good health, material and financial prosperity and even fruitfulness in ministry, they are but a foretaste of the true blessings to come. Success in a fallen world is hollow and ultimately worthless to those whose hearts are fixed on the kingdom to come and the certain knowledge that this fallen world with its attractions is swiftly passing away.

Similarly, the true Christian, whose heart is fixed on Christ, does not count the sufferings and hardships of this world to be of any ultimate consequence, because he or she knows that this world is passing away and whatever difficulties may befall them in it will quickly amount to nothing when their confident faith in the return of Jesus is realised and His kingdom replaces the present kingdom (whose real ruler is Satan).

The Gospel: Re-contextualised, Not Re-defined

In preaching to the Epicurean and Stoic followers in Athens, Paul engaged in the Greek way of thinking. When speaking to Jews he presented Jesus in his original Jewish context.[4] In fact some of the pre-Nicean fathers believed that what was best of monotheistic Greek philosophy, particularly the Socratic ideas and even some Platonic thought, helped prepare the Greek world for the coming of Jesus, in the same way that the Pentateuch (the first five books of the Bible) prepared the Jews.

On the basis of Paul's example and exhortation in 1 Corinthians chapter 9, we have a clear biblical basis to **re-contextualise** the gospel; that is to present it in a context in which it is digestible to people of a different culture, providing we do not **re-define** its meaning.

An example of this would be when Bible translators sought to translate the scriptures into a tribal language in equatorial Africa where the people had never seen snow. They translated Isaiah chapter 1:18 which reads, "Your sins shall be white as snow," as reading, "Your sins shall be white as coconut." Although a paraphrase is never desirable, contextualisation can be a practical necessity. Saying "coconut" instead of "snow" only re-contextualises, it does not redefine or alter the meaning.

The world in which we live, however, is currently witnessing a fundamental re-definition of the gospel in the light of the modern consumerist world view. For instance, the trend towards having women pastors directly reflects the feminism of the secular world in the Church.

The extreme emphasis on deliverance which supposedly gives 'instant cures' for sin etc, is a direct reflection of the microwave oven, T.V. dinner, and fast food mentality, where things that once required time and work now become instantly available. Again it nullifies the teaching of scripture about the Cross through which we crucify the flesh and persevere against our old nature.

The Church growth formulas associated with Peter Wagner and Bill Hybels, which in effect imply that Church growth will mainly come from having the right programme, originates from the view that in a hi-tech economy the key to having a computer do what we want is getting the right software programme. If you get the right software programme, your computer system will give you the right results.

The 'possibility thinking' of Robert Schuller from the Crystal Cathedral clearly has more in common with Dale Carnegie and Norman Vincent Peale's 'positive thinking' than it does with the biblical exhortations of what Christian life and faith should be.

The viability of faith-prosperity preaching is strongly related to modern consumerism. Fuelled by the advertising industry, we are continually bombarded with messages designed to induce us to consume. Easy credit creates the illusion that it is all simple and the cleverness of advertising psychology seduces us into thinking our needs can be met if we possess certain things.

Inevitably church members begin to follow this same line of thinking. Instead of Christians seeking the Lord about which church He would have them be members of in order to meet the needs of others, they engage in comparative 'shopping' trying to see which Church will meet their needs. *Agape* love always puts self last, and in God's economy one important way He meets our needs is by using us first to help others. "He who waters, will himself be watered."[5]

Therefore churches which preach the Cross, holiness, repentance, and a crucified life, are unable to compete 'in the marketplace' with those that preach an unbalanced extreme of health, wealth and prosperity. These churches tell Christians the lie that they don't have to suffer and that God wants them all rich in this world, instead of trusting in the world to come.

As Paul warned Timothy, the last days would see such deception perpetrated against the Church:

"For the time will come when they will
not endure sound doctrine; but wanting
to have their ears tickled, they will
accumulate for themselves teachers
in accordance to their own desires;
and will turn away their ears from
the truth, and will turn aside to myths."
2 Timothy 4:3,4

As Paul writes elsewhere, these Christians refuse to receive a knowledge of the truth—they want to be deceived, or as he told Timothy: "They turn aside to the myths because they desire to do so".[6] Those who want to be deceived will be. Not just by the devil or by the false teachers and false prophets they ordain for themselves, but by the Lord Himself.[7]

We are called to re-contextualise the gospel. We are forbidden to re-define it. We are called to bring the gospel into the world not the world into the gospel.

Faith In Jesus, Or Faith In Faith?

Kenneth Hagin in one of his books on faith (which seem to be handbooks on the subject for all the prosperity preachers) wrote: "Faith Sees the Answer", but the Word of God says that faith does not necessarily see the answer. It only sees the **source** of the answer. We walk by faith, not by sight.[8] The faith of Hagin and the faith of the Bible are mutually exclusive.

When prosperity preacher Fredrick Price says that it is not Jesus who heals us, but our faith, we must ask what is God's version of faith according to His definition. It is "the substance of things hoped for, and assurance of things unseen." That is to say since God's faith equals future fact, what does that mean for living a life of faith for us now?

The answer to this question is found in Hebrews chapter 11, the faith chapter of the New Testament. Here we read more about faith than in all the rest of the New Testament put together.

The chapter commences with an extensive list of the heroes of the Old Testament; heroes as examples of what we should be. It certainly does *not* hold up to us for emulation the television evangelists.

It describes the faith life as going through a realistic combination of good and bad things; it is not necessarily a life of continual misery, but neither is it a life of continual ease and prosperity, but a combination of both.

The chapter concludes with this powerful description of true faith lived out:

> **"Others were tortured, not accepting
> their release, in order that they
> might obtain a better resurrection;
> and others experienced mockings and
> scourgings, yes, also chains and
> imprisonment. They were stoned, they
> were sawn in two, they were tempted,
> they were put to death with the sword;
> they went about in sheepskins, in**

goatskins, being destitute, afflicted,
ill-treated (men of whom the world was
not worthy), wandering in deserts and
and mountains and caves and holes in
the ground. And all these, having
gained approval through their faith,
did not receive what was promised,
because God had provided something better
for us, so that apart from us they should
not be made perfect."
Hebrews 11:35-40

We are told that these true models of faith were people who accepted suffering, torture, death, poverty, hunger and homelessness precisely because of their faith.

We are also told that Jesus was a Man of Sorrows acquainted with grief[9] and that as his servants we are not above our Master.[10] Paul's main thrust to his readers was the same as that of Christ's in terms of death to self. Moreover this death to self was not simply to overcome the old nature, but was to be expressed in laying our lives down for others. As Paul writes, quoting from Psalm 44:

"For thy sake we are being put to death
all day long; we were considered as
sheep to be slaughtered."
Romans 8:36

Or as Paul also writes:
"I am conscious of nothing against myself,
yet I am not by this acquitted; but the
one who examines me is the Lord. Therefore
do not go on passing judgment before the
time, but wait until the Lord comes who
will both bring to light the things hidden
in the darkness and disclose the motives
of men's hearts; and then each man's praise
will come to him from God.

Now these things, brethren, I have
figuratively applied to myself and Apollos for
your sakes, that in us you might learn not to
exceed what is written, in order that no one
of you might become arrogant in behalf of one
against the other.
For who regards you as superior? And what
do you have that you did not receive?
But if you did receive it, why do you boast
as if you had not received it? You are already
filled, you have already become rich, you have
become kings without us; and I would indeed
that you had become kings so that we also might
reign with you.
For, I think, God has exhibited us apostles
last of all, as men condemned to death;
because we have become a spectacle to the
world, both to angels and to men.
We are fools for Christ's sake, but you
are prudent in Christ; we are weak, but
you are strong; you are distinguished,
but we are without honour.
To this present hour we are both hungry
and thirsty, and are poorly clothed, and
are roughly treated, and are homeless;
and we toil, working with our own hand;
when we are reviled, we bless; when we
are persecuted, we endure;
when we are slandered, we try to conciliate;
we have become as the scum of the world,
the dregs of all things, even until now."
1 Corinthians 4:4-13

Just as Jesus said, we cannot serve God and Mammon and
those who covet cannot enter into the Kingdom of Heaven. Paul

writes:

> "And if we have food and covering, with
> these we shall be content."
> 1 Timothy 6:8

The Word of God tells us godliness is only a means of great gain when accompanied by contentment[11] and Paul commands that if our basic needs are met, we should be content. Yet the prosperity preachers tell us 'name it and claim it' and if we don't get it, it is because of our lack of faith or because there is sin in our lives.

Far from showing us a faith that tells us to 'blab it and grab it', and that claims it is God's purpose for us to have whatever we ask for, including our desire for riches, Paul tells us that those who want to get rich will lose their faith.[12]

What do Kenneth Hagin, Kenneth Copeland, John Avanzini, Frederick Price, Oral Roberts, Charles Capps, Marilyn Hickey and Jill Austin, Robert Tilton, Casey Treat, and those who give assent to what they say, like Roberts Liardon, know that St Paul did not?

I dare to say that they know nothing!

Whatever We Ask?

It was Satan who originally handled scripture the way the prosperity preachers do. In the wilderness, when he tempted Jesus, he took certain verses out of context and turned their meanings upside down.

We are plainly told in 1 John chapter 5:14,15 that it is when we ask in accordance with **God's** will that we will have the things we ask for. Contrary to the lies of Satan voiced through his servants, the prosperity preachers, the Word of God never gives us a blank cheque to ask according to **our** will.

Additionally, we are specifically warned that if we ask for things with materialistic motives, we will not receive them.[13]

Which Faith Shall We Choose?

It is impossible to reconcile the faith taught in the Word of God with the faith taught by the prosperity preachers. They are two different faiths. One is genuine from the fount of all blessing, and one is a counterfeit from the pit of destruction. It also appears that it is a faith which the prosperity preachers do not seem to actually believe themselves.

Frederick Price teaches that since our bodies are the temple of the Holy Spirit, the Holy Spirit does not want to dwell in a broken down house. Thus he puts those Christians who are sick under condemnation. Yet his own wife is reported to have been diagnosed with cancer. Four hours after Oral Roberts claimed a complete healing on television at the hands of Paul Crouch, he was in hospital with a major coronary. While Kenneth Hagin claims that he has not had a headache in forty-five years, he has had four major cardiovascular failures.[14]

The choice is clear. Is it to be faith in Christ as written in the Word of God by men who laid their lives down for the sake of their faith, or faith in faith written in cheap paperbacks by the kinds of false prophets and false teachers that Jesus warned us would come in the last days to deceive the elect?[15]

Prosperity preacher Hobart Freeman blamed his son-in-law's lack of faith for the death of his grandchild. He is known to be responsible for the deaths of at least ninety-seven people who were persuaded by him not to get medical attention. Finally he died himself.[16]

We cannot believe the gospel of Jesus Christ as it is taught in the Bible and the gospel of Mammon taught by the prosperity preachers. One will lead us to eternal life, the other into deception and to the judgement of a holy God.

We note that Jesus only did what He saw His Father doing, and in Luke chapter 5:17 the 'power' had to be present for Him to perform healings. We may always pray for the sick and anoint them with oil, but to command an invalid to get out of a wheelchair in the name of Jesus requires the power and leading of the Holy Spirit to be present.

Jesus did teach that signs would accompany believers. He taught that among other signs his followers would lay hands on the sick who would be healed. But this same verse also says that they would pick up serpents, be bitten and not die.

In Acts chapter 28 Paul was bitten by a poisonous serpent and did not die, because it was the will of the Lord in that given situation. But today we see the primitive Baptists in the American Appalachians picking up snakes on the basis of this same verse, being bitten and dropping dead. Why? Because they act not in faith, but in ignorance and presumption.

Those who believe that at their own discretion they have the power of Christ and can lay hands on the sick and see them healed in every instance are no better and no different from those who pick up snakes and allow themselves to be bitten in order to prove their faith.

Christians who go about arbitrarily commanding the sick to be healed and the dead to be raised are under the same delusion as those who prophesy and give people 'words' when the Holy Spirit has given them neither prophecy nor 'word'. These are very often the same people who think they are praying in tongues, when such is not the case except in the ignorance of their own minds.

I accept prophecies, tongues and healings—but only when God gives them, and not when men or women think themselves in possession of some 'authority' to use those gifts indiscriminately. When the Holy Spirit is not leading and empowering someone to use spiritual gifts in a given situation and someone tries to use them anyway they are, at best, a gift that is being misused. More frequently they are not a gift at all but as Jeremiah wrote: "the deception and futility of their own minds."[17]

Jesus plainly used the example of the Good Samaritan giving medical attention to an injured man as an example of how Christians should behave. Then later we read that Paul left Trophimus sick at Miletus.[18] We rely on the Lord, not medicine;

yet most healings in the Bible were for injuries or diseases for which there was no cure available. It is usually the same today.

Note that both Jesus and Paul left people sick and Luke practised medicine.

Once more we ask: what do the faith prosperity preachers know that Jesus, Paul and Luke did not? Once again—the answer is nothing.

A False Faith That Murders True Faith

There is perhaps only one thing more cruel in the Body of Christ than when the faith-prosperity teachers would in effect have us believe that those faithful Christians who are suffering and dying for their faith in Communist and Muslim countries are the carnal victims of their own lack of faith.

The only thing that a dying Christian and their family ultimately has on their death bed is their faith in Jesus, yet these self aggrandizing con-men even want to take that. A weak and compromising Church may stand for it, but a powerful and uncompromisingly holy God certainly will not.

Is Healing In The Atonement?

Today no issue causes more controversy in the Church than the question of healing and whether or not it is part of the Atonement of Jesus.

First of all I acknowledge that there is one category in which practically all Christians would believe healing is in the Atonement. We read of it in James chapter 5:14,15 and in Psalm 31:10. It is when a given illness is a direct result of unconfessed sin, and when that sin is confessed and repented of healing comes as an unambiguous direct result. In this case healing can be said to be in the Atonement.

But to understand this complicated question, we must go back to Isaiah chapter 53:5: "By His stripes we are healed." The context here is of healing from iniquity. This verse is cited twice in the New Testament. The first time in Romans chapter 4:25 where the context is again Jesus' suffering for our sins. The Greek term 'healing' (being *therapis* from the Hebrew *rapha*) does not even appear in the text and the context in which it is quoted again deals with sin, not illness.

The second quotation is found in 1 Peter 2:24,25. Yet again the context is that of healing from sin. So we see that neither New Testament reference to this verse even mentions illness.

I do allow that the Hebrew term *chole* in the preceding verse of Isaiah chapter 53:4, which sets the original context, does carry the connotation of bodily sickness. Yet this is nowhere the primary New Testament focus of the text. We again note that Paul was sick and left others sick and did not heal all those who came to him in search of healing. The healing of Peter's mother in law is in the context of release from demonic power (Matthew 8:14-17).

We must understand Isaiah chapter 53 verse 4 in the context of the entire chapter and also in the context of what the New Testament says elsewhere about the chapter, such as in Acts chapter 8 (which also deals with salvation from sin) and the broader New Testament teaching on receiving glorified bodies found in 1 Corinthians chapter 15.

In other words, healing is indeed in the atonement in a final and ultimate sense, but it is only fully realised in the resurrection when we shall each receive new bodies that will not become old or sick. If this is not the meaning, then why do the prosperity preachers themselves grow old and sick just as all men do?

Once again the root problem is over-realised eschatology. The kingdom is now, but not yet. These want the kingdom now and, like the dominionists, they claim to have a '*gnosis*' apart from the straightforward teaching of the Bible, in order to justify their position. Thus we are reminded once again that these two errors are both manifestations of the same root error.

The kingdom is restored to Israel, not the Church, and it happens with the return of Christ, not before it. Any healings we have before the resurrection are simply the blessings of God representing just a foretaste of the immortal bodies we shall receive when Jesus returns.

Let's Be Realistic

Most of us would agree that we would rather see Christians having money and power than unsaved people. Hopefully, if it is Christians who prosper, a fair percentage of their wealth will go to the work of the Lord in financing missions and evangelism and helping the needy.

Yet for those who have the privilege of earning their bread from the ministry of the gospel we must ask: "Isn't a middle class lifestyle good enough?" A middle class lifestyle is far **more** than at least seventy five percent of the people in the world are ever going to have.

Is it any wonder then, when the world sees the limousine lifestyle and the mansions and the excesses of the prosperity preachers they immediately dismiss the gospel of salvation as a swindle and a fraud.

If a Christian prospers in business or his profession, his stewardship is between the Lord and himself, but for those who have a high profile in the ministry, the testimony of their lifestyle affects the entire Church and also the image that the unsaved world sees. Remember, Jesus drove the moneychangers out of the Temple because they were profiteering from the blood of the Lamb.

That is why Jim Bakker went to jail. Judgment always begins at the House of God[19] and Jesus is still driving out those who profiteer from the blood of the Lamb. Christ would not stand for His Father's house being made into a den of robbers two thousand years ago and, despite the pseudo-spiritual boasting of false teachers, He will not stand for it today.

Why Has Satan Raised Them Up?

There are at least six clear reasons why the devil has raised up faith-prosperity preachers at the present time in history, aside from the fact that their errors are part and parcel of over-realised eschatology.

First—Some of these men began as sincere and gifted ministers of the gospel whom God called, God blessed and God used. As Satan therefore desires to sift us all like wheat, he wanted to destroy them, their testimonies, and their ministries. Usually, this situation can be achieved by spiritual pride, the love of money or immorality, or some combination of the three.

Second—In 1 Corinthians chapter 14:24 speaking about spiritual gifts, Paul puts an unsaved person and an ungifted person who does not operate in the gifts of the Spirit (*idiotai* in Greek) in the same category. Why does he do this?

The context tells us that the reason is that those who practise the gifts of the Spirit are to do so in such a manner as the Holy Spirit will use them to bring conviction both to the unsaved and the ungifted, so that the unsaved will want to get saved and that those who do not have charismatic gifts of the Spirit will desire them.

Instead when conservative evangelicals who take a cesssationist line (not giving place to the charismatic gifts) see the corruption and perversion of scriptures by the prosperity preachers and the public scandals which demean the reputation of the gospel in the eyes of a dying world, it causes them to reject the gifts of the Spirit because of the disgraceful example of those who emphasise them most. Almost all of the scandals that have rocked the Church in the last ten years have been among charismatic and pentecostal Christians.

Third—Satan is able to use the bad name that these men give the gospel to undermine its credibility and presentability to those who are perishing without it. When unsaved people see the money grubbing lives and manipulation of prosperity preachers, it causes them to view the gospel of Jesus as a form of fraud and extortion. Jesus warned that the sons of this age are more shrewd than the sons of light.[20] We can see how correct He was.

Restorationism and faith-prosperity are theologically linked to each other. Both are based on the same doctrinal errors emanating from over-realised eschatology. When unsaved people see the kind of money preaching that Rick Godwin indulged in at Birmingham, England, when he related how much people should contribute to his ministry in relation to the value they place on the lives of their children, even pagans view this kind of perversion of the Christian message with contempt.

There are very few unsaved people who would be stupid enough to send money to Robert Tilton, John Avanzini, Kenneth Hagin, or Benny Hinn. Unsaved people very reasonably conclude that it takes a born again Christian to be that undiscerning and naive. In short, when the lost souls of secular society see regenerate believers in Jesus sending money to faith-prosperity preachers it damages the credibility of our witness, the believability of the Bible and they rightly think we are all crazy.

The book of Revelation speaks of Satan's two modes of attack in the characters of the serpent and the dragon. The dragon is Satan's manifestation as a persecutor, but the serpent is his manifestation as a seducer (as the serpent's seduction of Eve typifies the spiritual seduction of Israel and the Church). Yet Jesus exhorts us to be as innocent as doves, but wise as serpents.[21] We are to be as shrewd as Satan is himself, but only in the power and wisdom of God.

The comedian W.C.Fields once said: "Never give a sucker an even break." We can be sure that the devil never will, and neither will his servants—the prosperity preachers sent by him to deceive the Church in the last days.

Fourth—While honest ministries and missions are starved for cash to do the legitimate work of the Lord, Satan uses the faith-prosperity teachers to divert huge sums away from that work and into the coffers of their own organisations. Honest works of the Lord all struggle financially just to expand the sphere of their work to reach and help larger numbers of people particularly in relation to preaching the Gospel and aid to the poor.

Only God knows how much of the true work of Jesus could have been done with the unimaginable fortunes ploughed into Heritage U.S.A.—Jim Bakker's Christian Disneyland, which according to some estimates would have been the third largest theme park in the U.S.A.

Fifth—The scandals and corruption of the faith-prosperity preachers serve Satan's interest in provoking persecution of the Church by governments. They usually restrict the use of the airwaves to preach the gospel to the lost. Television and radio are powerful media which Satan is using for evil—and he is also dedicated to ensuring that the prosperity preachers corrupt them as a medium that God could have used for good.

When the public sees the outrageous scandals, manipulation, hype and gimmickry used by prosperity preachers, they demand that governments restrict the uses of the airwaves even for the honest work of the gospel, and that they should remove tax exempt status from all Christian ministries and organisations. This reduces our ability to obey Jesus' final command contained in His last words.[22]

Sixth—A final reason Satan has raised up faith-prosperity preaching at this time, is to destroy real faith. The Bible speaks clearly and directly of those who will fall away in the last days and betray one another. It is certain that those who have been fed a diet of lies which tell them that they will be rich and not suffer will be the first to lose their faith when crises come into their lives. It is also these who will be the first to fall away and betray faithful Christians when persecution arises against the Church in the West, as it surely will.

I am convinced that the Lord is using these false teachers, in order to separate the wheat from the chaff. I also believe the same of phenomena such as Toronto and Pensacola are not merely deceptions from Satan, but judgements from God. Jesus called Himself "the Truth",[23] therefore when people do not love truth they do not love Jesus.

The Real Victims

In God's idea of Christian economy and community, the educated Christian should look out for the interests of the uneducated. The wealthy should look out for the interests of the poor and the clever should look out for the interests of the simple. As we read in Proverbs 14:31a:

He who oppresses the poor reproaches his Maker.

When the poor are exploited, God takes it as a personal offence.

A disproportionately large number of those who are drawn into supporting faith-prosperity preachers and their ministries are from the less educated and less affluent social classes whose interests the Church should be most protecting.

We note Morris Cerullo's formula letters promising victory over debt through a series of appeals in which the recipients are urged "to listen to the prophet of God and give more than you can afford to."

It is appalling that the shepherds, who will one day give account to Christ for the welfare of their sheep, will not stand against this kind of outrage.

Worse still, as Christianity declines in the West, the same corruption can be found spreading in Eastern Europe and the developing world where people are generally poor. The poor countries have become targets of the same kind of Mammon worshipping counterfeits of Christianity that have turned most of the Church in the Western world into something approaching the Church of Laodicea.[24]

So now that the main future of the gospel is demographically in the hands of the believers in poor countries and it is these whom Satan is trying to undermine using the same prosperity preaching he has already used to torpedo gospel presentation in the West.

Can A Shepherd Still Guard His Sheep?

Pastors will give account one day to Christ for how they have cared for the sheep whom Christ has entrusted to them.[25] Pastors are told directly to know the condition of their flocks:

Know well the condition of your flocks,
And pay attention to your herds.
Proverbs 27:23

While a pastor may be responsible for teaching the truth in his own church, the time is long past—due to the explosion in Christian media and merchandising—when he can truly know the condition of his flock because he can no longer monitor what they receive from elsewhere.

Even a faithful pastor, who rightly divides the Word of God, will have people in his church for whose souls he is responsible before God, who will be reading paperbacks, listening to tapes, watching videos, seeing things on television, hearing things on radio and attending conferences where all manner of doctrine is being taught—including dangerous things contrary to the Word of God—that he would never allow to be taught from his own pulpit.

Nonetheless, as far as God is concerned, the pastor remains responsible for the condition of his flock. Honest pastors must be willing to stand up against errors and denounce them from their pulpits and, where necessary, name those who persist in seducing the Church, just as the Apostles and prophets did in their day.[26] Otherwise their flocks will be ravaged and their churches possibly split as factions within the church take these errors on board. Christ will still hold them accountable for not acting to protect His sheep if they say nothing.

But today we see the opposite of what God expects. Jack Hayford has been an honest minister of the gospel whom I have always respected. He was one of those not given to peddling the Word of God.[27]

Yet when Dr James Dobson warned that Oral Roberts had lost his sanity when Roberts claimed that God told him He would kill him if he could not raise eight million dollars within a specified time,[28] Jack Hayford warned against going on 'witch hunts' while Robert Liardon said that it was the Christians who criticised Oral Roberts who were the crazy ones.

Benny Hinn and Kenneth Copeland believe that Jesus became a Satanic being in hell of one nature with Satan and Oral Roberts made Christianity seem like the domain of the mentally deranged in the eyes of the public. Yet Jack Hayford defended Oral Roberts,

Kenneth Copeland, Frederick Price and others as "thoroughly Christian and soundly biblical."

When men teach hellish lies about Jesus saying that He became a satanic being in hell of one nature with the devil, they are neither thoroughly Christian nor soundly biblical. Moreover, when they do it on television in front of millions, those who challenge such blasphemy can hardly be described as participating in 'witch hunts'—the heretics are already in their living rooms.

Edmund Burke said that "the only thing necessary for evil men to triumph is for good men to do nothing." The Christian world has seen the results of what happens when otherwise good men like Jack Hayford 'do nothing' and prosperity preachers are allowed to plunge the gospel of Jesus Christ and the testimony and reputation of the Body of Christ into disrepute.

The question remains: how much more damage will we allow Satan to inflict on the cause of Christ by listening to the well-intentioned but thoroughly unbiblical advice of decent, but misguided men, instead of the clear declarations of the Word of God?[29]

I urge that believers who follow such false teaching be exhorted with great patience and instruction (*macrotheumia* in Greek). But note that later in the same chapter, Paul is not so benevolent in dealing with the false teachers themselves (2 Timothy 4:14-15). Who is right—the apostle Paul or Jack Hayford?

What About The Miracles?

In John chapter 5 Jesus tells us that the works that the Father has given Him to do—which include signs and wonders—bear witness to Him.[30] Jesus also said that His followers would do even greater works[31]—but again in order to bear witness to Jesus, not to the ministry of man.

We cannot be sure that Jesus had any more than five hundred committed converts. Countless servants of the gospel have had far more converts than Jesus. Indeed, greater works have been done and are being done. In Hebrews chapter 2 we read that signs, wonders, miracles and gifts of the Holy Spirit bear witness to the truth of the gospel we have heard. But the emphasis is on bearing witness to the gospel, not to human ministry.

The signs of Christ's likeness are a Christ-like life, never signs and wonders. As we have noted, Paul's proof of his position in Christ was his willingness to suffer as Christ did for the sake of others. In Hebrews chapter 5:8-9 we read that Jesus, who did not need to suffer for His own sake because He had no fallen nature, needed to be perfected by suffering for our sakes. Here was the proof of Christ's calling, here was the proof of Paul's calling, and here is the proof of those who are truly called today.

Miracles prove nothing about anyone except the power of Jesus and the authenticity of His salvation. They never say anything about the ministry of any other man or woman.

On the contrary, Jesus specifically warned against thinking that they were proof of someone's faithfulness or ministry. As He Himself told us:

"Many will say to Me on that day, 'Lord, Lord, did we not prophesy in Your name, and in Your name cast out demons, and in Your name perform many miracles?'"
Matthew 7:22

Jesus never said that we will know someone by their gifts. He said: "You will know them by their fruit."[32]

We must remember that after he had backslidden, King Saul continued to prophesy and people were baffled by this when they asked: "Is Saul among the prophets?" [33] Although the context deals with a different subject, the principle we read in Romans chapter 11:29 is that "the gifts and calling of God are without repentance."

Once again signs, wonders and miracles prove a lot about Jesus, they prove a lot about the validity of the gospel, and they prove a great deal about the power and faithfulness of God, but they prove absolutely nothing about the minister who performs the miracles or the ministries which boast of them. It was not his ability and gifting to do signs and wonders that Paul boasted of, and he rebukes those who look for outward things as cause to boast.[34] In the natural realm and in terms of ministry, Paul had a lot more to boast about than the arrogant boasting of faith-prosperity preachers and restorationists, but he didn't. Paul said as far as he was concerned, the only things that he had worth boasting about were not his miracles, his ministry, his Jewish background and his Pharisaic theological education but his weakness![35]

When we compare the ministry of Paul with the ministries of the faith-prosperity preachers, and when we compare the thing he boasted about with what they boast about, and then when we see the impact of his ministry on a world of sin compared to theirs—we must seriously ask, "do these people know what true power is?"

The Word of God is clear. We should not marvel at the gifts and, much less, the gifted, but rather we should marvel at the Giver.

Are All The Miracles Really Miracles?

There are miracles which are purely spiritual, the greatest of these being salvation. There are also miracles which are both spiritual and physical which we call 'signs and wonders'.

It is unfortunately necessary first of all to reconcile ourselves to the fact that much of what is called healing is not healing at all, and the same is certainly true of much of what we call being 'slain in the Spirit'.

I do not reject the biblical basis for this phenomena as there are documented occasions when the power of Jesus came on someone and they fell as if dead,[36] but much of what presently passes for being 'slain in the Spirit' is purely psychological, or people being pushed down or knocked out in order to stage a show.

This is certainly not what was happening when this phenomenon accompanied the ministries of John Wesley and George Whitfield because they were true charismatics, who based their ministry on the Word—unlike the 'charismaniacs' of our own day who invent their doctrines and practices in order to please themselves and to impress others.

Martial arts experts who have become Christians and Christian medical doctors have watched videos of prosperity preachers laying hands on people and were easily able to identify these people as applying pressure on peripheral cervical nerves which would make anyone collapse.

'Leg-pulling' is another of these absurdities where even secular television documentaries have captured the sleight-of-hand machinations of the so-called 'faith healers'. I do not reject the fact that Jesus can, and does heal people today as He did in scripture, and neither do I reject that there are Christians in the Body of Christ today upon whom God has graciously bestowed the gifts of healing.

I do believe, however, that, as a Christian orthopaedic surgeon in Australia wrote, the medical condition of one leg being shorter than the other is usually due either to a severed femur, or a congenital condition. This is something which most ordinary doctors rarely if ever see, and which even most orthopaedic specialists would only encounter a few times in the entire course of their careers.

From conception, human beings develop with 'bi-lateral symmetry'—that is our left and right sides are mirror images. Nonetheless there are always slight differences between, say, the left ear and the right, the left and the right nostril etc. Slight differences do not normally constitute a medical deformity.

I do not deny this medical condition exists, because medical science assures us it does. Neither do I deny that there may be people who have been healed of it through prayer. What I do not believe is that a condition which is relatively rare and usually a minor disorder according to recognised medical experts, is so suddenly commonplace at the meetings of faith-prosperity preachers. Not only are they pulling the legs of the people who they have talked into thinking that they suffer from this disorder, but they are also 'pulling the legs' of everyone else.

Are All Miracles Done In The Name
Of Christianity From Christ?

God makes it clear in Isaiah chapter 42:8 that He will not give His glory to another. We therefore know that the miracles that are alleged to take place in places like Fatima, Lourdes, Knock and Megjurigore are either bogus or demonic. God will not perform a miracle and let Mary or anyone else have the glory.

More striking, however, are the warnings of both Jesus and St Paul of the deception that would come in the last days involving signs and wonders which are designed to trick the elect.[37] That is to say the devil will use signs and wonders in order to deceive Christians.

In 2 Timothy chapter 3:1-9 Paul tells us that those engaging in this deception will create difficult times for the Church, just as Benny Hinn and others are doing today. Paul describes these men as being boastful and arrogant and says that they have a form of godliness but not its real power and he commands that such men be avoided.[38] He also warns that women will be particularly vulnerable to this kind of spiritual seduction just as Eve was in the garden.[39]

Paul commands that we avoid men such as these, because they have depraved minds and they oppose the truth. He also predicts by the Holy Spirit that their folly will be obvious to all, just as we have seen the folly of Larry Lee, Robert Tilton and Benny Hinn exposed by the secular media on television.

Above all Paul highlights the fact that the deception that these men will perpetrate will be in the character of Jannes and Jambres.[40]

Who were Jannes and Jambres, and what were the keys to their deception? They were the magicians of Pharaoh in Exodus chapter 7 who were able to counterfeit the miracles of Moses and Aaron, just as the Antichrist and False Prophet will counterfeit the miracles of Jesus and His witnesses.[41]

It is precisely this background that Revelation chapter 13:14 draws on in warning us how the Antichrist (whose existence restorationists deny) will deceive the nations:

"And he deceives those who dwell on the earth because of the signs which it was given him to perform in the presence of the beast telling those who dwell on the earth to make an image to the beast who had the wound of the sword and has come to life."

When Kingdom Now preachers say that there will be no Antichrist, and when faith-prosperity preachers make 'signs and wonders' the proof of the pudding; when triumphalists teach that Christ returns to the Church before He returns for it, we cannot say that the deception foretold in Revelation chapter 13 will only take place against the unsaved. In the light of the treachery and heresy of the prosperity preachers, thinly camouflaged as Christ-likeness, we must now ask—"will these deceptions be directed against the elect"?

Asian Evangelist to the Hindus, Thomas Chakko, after viewing videos of Toronto featuring Rodney Howard-Browne and Kenneth Copeland, warned that such manifestations are identical to Kundalini Yoga and described the Toronto experience as eastern religion infiltrating western Christendom.

Romany Gypsies who become Christians call Toronto manifestations "duckering", something they describe as what they did before they were born-again—using the occult to get money out of people.

These manifestations however find a natural bedfellow in false doctrines of Kingdom Now theology. Dominionists, charismatic and pentecostal christians who draw their eschatology from Gary North, David Chilton and Rouses Rushdooney match this overrealised eschatology with Toronto/Pensacola style lunacy. Kevin Connor in Melbourne Australia, true to form, embraced the Toronto Experience. Such phenomena also found the endorsement of CBN founder Pat Robertson.

The above becomes especially true in view of the rapprochement that politically motivated evangelical leaders like Pat

Robertson have made with Rome (with his new found reconstructionist over-realised eschatology). We must remember that not only does the Pontiff of Rome—whom we call the Pope—have the same title as the imperial emperor of pagan Rome, who was also called the Pontiff (*pontifex maximus,* the emperor worship of imperial Rome typifies and foreshadows the worship of the ultimate Antichrist), but he has another title.

The term Antichrist in Greek does not simply mean against Christ, but means vicar, or the one who was in place of Christ and that is exactly what the Roman Catholic church teaches that their Pontiff is—"The Vicar of Christ".

This is not to suggest that the Pope is **the** Antichrist, but by definition he is certainly "an" antichrist and he typifies the one who is coming and who may already be alive.

The lynchpin in all of this is, of course, money. The prosperity preachers worship mammon and preach money. Pat Robertson now leans towards a kingdom theology which over identifies American capitalism with biblical teaching about the kingdom of God. Finally the Vatican is and remains a financial institution whose bank is actually called "The Ministry of Religious Works". It also owns other banks, primarily in Italy, such as "the Bank of the Holy Spirit".

What we have in the convergence of these interests is ecumenical compromise; compromise with false prosperity doctrine and adherence to triumphalism. A worldy manifestation of a spiritually blind evangelical church whose priorities are determined by the interests of money and politics and whose view of biblical doctrine becomes functionally subordinate to people's opinions which demand that scripture be re-interpreted accordingly. This is the type of church found in Laodicea and at Babylon.[42]

The signs and wonders deception is underscored and supported by a number of other deceptions that merge together to perpetrate an unimaginable level of seduction that goes beyond simply deceiving the world. The world is already deceived. Satan wants to deceive the Church—and he does this by counterfeits. Jesus did true miracles so Satan will counterfeit them. The elect of

Jesus also do miracles and he must counterfeit these also.

The only question concerning the apparent 'signs' of men like Benny Hinn is, are their miracles genuine gifts that are being misused, (as with King Saul who—like the Pope and pagan emperors—also typifies the antichrist in certain aspects), or are they spiritual counterfeits done by the prince of the power of the air, in the spirit and character of Jannes and Jambres as Paul warned us?

Jesus Himself specifically warns of those who will use signs and wonders in the last days to try and deceive true Christians.[43] In the charismatic and pentecostal movements too often there is little care for the prayerful study of the scriptures, and still less care about the warnings of scripture. When we are warned against things we would rather ignore, it is easy to see why it is that in order to defend against deception, Paul warns Timothy that his only sure protection is the Word of God.[44] "For these evil men and impostors will proceed from bad to worse deceiving, and being deceived."[45] In the previous verse the apostle even suggests that these scoundrels will persecute godly Christians.

As Paul predicted, since the scandals of Jim and Tammy Bakker and Jimmy Swaggart, things have gone from bad to worse. In their heyday even these fallen brethren would not have sunk to the level of Bible twisting since undertaken by Robert Tilton, Oral Roberts and Benny Hinn.

Yet instead of looking to the Word of God, some people look for a sign. Certainly signs have their place, but their place is never to replace the doctrines of God's Word or the message of repentance.

It is no wonder that Jesus said: "It is a wicked generation that seeks a sign."[46] It is sobering to think that we have become that wicked generation!

Yet Another Gospel?

As we have seen in our treatment of Jesus' triumphal entry into Jerusalem, the Jews of His day had three wrong ideas about the gospel which we in the church share today: a Kingdom Now gospel, a prosperity gospel, and a signs and wonders gospel.

As is typical, those arriving at these conclusions do so through false exegesis. We see the Restorationist preacher Andrew Shearman distorting the original meaning of the text of Matthew chapter 11:12 which says:

"And from the days of John the Baptist
until now the kingdom of heaven suffers
violence, and violent men take it by force."

Shearman teaches pentecostals that this means a triumphalist movement of violent Christians establishing the kingdom. Yet the original context and Greek definition of the word for violent (*biazetai*) renders Shearman's view ridiculous. This same passage is repeated in Luke chapter 16:16 where the same word is translated in most English Bibles as "forcing their way into".

The text itself, therefore, teaches that the law and prophets teach us about our condemnation, or as it says in Galatians, "the law is our tutor"[47] to teach us about our need for someone to save us from the kind of judgment that John the Baptist preached about. As we read in Psalm 19:7 it is the law of God which presses our souls to convert because it condemns us and shows us that we need to be saved.

The picture is like that of a ferry boat having a casino, a discotheque and a pub on board. The Christians are outside in the cold night air seated in lifeboats which correspond to the Church. If the Christians try to tell people that being in the lifeboats will give them a better cruise, even the people they persuade to get into the lifeboats will soon tire of it when the sea becomes rough and the night cold and the rain wet and will return back to the pleasures of the casino and the discotheque.

If, however, the Christians warn the people that the ferry is sinking and they are doomed, they will force their way into the lifeboats violently. This is the meaning of "*biazetai*". It means that people knowing they are condemned (because of the law) will press their way into the Church, the only way of salvation, the same as the lifeboats are the only way of salvation for those on the sinking ferry.

Shearman rejects the meaning of the text itself and invents his own in order to propound his own Kingdom Now ideas.

What Do The Heretics Know That Jesus Didn't?

Jesus refused to put on the kind of show that the Jews wanted on Palm Sunday. Instead He cleansed the Temple. Only after dealing with the corruption in the House of God did He perform Signs and Wonders. As the Scripture says: "these signs shall follow." The signs are not the message or the emphasis in themselves.

Yet today we see prosperity-preachers engaging in the very thing Jesus refused to do—putting on a show instead of preaching repentance. In his English advertising, Morris Cerullo represented the entire thrust of his version of the gospel as signs and wonders in a billboard campaign.

With his blowing on people and ranting around the stage, Benny Hinn appears more like a television hypnotist than like Jesus or the Apostles. Indeed that is probably what he actually is.[48] Hinn reduces the ministry of the gospel to the level of cheap exhibitionism that Jesus refused to allow.

When Jesus performed a miracle, unless there was a special reason, He usually told people to keep it quiet or not to tell anyone or to keep it to themselves and give God the thanks and the glory. Christ would not allow signs and wonders to eclipse His message of repentance, and He would not allow His ministry to be turned into a circus spectacle to provide the entertainment the Jews expected.

The Antichrist on the other hand will certainly engage in such ploys.

Conclusions

There is a prosperity that God promises to His people. But it is not the prosperity of this world. One way or another God will meet our needs—on His terms, not ours. But He has never promised to meet our wants in this fallen world. We are called to live in it like sojourners, holding it lightly even though we are promised it one day.[49]

Our example of faith is rather to be like father Abraham[50] who lived as an alien in the land promised to him because he knew he could not truly inherit it in this life. Instead he was looking for a city whose architect and builder is God.[51] As the writer of Hebrews also tells us:

> "All these died in faith, without receiving the promises, but having seen them and having welcomed them from a distance, and having confessed that they were strangers and exiles on the earth."[52]

We cannot have both the faith of Hebrews and that of Hagin. We must choose. Those Christians who do not love the truth, but persist in following men who teach error—instead of what God knows they need to hear—are not only being deceived by the devil, but also by themselves and by the pseudo-Christian gurus they choose to follow. As I have said, if they do not stop now before it is too late, the time will come when the Lord Himself will deceive them, since deception is what they choose.

1 John chapter 2 warns us about the Antichrist by first exhorting us not to love the world. If we love the world, we will be deceived and Prosperity preaching is nothing if not a love of the world ruled over by the god of this world. As the Spirit of God warns us through the writings of Paul:

> "For the mystery of lawlessness is
> already at work; only he who now
> restrains will do so until he is
> taken out of the way.
> And then that lawless one will be
> revealed whom the Lord will slay
> with the breath of His mouth and
> bring to an end by the appearance
> of His coming; that is, the one whose coming
> is in accord with the activity of Satan,
> with all power and signs and false
> wonders, and with all the deception

of wickedness for those who perish,
because they did not receive the
love of the truth so as to be saved.
And for this reason God will send upon
them a deluding influence so that they
might believe what is false, in order
that they all may be judged who did not
believe the truth, but took pleasure
in wickedness."
2 Thessalonians 2:7-12

Faith-prosperity preaching is neither the faith of the Bible nor the prosperity that the Bible promises. It is not the gospel of Jesus, but the gospel of mammon. It is a deception that will poison your soul and murder your spirit. If you want to be deceived instead of loving the truth, the Lord Himself will deceive you. Yet He loves you and so He beckons you to return to the true teachings of His Word.

The return of Jesus, or your going to meet him, will either be your best dream or your worst nightmare. Many who think they are following the real Jesus are following a Jesus that does not exist. Because the real Jesus loves you, He wants you to believe Him, and not the lies and hype of the world.

Those who persist in this deception will be destroyed by it. The only viable alternative is that we return to the real Jesus of the gospel and abandon the fictional one of the faith-prosperity preachers while there is still time.

If you are following faith-prosperity preaching,
THE DEVIL IS TAKING YOU FOR A RIDE.

Notes on ch.8

1. Hebrews 7:22; 8:6; 12:24.
? 1 Corinthians 4:9-13; 2 Corinthians5:8; Philippians 1:21-23.
2 Benny Hinn, "Benny Hinn" Programme on TBN, 3 November, 1990. Cited in Hank Hanegraaff, *Christianity in Crisis*, Nelson Word, Milton Keynes. 1993: 97-102.
3. Benny Hinn recorded onto Audiotape 1, side 1, of Hank Hanegraaff, *Christianity in Crisis*, Harvest House Publishers, Oregon. 1993.
4 1 Corinthians 9:19-23.
5. Proverbs 11:25.
6. 2 Timothy 4:3-4.
7. 1 Thessalonians 2:11.
8. 2 Corinthians 5:7.
9. Isaiah 53:3.
10. Matthew 10:24.
11. 1 Timothy 6:6.
12. 1 Timothy 6:9.
13. James 4:3.
14. Hank Hanegraaff, *Christianity in Crisis*, Nelson Word, Milton Keynes. 1993:237-238.
   Further reading: Dave Hunt and T.A. McMahon, *The Seduction of Christianity*, Harvest House Publishers, Oregon. 1985.
   D. R. McConnell, *A Different Gospel*, Hendrickson Publishers, Massachusetts. 1988, 1995.
15. Matthew 24:24.
16. A routine medical operation could have saved the boys' life. Hobart Freeman's rejection of medicine also led to his own apparently premature death in 1984. Bruce Barron, *The Health and Wealth Gospel*, Intervarsity Press, Downers Grove, IL. 1987:14-34.
17. Jeremiah 7:24.
18. 2 Timothy 4:20.
19. Ezekiel 9:6, 1 Peter 4:17.
20. Luke 16:8.
21. Matthew 10:16.
22. Acts 1:6-10.
23. John 14:6.
24. Revelation 3:14-22.
25. 1 Peter 5:4.
26. Jeremiah 28:15; 1 Timothy 1:20; 2 Timothy4:14; 3 John 9.
27. 2 Corinthians 2:17.
28. On January 4, 1987, Oral Roberts attempted to raise funds by telling his followers that if he did not raise 8 million dollars by March, God was going to take his life. David Lane, president and general manager of WFAA-TV in

Dallas, quoted in Associated Press dispatch from Tulsa, Oklahoma, printed as: "TV Ban Won't End Oral Roberts' Vow of 'Cash or Death.'" Toronto Star (14 January 1987), All; and "Despite TV Stations' Protests, Oral Roberts Won't Stop Life-or-Death Appeal for Funds," Orange Country Register(California) (14January 1987), A19. Cited in Hank Hanegraaff, *Christianity in Crisis*, Nelson Word, Milton Keynes. 1993:196.

In a follow-up direct mail letter, Roberts confirmed that there was only until 31 March to raise the remaining 1.5 million dollars. "Just 30 days left!" was written in handwriting at the top of the page. Ibid.,196

29. 2 Timothy 4:2-4.

30. John 5:36.

31. John 14:12.

32. Matthew 7:16.

33 1 Sam 19:23-24

34. 2 Corinthians 10:7-18.

35. 2 Corinthians 11:30.

36. Mark 9:26; Revelation 1:17.

37. Matthew 24:24; 2 Thessalonians 2:9.

38. 2 Timothy 3:2-5.

39. 2 Timothy 3:6.

40. 2 Timothy 3:8.

41. 2 Thessalonians 2:9.

42. Revelation 3:14-22.

43. Matthew 24:24.

44. 2 Timothy 3:14.

45. 2 Timothy 3:13.

46. Luke 11:29.

47. Galatians3:24.

48 See *The Signs and Wonder Movement Exposed*: Glover, Haville, Hand and Foster

49. Matthew 5:5.

50. Hebrews 11:19.

51. Hebrews 11:10.

52. Hebrews 11:13.

Chapter 9

Lie 4: Gnosticism and the New Age

The Rebirth Of Gnosticism

Alexandria was the crossroads where Hellenism, Judaism, and Christianity converged to meet the religions and philosophies of the Orient. There were both Hellenistic and eastern expressions of Gnosticism influencing Christendom in the early centuries of the Church dating back again to Philo but climaxing under Origen.

The Greek versions of Gnosticism were tied to the philosophical concepts of Dualism. The Greeks could accept the *logos* or the Word as being the creative agent and even the instrument of salvation of a supreme being. However, they could not accept the idea that the "Word became flesh".[1] The Greek Gnosticism at the time of the early Church was cemented to the Dualistic world view of the Greeks which said everything material (such as flesh) was automatically evil simply because it was material, often viewing the material world as the creation of an inferior or evil god while the spiritual realm was the domain of the higher god. Incidentally, the new creation narrative in the prologue of John' Gospel is in fact a midrashic replay of the creation narrative in Genesis which draws upon the Hebrew concept of *dvar* (word or *mamra* in Aramaic), the Greek equivalent being *logos*.

The faith teaching which Kenneth Copeland, Fredrick Price, Kenneth Hagin and others borrow from the teachings of E.W. Kenyon was something Kenyon himself acquired from Mary Baker Eddy, the founder of Christian Science. The entire 'hyper faith' view that "my body is lying to me" (confessing things by faith, no matter what is true in the natural world, have this Gnostic orientation: that the physical world is irrelevant and only the spiritual realm matters, and what is declared in the spiritual realm will automatically have practical consequences in the physical world.

The gospel, however, stands completely against this Greek world view. The material world was not created evil by a 'lesser god' but was created by the one true God and is fallen. In order for redemption to be possible, it was not enough to 'declare' something in the spiritual realm, but rather that the God who is Spirit had to become flesh, taking on a material body and overcoming the fall upon the Cross .[2]

The licentiousness and carnality often found among hyper-charismatic and hyper-Pentecostal faith preachers are a natural by-product of such Gnosticism. It has the same root origin as the antinomian heresy of the early church. Antinomianism taught that "It does not matter what we do in the flesh because the flesh is part of the fallen world. It only matters what the spirit does which is part of the spiritual world as a result of the new creation, the new birth." Paul spoke directly against this in his epistle to the Corinthians where he reminds them of their fleshly body being the temple of the Holy Spirit.[3]

Gnosticism, Dualism, And Crazy Eschatology

The root of Gnosticism was the concept "You are God". The biblical teaching is rather different, saying: "We shall be as He is." Dominionism and its faith-prosperity counterpart, says: "We are now like He is" in some kind of already complete sense, apart from the return of Christ. Hence we hear Morris Cerullo stating boldly: "When you look at me, you are not looking at Morris Cerullo, you are looking at Jesus Christ."[4] Once more, this is over-realised eschatology.

For these people the cross is a past, static event and not a current dynamic one. In other words, the purpose of the cross is over and the true emphasis on picking up our cross and following Jesus, and continuing to die with Him until He returns, is replaced by this over-realised eschatology. There is little, if any, emphasis on a crucified life. Instead the emphasis is on being 'King's kids' and as such, that there is no need to suffer in this world.

Among other things, this wrong view of Christianity demands two things. First it demands a Gnostic dualism which tries to deny the reality of illness, financial hardship, persecution and suffering, along the same warped lines as Christian Science, which is largely where it originates.

Secondly, it requires a *gnosis*, an 'inner revelation' which in turn requires bizarre methods of interpreting Scripture.

We continually find this train of thought in the teachings of Kenneth Hagin, Kenneth Copeland, Fred Price, Benny Hinn and others who claim new revelations that God has given them, precisely as the gnostic heretics did in the early Church. Those who do not possess the gnosis are called 'rebels' or 'deceived brethren'. Hence, like the Gnostics in the early Church, those who follow such people become victims of personality cults or, in the cases of Restoration churches, personality cults interwoven with heavy shepherding—they are natural bedfellows.

These people always copy from each other and quote each other. As Jeremiah declares: "They steal from each other...".[5] We always see Hagin and Copeland speaking the way the Apostles of restorationism do saying: "The Lord showed me...", and "The Lord told me this secret for success..." They then proceed to divorce certain verses or passages of scripture from their contexts in order to construct an artificial theology to support these gnostic 'revelations'.

The Real Nature Of Gnosticism

This is the nature of Gnosticism—a secret mystical knowledge subjectively revealed. So for others to come to the truth, they must come to and go through the person with the *gnosis*. Gnosticism bears the mark of antichrist because it puts man in the place of God. The faith prosperity heretics who teach faith in faith camouflaged as faith in God mislead people into believing that we can speak into being things which do not exist, just as God did.

This heresy is vividly demonstrated in David Yonggi Cho's

book *The Fourth Dimension*[6] where he discusses visualisation. He speaks of visualising what you want and speaking it into being—just as Buddhists have done for centuries—only now, it seems, Jesus has shown him it should be done by Christians. Similarly we see the prosperity teachers preaching "you do not have a god in you, you are one", which they prove to their satisfaction by taking certain passages of scripture out of their context.

One of the most apostate deceivers in the world today is without doubt South African money preacher Ray Macauley who appears to teach that building the Tower of Babel is God's model for Christian unity. McCauley has published his own version of the Bible which totally redefines the teaching and meaning of the creation narrative in Genesis. He has also repeatedly imported the erroneous teaching of anti-Israel preacher Rick Godwin into South Africa.

Gnosticism was rampant in the Orient and eastern Mediterranean during the first centuries of Christianity and it is making a triumphant comeback today. In the ancient world, as today, it came in a multitude of forms, expressions, trends, fads, cults and strains, combined with a multitude of different religions and philosophies. But it all had the same essence—secret knowledge revealed through a cult figure, "You are God" teaching and usually a dualistic view of reality which tries to mimic the biblical view as closely as possible. Making it appear as part and parcel of the flesh/spirit conflict that the Bible actually does teach, but which is in fact completely different.

Gnosticism is tied to the Hellenistic concept of dualism which teaches that the physical world is not simply fallen but inherently bad. Hence the common fruit of Gnosticism is always either stoicism and legalism on one hand or licentiousness and anti-nomianism on the other.

Roman Catholic perversions such as celibacy and transubstantiation are philosophically derived from dualist concepts in pagan thought—particularly Aristotelianism (which Thomas Aquinas adopted when he reinterpreted Christianity as an Aristotelian religion).

These ideas stand in stark contrast to the gospel message where God becomes a man to redeem all of the creation—including physical matter. It begins with the crucifixion and resurrection but is set to find its ultimate fulfilment at the return of Christ. As Paul wrote: "For we know that the whole creation groans and suffers the pains of childbirth together until now. And not only this, but also we ourselves, having the first fruits of the Spirit, even we ourselves groan within ourselves, waiting eagerly for our adoption as sons, the redemption of our body."[7]

Gnostic Hermeneutics In The Church

From this gnostic mindset there evolved an entirely unscriptural method of interpreting the Bible. It is based on revelation and *eisegesis* (that is, reading something *into* the text that it does not say as opposed to *exegesis* which is drawing something *out from* the text) and not on the grammatical and historical exegesis nor midrashic Jewish exegesis.

In Biblical hermeneutics, we never base a doctrine on a type or allegory. What Scripture does is to use typology and allegory to illustrate and illuminate doctrine in order to amplify it in such a manner as to reveal a greater depth of understanding.

For instance, in 1 Corinthians chapter 5, Paul uses the typology and symbolism of the Jewish passover to explain the New Testament doctrine of atonement—that Jesus died for our sins and that He is the actual meaning—or anti-type—of the passover lamb. Nowhere does the New Testament base the doctrine of atonement on the symbolism of the Jewish passover. What it does do, however, is to use the symbolism of the passover and its rituals as a way of demonstrating and explaining on a deeper level the meaning of the sacrifice of Jesus for our sins as the Lamb of God "who takes away the sins of the world".[8]

In the Gnostic hermeneutics that came into the early Church, however, the influx of Greek ideas regarding allegory progressively usurped and eventually replaced the Hebraic ones. This had its origins in the teachings of Philo who began combining Greek and

Jewish methods of allegory. Admittedly, at times the link between the two concepts could seem, on the surface, to be similar. This is demonstrated in the development of apocalyptic writing as a Jewish literary style during the inter-testamental period (that is the time between the writing of Malachi, and the New Testament). There **were** similarities between Jewish and Greek apocalyptic literature. However, there is no Biblical basis for determining doctrinal truth on the basis of types, allegories, metaphors, figures, or symbols. These things are only intended as illustrations of truth, not the basis for it.

Gnostic hermeneutics, however, again drawing on Hellenistic models, would see someone claiming to have a *gnosis*, or subjective revelation into the symbolism/typology/allegory and would then base a doctrinal conclusion upon such 'knowledge', re-interpreting the plainly stated meanings of Scripture in light of the *gnosis* and confusing the descriptive with the prescriptive.

Roman Catholicism is one very well known example which is based on Gnosticism. In the Magnificat contained in Luke's gospel, Mary plainly states that her "spirit rejoices in God my Saviour", thus confessing her need to be saved from sin. The Pope erroneously claims to have a *gnosis* as the heir of Peter. Speaking *Ex Cathedra* through the *magisterium* of the Roman church, the Pope can contradict Mary and proclaim "the Immaculate Conception", demanding that, contrary to what is plainly stated in the gospel by Mary herself, she had no sin and therefore needed no Saviour. Hence, the plain meaning of Scripture is ignored. To Catholics it is only important what the person with the *gnosis* says about it, and that the *gnosis* can only be found in the Pope as the heir of Peter.

In Hassidic Judaism, the rival Hassidic sects claim that their rabbi (called a **Rebbe** or **Tsadik**) has a *gnosis* through the re-incarnated spirit of **Bal Shem Tov** (called the **Besch**) which came down through his followers such as Rabbi Isaac Luria. Hassidic Judaism propounds **Zohar** (mystical Judaism), particularly Kabballah. The Kabbalistic views of God closely follow the ancient gnostic concepts of the *demi-urge*. God is called the **Ein-Sof**, having no essence, only attributes or emanations.

In Hassidic Judaism there are two ways to this god—either through *Torah*, or by *Tsadik* who through a Kabbalistic *gnosis* can go directly to God. Hence, when he goes to God through *Torah* (viewed Kabbalistically), his followers go to God through him.

Thus, in Hassidic Judaism (as in Roman Catholicism), it is not important what the *Torah* (the first five books of the bible) actually says, but rather what the *Tsadik* who has the *gnosis* says about it.

In Shia Islam, the intermediary is called the *Imam*. The Koran is viewed through the prism of what the Imam says about it. In Sufi Islam, it is the *Suf* who pronounces Allah's word. He goes to Allah directly, his followers go to Allah through him.

In Hinduism, it is the *Brahmin* priests—the highest order of the caste system—or the guru who go to Vishnu, Krishna, Shiva and Rama, directly. Once again their followers enter the presence of the supernatural through them.

With the Mormon cult, it is their priesthood and their revelators, while in the Jehovah's Witnesses, it is their governing board following the teachings of C.T. Russell and Judge Rutherford. In its studies in scripture, the Jehovah's Witness cult maintains that someone could read the Bible and understand nothing but if they read the cult's own studies in scripture, they will understand everything—it becomes the Bible in an 'arranged form', thus it is not important what the scriptures say but what their leaders say about scripture.

In Zoroastrianism, all knowledge is in the hands of the priesthood. In Tibetan Buddhism, it is the Dalai Lama whom they see as the reincarnation of the Buddha and who is worshipped as God incarnate.

In even the most primitive religions, it is the shaman, witch-doctor, or medicine man, while with spiritism, it is the diviner or spirit medium who leads the adept into mysteries.

As I have demonstrated, the root of all of this kind of thinking is Gnosticism and most of it has its origins in the ancient Orient where it met and married Christendom at Alexandria. For political reasons in the early Church the Alexandrian school of theology won over the rival Antiochan school of theology and was imported into the west by Augustine of Hippo who began imitating Gnostic methods of biblical interpretation by basing doctrine on typology and allegory.

In the parable of the Good Samaritan Augustine would argue not only that the robbery victim represented fallen man and that the Levite and priest represent the inability of the law to save him, but went beyond this reasonable application of the text to state that the innkeeper was St Paul and so began giving conjectured meanings to every detail of the parable. Regrettably, he later began inventing doctrine on a similar basis saying that because God apparently used violence to convert St Paul, the Church could use violence in forcing people to become 'christians' which opened the door for the misery of the Middle Ages, with its Papal wars, unholy crusades and inquisitions.

As we have noted, such hermeneutics reached their climax in mediaeval scholasticism during the Renaissance, with the grammatical and historical exegesis of humanism and the Reformation following later as a reaction against it.

If, then, all of these things have Gnosticism at their core our question to a devotee would be, "Who is your Pope?" or "Who is your Guru?" or "Who is your Tsadik?", or "Who is your Imam?" To a modern devotee of restorationism and triumphalism. The question is, "Who is your apostle?" or "Who is your prophet?" Remember, to these people it is not important what the Word of God actually says, but rather what the person claiming to be a prophet or an apostle, or having the *gnosis*, says about it.

The Late John Wimber—A True Gnostic

We see this clearly in the Gnostic hermeneutics of Jack Deere and the late John Wimber. The basis of most Kingdom Now theology as illustrated by these men is their interpretation of Joel chapter 2. Joel, like all of the Old Testament prophets, prophesies in three times frames: his own time, the first coming of Jesus and also for the last days. Joel's vision is partially fulfilled on the day of

Pentecost but will be ultimately fulfilled, as Peter says in Acts chapter 2, in the last days. However, the text also has some meaning for Joel's own time. The army described in the book of Joel as the "great army of the Lord which will do great things", and as an army of devouring locusts, does in its historical setting point to Nebuchadnezzar's army. His army was used by God to judge the sin of His own people but was itself destroyed by the rise of the Persian empire. The important point to grasp is that whatever Joel's army means eschatologically (in the end times), it will always be in the character of an agent of judgment.

The late John Wimber takes the conclusion of Joel chapter 2 from verses 28-32, rightly referring to it, as Peter did, as the "latter day rain" or a "mighty outpouring of the Holy Spirit at the end of days". As we noted in our section dealing with the typology of the Jewish calendar, this has a particular meaning for Israel and the Jews as well as for the Church. However, John Wimber cuts out the middle of the chapter and teaches that the Church 'triumphant' *is* this victorious army of locusts that will do the devouring and turn Paradise into a scorched land.[9] Yet, before His Spirit is poured out in verse 28, God says He will restore what the storming locusts have eaten, and that He will utterly destroy this locust army (as He did Nebuchadnezzar's) and its stench will go up to Heaven.[10]

So, although the text says that it is an evil army of judgement that God will utterly destroy, casting it into the sea, where its stench will reach up to Heaven; John Wimber, following the Gnostic practice of cancelling the plain meaning (as the Pope does with Mary's need for a Saviour) in light of what he believes God showed him, says that this mighty army represents the dominionist Christians who will first conquer the Church and then conquer the earth, subduing it before the return of Christ and presenting it to Him fully subjugated.

In one sense, John Wimber may have been right! He and his followers are locusts who are destroying the Church. But, the text clearly states that these locusts represent an evil force that God will totally exterminate. If someone wishes to be part of a great army that God will lay waste, with its stench rising to the heavens, all they need to do is to join the Vineyard Fellowship.

As It Was In The Beginning—Is Now...

There were two forms of Gnosticism in the early Church. The pagan form, with a wide variety of strains and variations within it, and the form that got into the Church under the leadership of figures such as Basiledes and Valentinus.

Today it is the same. The pagan kind of Gnosticism overtaking much of the western world is the New Age movement. It comes in Hindu packaging but its core is purely Gnostic. The kind of Gnosticism coming into the church, however, is restorationism, Kingdom Now theology and dominionism.

New Age Christianity

One form of error acts as a magnet for others. A new kind of paradigm is being created because societies have shifted from an agricultural to an industrial focus in the developing world and are shifting from an industrial economy to an information based hi-tech economy in the developed world. Such changes invariably bring about a change in people's world view.

At the end of the middle ages the Renaissance rediscovered Greco-Roman culture causing a paradigm shift. Similarly such a change happened in the aftermath of the Renaissance when humanism and the Protestant Reformation were born. Another such change took place with the advent of the Industrial Revolution. At each of these transformations—or paradigm shifts—people tried to explain Christian theology in a new way for people with a newer way of thinking. Some of these, like John Wesley and his Methodists, got much of this process right. They **re-contextualised** the gospel message without **re-defining** it thus giving it renewed power in industrial England. Others, like Luther, got much of it right but also certain other aspects wrong when the Holy Roman Empire collapsed and the nation state emerged.

Capitalism replaced feudalism and a string of new inventions, especially the printing press (allowing Bibles to be mass produced) radically changed people's thinking throughout western Europe. At the close of the Dark Ages still others got it completely wrong, especially Thomas Aquinas who re-wrote Christianity as a religion based on Aristotle's philosophy. Before him, Augustine had already re-defined it in light of Plato's philosophy. This became medieval scholasticism against which the early Christian humanists, followed by the Reformers, reacted.

Once more today, with the hi-tech revolution, new forms of technology and communication are forcing the birth of a new world view. The challenge for responsible Christian leaders is to re-contextualise the gospel message and Christian doctrine for the new world view without changing it's meaning. Unfortunately, in popular charismatic and pentecostal circles, Christianity is being *re-defined* in light of the new world view. People like John Wimber have been at the forefront of adopting this paradigm shift and bringing it into the church. Philosophically the problem is that the emerging new world view is no longer the kind of scientific rationalism that led to people thinking that faith in God and the supernatural were unreasonable. These views produced liberal theology with its higher criticism and the existential ideas being incorporated into nominal protestantism.

The new world view today is in fact New Age. The New Age movement is essentially eastern Gnosticism and comes in the packaging of various forms of oriental mysticism such as visualization and shamanism.

A premise which underlines faulty church growth ideas is that the Vineyard paradigm shift models, so prominent among American Fuller Theological Seminary graduates (although Fuller also has its share of more biblical and realistic missiologists such as Dr. Arthur Glasser) is that instead of throwing back the avalanche of eastern religion and New Age which is challenging the future of western Christianity, the Vineyard paradigm shift instead embraces it and imports it into the Church. This can be clearly seen in the wholesale embracing of the mystical Toronto Experience and its American counterpart taking place at Brownsville, Pensacola.

Increasingly there is a marriage of occult belief and science. The two began to separate after the Enlightenment (18th century philosophical movement characterised by reliance upon reason.) but now we see a new merger between them. The ancient Greeks drew no distinction between Astrology and Astronomy. Superstition and science were viewed as the same. Neither did the ancient world draw a distinction between alchemy and chemistry—science and the occult were homogeneous in their thinking. So too were folk medicine and healing arts. Magic was indistinguishable from the sciences of physiology and pharmacology.

Now with the new world view science and the occult again come together, a fact demonstrated by holistic medicine and aspects of theoretical particle physics. William De Artega is an exponent of this new synthesis whose ideas we will examine next.

In the near future biogenetic engineering and virtual reality technology will take on an increasing metaphysical dimension. I believe there will be a popular drive to attempt to use molecular biology and cloning to make a form of reincarnation a reality. So people will begin to create not only their own reality but their own spiritual reality and belief system through the use of virtual reality. In this new world view things which are purely subjective will take on a virtual reality and therefore appear indistinguishable from true objective reality in people's thinking.

William De Artega

William De Artega has tried to construct an argument in defence of this paradigm shift. He first attempts to produce a justification for the subjective becoming treated as the objective from philosophical and metaphysical ideas. He then attempts to extrapolate a similar idea from particle physics. Physics treats light as both waves and particles. It also has to point out that the presence of a human observer affects the outcome of observations. De Artega claims that physics is therefore no longer able to use the old rational position about reality. He goes on to assert that, by analogy, cessationism equals the old materialistic rationalism. False teachers such as money preacher Marilyn Hickey and retiring Elim leader Wynn Lewis have endorsed De Artega for his attacks on Dave Hunt, author of such works as *The Seduction of Christianity* and *Beyond Seduction* as a cessationist.

De Artega's premise is hollow. To claim that cessationism (the belief that the gifts of the spirit died out in the early church) is the product of a cause and effect rationalist view of the material universe is simply not so. The Reformers disliked the miraculous in reaction to the bogus miracles of medieval Roman Catholicism. These featured charlatans merchandising alleged relics (not at all unlike Morris Cerullo's £25 Holy Ghost Miracle Handkerchiefs to remove debt). While the Reformers were indeed humanists who had a humanist perspective to their faith intellectually, they were **Christian** humanists fathered by such humanist scholars such as Erasmus of Rotterdam. Note that the Reformers never rejected the historic truth of the miracles of Jesus as recorded in scripture.

The modern doctrinal errors of cessationism owe much more to B.B.Warfield who, again in reaction to the bogus miracle preachers of **his** day, threw out both the baby and the bathwater and who in reaction to the advent of liberal theology sought a return to a rigid Protestantism and a stoic view such as that held by the Reformers. It is possible to connect cessationism with the anti-supernatural rationalism of the old Newtonian material world view in a philosophical sense. However, one would have to exaggerate the connection beyond the historical evidence in order to link cessationism with anti-supernaturalist rationalism in a theological sense. While I affirm that cessationism is unscriptural and the Reformers were misguided on this point, De Artega has no reason to place evangelical cessationism in the same category as the negation of charismatic gifts by non-evangelical liberal Protestantism.

I accept that with the introduction of Einstein's theory of relativity—and the new era of particle physics—a revolution is underway regarding the way in which we understand the properties of matter and energy and the dynamics between them. However, to misuse this as a scientific basis to interpret the definition of objective truth on the basis of a subjective point of view is both bad science and bad theology. In fact it borders on the occult. It also helps push his version of evangelical Christianity closer to Roman Catholicism as his perspective effectively endorses the error of "Aristotelian Accidents" (which is the philosophical basis of transubstantiation). This is of course an illogical and wholly unbiblical belief system, the demise of which was produced by the age of science. The Roman doctrine of transubstantiation depends upon an acceptance of 'Aristotelian Accidents' where the substance is alleged to have changed while its appearances remain the same. As with De Artega this in turn depends upon the confusion over or substitution of objective truth with subjective belief.

This also fits the 'faith confessionism' and the "my body is lying to me" deceptions of the Hagin/Copeland school of apostasy which similarly demand the subjective misinterpretation of objective facts (such as medical symptoms).

Another expression of this same deception is the positive thinking Christianity that Robert Schuller borrowed from Norman Vincent Peele. This combines a deluded Christian message with popular psychology and owes more to these 'philosophers' than Matthew, Mark, Luke or John. It also relates to Greek dualism, a polemic against which is found in John 1:14 where "the Word became flesh".

The Greeks had a dualistic view of the universe which saw the physical realm as the domain of lesser gods, demiurges, or evil spirits—while the spiritual realm was the domain of the higher god (*theon*) or higher deities which were seen as "without passions". Thus while the visible creation is subject to an invisible God, He is by His own choice capable of suffering and displaying emotion. Thus we see that objective reality is never negated by purely subjective considerations.

As we have already seen, John Wimber's teaching on Joel's Army and 'manifest sons' teaching have further common ground in their joint defiance of 2 Peter chapter 1:20. Heresy finds its natural complement and will often find its natural ally against biblical truth.

De Artega goes from being implausible to dishonest, however, when he labels Dave Hunt a cessationist. This he certainly is not. It is well known that Dave Hunt came into conflict with his own Brethren church background over the issue of charismatic gifts, and knowing Dave Hunt personally, I can testify he holds to a pneumatology which gives place to an ongoing ministry of the Holy Spirit including the gifts. Dave Hunt is therefore manifestly not a cessationist.

Toronto And Pensacola

If we remember that the fruit of the Spirit is self-control and not the lack of it,[11] we see that the fruit of Toronto and Pensacola is not the fruit of the Spirit. These claims have now had some years to show their truth but have not borne fruit, only disagreement and argument. In fact what is seen has had the opposite impact on our Christian witness. Its proponents realising it has not bought revival have foolishly stated it is rather a "refreshing that will lead to revival when large numbers of people will repent". However, in Acts chapter 3:19, the very verse they quote as the basis for this assertion, the text says not to have a refreshing that the repentance will come, but to repent *that* the refreshing may come. The verse says the very opposite of what these unfortunate people foolishly think. Not only can most pro-Toronto pastors not read Hebrew or Greek, but one wonders if they are able to read English.

Jesus never said that one would know a phenomenon by its fruit, but a person by their fruit. A phenomenon is known by whether or not it agrees with scripture and—as we have seen—the excesses of Toronto and Pensacola and the doctrines of its leaders certainly do not.

When challenged biblically the most common response noted is that one is accused of being a Pharisee. In fact they themselves are pharisees because they operate in the exact manner the Pharisees of Jesus' day did according to the Lord's own charge against them. Not having a biblical basis for what they teach and do, they teach as precepts of God the inventions of men.

Christians are commanded not to exceed that which is written[12] and to test all things and hold to what is true. Instead these people engage in practices alien to scripture and spout lunacy which has no biblical basis—other than twisting verses out of context as Satan did.[13] Instead of testing what is true, John Arnott describes the phenomenon as a river that one needs to jump into and experience without undertaking any critical or biblical analysis of it. Clearly one cannot believe both Jesus Christ and John Arnott.

False religious practice will always lead to immorality and inevitably this has happened with the moral perversions associated with the Toronto Blessing. The most gross perversion of all is that which pictures the believer as having sexual relations with Jesus personally. The Church is a corporate Bride and Jesus is never portrayed in Scripture as a personal lover. Yet the wife of Mike Sullivan, Pastor of the Metro Vineyard church in America, claims to have had dreams of Jesus kissing her passionately and the Holy Spirit whispering in her ears "I want you". There are video tapes showing Christian women appearing to experience sexual orgasms in Toronto meetings. Such ideas of "having sex with God" are rooted in Hellenistic mysticism and eastern religion. Yet they are now called manifestations of God's Spirit.

Another typical response of pro-Toronto advocates is that those speaking against it are 'being negative'. This is—of course—drawn from the positive thinking psychology which Norman Vincent Peele and Robert Schuller have attempted to camouflage as orthodox Christianity, but which has no biblical basis in scriptural Christianity. Pensacola is nothing more than the American version of Toronto. It comes complete with the same sort of carnal manifestations. The leaders of Pensacola have had direct association with the heretical leadership of Toronto. Such Pensacola practices as burning incense in the model of a temple as a way to call down the Holy Spirit are scripturally absurd. What they are in fact doing is more in line with building a golden calf than watching and waiting for the true move of the *Shekinah*.

Claims of numbers saved at Pensacola are, by and large, wild exaggerations. Every indication is that, like Toronto, there is not much more to it than people who already claim to be Christians coming for an experience or coming to see a show. For all of the supposed talk of repentance and preaching of the gospel, any real evangelistic content is undermined by lunacy, false doctrine, and carnality. No revival came from Toronto and no revival will come from Pensacola.

The official Pensacola video called 'The Intercessors' demonstrates the folly—if not outright fraud—of what is trumpeted as 'revival'. It shows Pastor John Kilpatrick denigrating the Holy Spirit on no fewer than eight occasions by referring to Him as 'it'. Biblically the outpouring of the Spirit is the Spirit Himself. The carnal antics seen on this video are so outrageous that any unsaved person looking at it would simply mock. The spectacle of devotees rendered unable to walk by the 'anointing' of this drunken spirit, being carried around the church in a bizarre procession called 'intercession' by the leadership, can only be described as idiotic.

The video clearly demonstrates that contrary to popular belief there was no actual biblical preaching of the gospel to the lost. It is all a matter of cliches, such as "get your heart right with God" and experience chasing by undiscerning Christians. In short the whole experience was a fiasco which amounted to nothing more than deceived believers responding to altar calls.

There are true moves of God in David Wilkerson's Time Square church in New York and in the Calvary Chapels of Southern California. Neither the market research driven churches influenced by Peter Wagner nor the Toronto influenced fiasco in Pensacola are going to trigger repentance in America. As we have seen, throughout this book, such things are almost all part of one big deception.

America is heading for God's judgement. Only repentance can delay it, and in all probability nothing can stop it. However, such things as Pensacola can delay—or stop—a true repentance. When unsaved people see this craziness they see no reason to repent and become born-again Christians because after watching the shenanigans at Pensacola, becoming a born-again Christian simply means becoming a lunatic.

By mid 1997 the deception upon which Pensacola is built was publicly exposed. Initially its proponents attempted to claim it had no connection or continuity with the Toronto experience or the antics of Kenneth Copeland or Rodney Howard-Browne. In fact, however, John Kilpatrick, the Pastor of Brownsville Assemblies of God Church in Pensacola, had his wife visit the airport Vineyard Church in Toronto at least twice after which she whole heartedly commended it. Steve Hill, the evangelist of Pensacola, visited Holy Trinity Brompton in London, as did the worship leader at Pensacola.

The videos show that the worship in Pensacola is essentially of the Vineyard type. Very few Vineyard hymns and choruses have any reference to the biblical gospel themes of the Cross or the Blood of Christ, but are devoid of sound doctrinal theology in their lyrics, sometimes to the point of perversion.[14] One hymn composed by a leading Toronto experience Vineyard pastor lauds Jesus as a personal lover. I repeat the point I made earlier, in scripture He is the lover of a corporate bride, never of individuals.

The music at Pensacola is repetitive and mesmerizing, which predisposes people to hypnotic suggestion. Moreover with no theology there is no true doxology (praise). What we see in Pensacola and, in many popular charismatic pentecostal churches today, is the worship of worship and the worship of experience being substituted for a scriptural worship of God.

John Kilpatrick boldly and assertively gave a recorded public prophetic prediction in April, 1997. In it he stated that God would bring down the ministry of *Christianity in Crisis* author Hank Hanegraaff within three months. As July approached and the prophecy had not happened, Kilpatrick was compelled to admit publicly that he had been wrong. Although he then tried to deny that his original statement was a prophecy, the fact remains that he prophesied falsely. By biblical definition he is a false prophet, one of those whom Jesus warned would come to deceive the elect in the last days and whom the Word of God commands Christians to ignore. Yet Kilpatrick's books are stocked in many christian bookstores.

Perhaps the most outstanding feature of Pensacola has been the readiness of its leaders to lie and deceive. As exposed by pentecostal minister Joseph Chambers, the leadership at Pensacola falsely claimed that revival had come resulting in crime going down and the police bringing arrested juvenile delinquents to the Church to be saved. The local Police Chief and the Sheriffs' department, stated that this is would be illegal to act in this way. They also pointed to crime statistics showing that the crime rate has actually **risen** in the area since the supposed revival began.

The adult population of Pensacola is not that large. Some would estimate it at about 218,000. If 100,000 people had been saved at Pensacola in the last two years, then something on the order of fifty per-cent of the adult population would have had to be born again since 1995. Investigative reporters on the streets, the crime statistics, and the testimony of pastors of other local evangelical churches conclusively show that this is utter nonsense. The Pensacola leadership also claimed that the number of school campus Christian fellowships went from three to over thirty, yet the superintendent of schools and the education department say that no such thing has happened.

On one very disturbing video John Kilpatrick was trying to justify the violent shaking of a teenage girl as a manifestation of the Holy Spirit. Kilpatrick claimed that he had known the girl, her sister, and their family for years, with a mother who was a teacher and a father who was a doctor, stating that their good family background was evidence that what was happening as the girl was vibrating must be of God. In fact the girl's parents had been separated for fifteen years and she came from a broken home having suffered the traumatic upbringing that growing up with separated parents produces, especially in view of the fact that such things are not ordinarily supposed to happen if the children were bought up in a Christian home.

Worst of all seems to be one Michael Brown—who made outlandish false prophecies at a Messianic Conference in Jerusalem several years ago which naturally failed to happen, even after he had people up the entire night waiting for the fire that never fell. In July of 1997Brown cancelled a mid week debate at a neutral venue in New York with me last year on short notice after I had already booked flights for my family and myself to travel over from England. He cancelled the meeting after becoming aware that I was in possession of Joe Chambers' videos showing John Kilpatrick lying about the family background of the vibrating girl mentioned earlier. The tapes also contained footage showing that what was misrepresented as large numbers being saved were actually hyper charismatic Christians responding to altar calls. Proof that there is no difference between Toronto and Pensacola either in their carnal excess or the willingness of some of their leaders to lie.

Perhaps unsurprisingly, Brown wanted to re-arrange the debate at a Pensacola church on a Sunday night when others could not attend. Brown was also apparently disturbed that I had accumulated proof of his Jerusalem fiasco and that I also held similar material on Brown from Long Island and Washington, D.C.

Pensacola Is All A Big Money Grabbing Con!

According to disclosures in the American press, the leaders of the Brownsville, Pensacola 'revival' have indulged in expensive lifestyles, and have set up their own non-profit corporations to sell revival related merchandise but failed to collect sales taxes. Rev. Carey Robertson, associate pastor, preaches: "Reach into your wallet and pull out the biggest thing you find." He suggests $100 as an acceptable figure. The Pensacola leaders claim some of the money goes to missions working to spread Christianity, but The Internal Revenue Service returns and financial statements contradict their figures. Robertson reportedly told "The News Journal": "If you are wondering where the money is going, don't give."

- Only 2% of the church's $6.6 million annual budget goes to missions after evangelist Steve Hill takes his 16% cut (about $1 million) for his "Together in the Harvest Ministries". The IRS return for Hill's organization shows that in 1996 he gave only $102,000 to missions. Hill himself has been shown to be untruthful both regarding his own background and about how he obtained the Toronto experience at Holy Trinity Brompton in London, England and imported it to Pensacola.

- John Kilpatrick is building a new $343,860 home in nearby Seminole, Alabama, and assets of his "Feast of Fire Ministries" include a $310,000 bus and 14 acres of land where he is building a second guest house costing $203,000.

- Steve Hill's ministry owns $877,930 in real estate including a 40 acre estate where he lives near Foley, Alabama.

The Associated Press release contained other material as well, but 120 pages of damaging disclosures about Pensacola are available on internet.

Things have not gone well for Pensacola of late. Hank Hanegraaff recently met with the leaders but his CRI organization put out a statement confirming his view of Pensacola had not changed.

First, Pensacola Pastor John Kilpatrick was forced to admit that he prophesied falsely that God would bring Hank down in three months, which then failed to happen.

Instead, God brought Kilpatrick down when he fell off a roof and wound up badly injured, confined to a wheelchair.

Most tragic of all was the reaction of American Assemblies of God General Superintendent Thomas Trask (who also issued minister's credentials to heretic Benny Hinn). Trask said the finances, though given by ordinary hard working Christians, are "an ecclesiastical matter" only.

This is the same attitude by the Assemblies of God leadership in the U.S.A. that allowed the last public financial scandal to happen when Assemblies of God minister Jim Bakker and his PTL club discredited the gospel in the eyes of tens of millions and made the term 'born again' into a household joke. The leadership refused to stop Bakker's Bible twisting, money sucking antics before it was too late.

While Assemblies of God leader Dr. George Wood opposed Toronto, and Assemblies of God academic William Nunley opposed Pensacola, it was business as usual for Trask, who is now involved in the biggest scandal to rock the Assemblies of God since Bakker and Swaggart. Unfortunately, at the time of writing it is unlikely that enough of the good men left in the American Assemblies of God will rise up and demand that Trask resign and so regain some of the denomination's lost credibility.

It is the case that thousands of ministers and churches have disassociated themselves from the American Assemblies of God in the last decade, including David Wilkerson. To date, however, the denomination's large size, plus the growth of pentecostalism among Hispanic and Asian Americans, have disguised the fragmentation and decline that is so obvious in the U.K. With Pensacola, however, the cracks are at last beginning to show.

Conclusions

In His final words Jesus called us to be His witnesses. We are to witness to a gospel of salvation who's credibility rests upon the objective historical fact of a literal bodily resurrection. The spiritual truth does not nullify the objective reality that Jesus died and rose again. The objective evidence reinforces the spiritual truth of who Jesus is and what He did. To this I gladly give witness. In His death He took our sin and in His resurrection He gave us His life. By believing in sacramental salvation the Roman Catholic church has a totally different gospel. Their sacraments are not simply emblems of salvation but the means of it. Roman Catholicism has long been captured by the eclectic influences of eastern religion that are now being welcomed into much of pentecostalism and the charismatic movement under the auspices of the late John Wimber's Vineyard heresy, the Branhamite Kansas City false prophets and the faith-prosperity money preachers. Because of ecumenical compromise and the incorporation of New Age eastern religious ideas such as visualization, another Gospel is being preached and we are no longer His witnesses in the sense He commanded in His final words.

Thus, what we see now in the paradigm shift is not a preserving and representation of biblical truth and the teachings of Jesus in a new context or framework (re-contextualization) for a newly emerging world view, but a re-definition of Christian truth along the lines of subjectivism, New Age, and eastern religion. This fits well with the ecumenical designs of Roman Catholicism which from its Constantinian roots is dominionistic and also Gnostic in its approach to Biblical interpretation. It also demands in its pagan sacramentalism that objective reality be subjugated to subjective belief.

Those being swayed by such things are being taken for a ride to Babylon. What they are being told is Christianity is rather New Age thinking in Christian guise. What they are told is the gospel of Jesus is in fact another gospel—a gospel of a Jesus resembling more the christ of New Age rather than the christ of Scripture. The late John Wimber, Robert Schuller, Marilyn Hickey, William De Artega or Kenneth Copeland may be those extending the invitation to come along for the ride—but Satan is definitely at the wheel.

Notes on Ch.9

1. John 1:14.
2. Philippians 2:6-8.
3. I Corinthians 6:19.
4. "Did you know that from the beginning of time the whole purpose of God was to reproduce Himself? ...Who are you? Come on, who are you? Come on say it: "Sons fo God!" Come on , say it!...And when we stand up here, brother, you're not looking at Morris Cerullo; you're looking at God. You're looking at Jesus." Morris Cerullo, "The Endtime Manifestation of the Sons of God" (San Diego: Morris Cerullo World Evangelism, Inc.,n.d.), audiotape 1, sides 1 and 2. Cited in: H. Hanegraaff, *Christianity in Crisis*, Nelson Word 1993:358.
5. Jeremiah 23:30-32.
6. Paul Yonggi Cho, *The Fourth Dimension*, vols 1 and 2, Bridge Publishing, South Plainfield NJ 1979, 1983
7. Romans 8:22-23.
8. John 1:29.
9. Joel 2:3.
10. Joel 2:20.
11. Galatians 5:23.
12. 1 Corinthians 4:6.
13. Matthew 4:1-11/Luke 4:1-13.
14. For a thorough investigation of the ideology behind Vineyard worship see: Martyn Percy, *Words, Wonders and Power—Understanding Contemporary Christian Revivalism*, SPCK, London. 1996:60-81.

Chapter 10

Lie 5: Ecumenism

The New Nomianism And Ecumenism

When the Church confuses preaching the gospel of the Kingdom of God with the theonomic and reconstructionist ideas of trying to establish it here on earth, it becomes too concerned with politics to see clearly enough to remain focussed on its true purpose—the preaching of the gospel.

We must remember that the largest revivals happening anywhere in the world are perhaps those taking place in Roman Catholic countries where the souls being saved see Rome as a false religion which prays to the dead, idolatrously worships transubstantiated elements, replaces the authority of God's Word with the traditions of men, forbids marriage amongst its priesthood (which Paul calls a doctrine of demons),[1] and teaches sacramental salvation instead of regenerational salvation.

The neo-reconstructionism of the evangelical right finds a natural ally in Roman Catholicism in its quest for theonomic entity, and it does so for three reasons.

First, from the time of Constantine and the early Papacy, Rome has always sought to establish itself as the theonomic dominion of Christ on earth.

Second, the Roman Catholic Church proves itself as a convenient political ally in that at least officially, it shares evangelical aversion to divorce, abortion and homosexuality.

Third, Roman Catholicism, like the restorationist over realised eschatology to which Pat Robertson is leaning, has Gnostic roots.

Evangelical political candidates therefore have to court the endorsement of the Roman Catholic Church and the votes of practising Catholics in their electoral endeavours.

The problem is that praying to the dead, the preaching of another way of salvation (which is 'another gospel') and the idolatry and superstition of Roman Catholicism are all abominations in the eyes of God. The Roman Church has always struggled to utilise its political influence for the suppression of the gospel.

Pope John Paul the second denounced evangelical Christians as "rapacious wolves." on his visit to Mexico not long ago.

Yet we see the sickening scene of a group of evangelical leaders—most of whom are identified with the political Christian right—having signed a concordat with the Roman Catholic Church, accepting this traditional and current enemy of the gospel as Christian. Those who signed this pact with Rome include Pat Robertson, Chuck Colson and Bill Bright of Campus Crusades for Christ and the leadership of the Southern Baptist Convention.[2]

The evangelicals who were signatories to the agreement also agreed not to present Roman Catholics with the gospel lest they be saved out of the false Christianity of Rome

The actions of Robertson, Bright, Colson, and the Southern Baptist leadership allow Roman Catholics to go to Hell without the new birth that Jesus taught is the only thing that will keep them from it. It encourages them to continue to practice praying to the dead (God calls this necromancy),[3] to believe in sacramental regeneration instead of new birth atonement,[4] to believe in suffering in purgatory for their own sins (thus denying the efficacy of the Cross and putting people into the bondage of fear that Christ died to free them from) and to practise a plethora of superstitions that God calls abominations.

This of course says nothing of the doctrine of the Mass which Roman Catholics are required to believe and which rejects the New Testament teaching that Jesus died once and for all as a perfect sacrifice—once again, rejecting the sufficiency of the cross. The mass teaches that Jesus dies again and again in direct rebellion against the clear teaching of the Word of God.[5]

Nor do they address the serious problems of the mandatory belief in Papal infallibility,[6] or the prayer to and veneration of Mary as a sinless being whom co-redeemed us.

True Christians, many of them ex-Catholics, have been murdered by Rome rather than make peace with these terrible lies that Robertson, Bright, and Colson have effectively condoned by calling a church that leads millions into hell with such lies 'Christian'.

Like the Christian Zionists (also partly driven by political considerations) in their accommodation of the false Judaism of the rabbis which rejects its own Messiah and persecutes Jewish believers—Robertson, Colson, and Bright now accommodate the false Christianity of Rome that persecutes converted Catholics in many countries. As the Christian Zionists send Jews to hell without Christ, Robertson, Colson, and Bright now send Catholics to hell without Christ.

It is only in increasingly post-Christian and neo-pagan countries like America—where traditional biblical Protestant Christianity is dying—that such betrayal of the gospel of Jesus, the authority and truth of God's Word, and the salvation of precious Catholic souls for whom Christ died is happening.

In Latin America, The Philippines, and even among the Catholic communities in America, Australia and Europe where Catholics are being saved, the basic trend is for them to "come out" of false religion, as the Word of God commands.[7]

Instead of Robertson, Colson, and Bright making themselves the spokesmen for what evangelical Christianity's view of Roman Catholicism should be, why were none of the millions of people who have been saved out of Roman Catholicism consulted?

The reason converted Catholics have not been consulted is because Rome decrees that these have left the "one true Church", are in mortal sin and will go to hell unless they return to Rome. By 'return' the Roman hierarchy mean a complete surrender to all Rome's dogma.

Furthermore, Rome admits in its ecumenical dialogues that the road to Christian unity is the road back to Rome (the age old political ambitions of the Vatican notwithstanding). For this reason Rome will never deal with evangelical theologians or leaders who have left the Roman Catholic Church, because converted Catholics know exactly what Rome is, and more importantly, what it is not.

In addition to betraying the cause of the salvation of Catholic people, these three men have stabbed in the back those millions of converted Roman Catholics who are now born again believers worshipping in evangelical churches.

Now huge numbers of Roman Catholics who have become evangelical Christians and who have left the church of Rome find themselves in a novel situation. They had realised that they could not remain in what scripture reveals to be a false religious system (as Spurgeon, Bunyan, Wesley, Whitfield and others have all said, including the Reformers—who were themselves from the intelligentsia of the Roman Catholic clergy). They have heard themselves being anathematised by Rome. They see Roman Catholicism leading their families into eternal judgment by preaching sacramental salvation instead of the new birth. But now they see their new 'evangelical' leaders aligning themselves with and accepting the same false church that persecuted them!

At a time when the Holy Spirit is moving powerfully throughout the Roman Catholic world, the Roman Catholic Church also finds itself in a new state. Having allies in the evangelical right, they can now encourage charismatic Catholics to continue praying in tongues to Mary, they can call people saved out of Catholicism back into it, and they can denounce the evangelisation of Roman Catholics with the endorsement and participation of recognised leaders of what is supposed to be the Bible-believing Body of Christ.

The key to much of this betrayal is undoubtedly the political considerations of a declining western evangelical Protestant Church infected with reconstructionism and compromise.

Sadly, but predictably, it is mainly the same ones who were deceived into trying to marry the doctrines of the Bible with the dogma of the Reagan government who are now trying to marry the doctrines of the Bible with its traditional enemy, the harlot Church of Rome.

Again this neo-reconstructionism and new-found ecumenism are both directly related to each other and indirectly related to the rise of Kingdom Now restorationism in terms of its theological roots; in fact they are simply another manifestation of the same trend, and are symptomatic of the same disease, caused by the same virus injected into the Church by the Father of Lies.

Man's Ideas And Compromises Do Not Work

The Ecumenical Missiologist Peter Wagner of Fuller Seminary in Pasadena, California, in conjunction with such Churches as Willow Creek in Illinois, reduced church growth to a matter of programmes and market research based on models of consumerism. As we have seen previously according to this philosophy one simply does market research to come up with a growth program which will see a church increase in size in imitation of secular market research. The new world view simply states: get the right software for your computer and your hardware will perform as you wish. So, church growth becomes a matter of man's programmes, often with little emphasis on the leading and sovereignty and timing of God. In the last few years Great Britain has seen a stream of such disappointing failures in the shape of the *JIM Challenge* and Reinhard Bonnke's *Minus to Plus* evangelistic programmes.[8]

Three essential points which debunk these ecumenical models of church growth are usually ignored by its proponents. The first of these is that the church growth movement as initially established by Wagner's predecessor, the late Dr. Donald MacGarvan, requires that conversions and transfer growth—that is people leaving one church for another—be statistically quantified. While there is evidence to suggest that the "Homogeneous unit" concept is a viable factor in evangelism, there is far less statistical evidence that it is a viable factor Ecclesiologically. There are instances where it may be a factor (particularly where there is a distinction in language or strong cultural differences), but there are many other circumstances in which it does not appear to be a factor at all.

We can say the "homogeneous unit" has a biblical root in 1 Corinthians chapter 9 where St. Paul becomes 'as all things to all people' in order to reach them. There are, additionally, too many other Churches which are both multi-ethnic, inter-cultural and comprised of born again Christians of too many diverse socio-economic and educational backgrounds to make the homogeneous unit into the kind of template for church growth which some have attempted. Using the first principle of church growth which demands that the growth figures be quantified on a statistical basis we would have to say that most church growth in the area of home missions probably—if not certainly—simply does not work. The most the figures often show is that by appealing to one sector of society transfer growth can be achieved by drawing people out of one church into another. This is itself a further manifestation of consumerism in the church where a self centered instead of a Christocentric idea of finding a church takes over from a model more based on biblical principle. Interestingly, the homogenous unit may be useful in relation to foreign mission, as it helps answer the historical problem of cultural imperialism.

On the question of finding a church a committed Christian should ask only two questions. The first is: "Where does God want me to be?" And the second is: "Where does God want to use me to help meet the needs of others?" True *agape* love always puts God first, others second (beginning with our families) and ourselves last. Instead, the spirit of 'consumer' church growth encourages people to ask: "Which church is going to meet my needs?"

The transfer growth that the church growth movement's own standards of statistical analysis reveal is not real growth at all. It is like taking money from one pocket and putting it into another and thinking one is financially better off. This kind of growth has no impact on sin and does not see many people saved. Furthermore it does nothing to hold back the wave of moral disintegration and New Age and eastern religious philosophy which is overtaking western society. Great Britain is already a post Christian, neo-pagan society, and the United States is not far from going down the same road.

The second factor which fundamentally mitigates against the ideas of ecumenical models of church growth is people such as Peter Wagner and his disciples who ignore the facts of church growth in Latin America and the Philippines—Latin America being the nearest area to the USA where authentic, conversion based, church growth is actually happening.

Much of church growth pre-supposition is founded on the notion—which while having a grain of truth in it is greatly overstated to the point of becoming erroneous—that by seeing how God is moving in one place, we can modify what is happening into a formula to make God move similarly elsewhere. How unfortunate it is when we forget that when the Apostles were made "fishers of men" they fished and fished and caught nothing until Jesus directed them where to cast their nets. Still, to what degree this concept has merit, Peter Wagner and other ecumenical evangelicals fail to correctly observe what is actually happening in Mexico, Brazil and Argentina. Latin America is the demographic epicentre of the Roman Catholic world today, just as western Europe was its centre in the 16th century, when the Reformation took place.

A third reason which underlines faulty church growth ideas is that the Vineyard paradigm shift models, so prominent among Fuller graduates (although Fuller also has its share of more biblical and realistic missiologists such as Dr. Arthur Glasser) is that instead of throwing back the avalanche of eastern religion and New Age which is challenging the future of western Christianity, the Vineyard paradigm shift instead embraces it and imports it into the Church.

Ecumenical compromise is the inevitable first step into inter-faith compromise. The Pope of Rome is already calling men like the Dalai Llama "a great spiritual leader" (even though he is worshipped as a re-incarnated Buddha by Tibetan Buddhists). The Pope has been involved in inter-faith rallies in places like Assisi,

Italy; in inter-faith forums with witch doctors, gurus, Imans and leaders of other eastern religions which worship other gods, which scripture calls demons.[9] Thus by entering into ecumenical unity with Rome, men like those named above mislead the Church into a unity that is intentionally blind to the fact that Rome and liberal Protestantism are also cultivating unity with religions that worship false gods. In Europe and America this trend is also becoming increasingly political in scope and will ultimately become a prelude to the rise of Babylon predicted in the Book of Revelation.
IS SATAN TAKING YOU FOR A RIDE?

Notes on ch.10
1. 1 Timothy 4:1-3.
2. Details in *The Woman Rides the Beast* by Dave Hunt.
3. Deuteronomy 18:11.
4. Galatians 1:6-9.
5. Hebrews 7:27; 9:19; 10:10.
6. Papal infallibility was proclaimed Ex Cathedra in 1854.
7. Revelation 18:4.
8. The evangelistic agencies involved with the 1994 Jim campaign reported 269 converts from 46 events, according to an Evangelical Alliance survey. Statistics cited in: Roland Howard, *Charismania - When Christian Fundamentalism Goes Wrong*, Mowbray, London 1997:128.
   In 1994 the German Charismatic evangelist Reinhart Bonnke distributed a booklet called 'Minus to Plus' to the majority of houses in Britain, and his publicity referred to millions of converts. However, a survey undertaken by the Evangelical Alliance reported that the campaign led to less than one convert per participating church. Ibid., 128.
9. Deuteronomy 32:17; 1 Corinthians 10:20.

Postscript

Some people will applaud me for having written this book, others will loathe me for it. Let God judge me as He sees fit; that is His responsibility. Yours is to ask Jesus to show you whether or not the things I have written are true.

When the religious hypocrites of Jesus' day were unable to attack what he said, they attacked him for saying those things. The reason was that they were exploiting God's people and when Jesus exposed their false doctrine and their corruption He threatened their financial and religious power.

Things have not changed much. Inevitably people will attack me for having written this book as a way of avoiding having to deal with what it actually says.

This was certainly the way the medieval papacy reacted to Martin Luther's ninety-five theses. The papal bull issued against him attacked Luther but could not contradict what he had written. Nor in fact could Jan Eck, one of Luther's cleverest opponents. So today none of Hank Hanegraaff's critics can dispute him theologically, let alone dispute the factual truth of his book *Christianity In Crisis* and *Counterfeit Revival*.

Unable to confront the issues, religious hypocrites tried to destroy Jesus, the Prophets and the Apostles for raising those issues. I am far from being an Apostle like Paul or Peter; I am also far from being a Prophet like Jeremiah, Daniel or Ezekiel; and above all I am very far from being what Jesus wants me to be. None the less, if that is the way a corrupt religious establishment treated them, I expect that to be the same manner in which they will treat me—or anyone else who takes the kind of stand that I believe God has led me to take.

Sadly, when William De Artega tried to construct an argument to refute the teachings of Dave Hunt, author of "The Seduction of Christianity", he could only do so by lying. De Artega found it necessary to misrepresent Dave Hunt as a cessationist, which he certainly is not. De Artega's falsehood brings to mind the ridiculous false allegations which were brought against Martin Luther. Truly there is nothing new under the sun.

Most tragic of all will be the sons of Jonathan. Jonathan knew that the house of Saul had gone mad, but when push came to shove, he was unable to leave the house of Saul for the house of David. As a result he died with Saul on Mt Gilboa.

There are many Christians in the character of Jonathan today. They will know what I say is right, they will harbour some sympathy for the fact that I say it, but they are too bound to a declining and failing Laodicean Church to stand against it to the degree where they will be able to have any significant impact.

There will be those who agree with what I say, but will not agree with the fact that I have said it—even though they know that it is the truth. They will read this book, bear witness with it, but the fear of man will prevent them from admitting it. That is their decision. I know that in writing this book I have done what God has required of me concerning these matters. It is before Him that I shall one day stand and have to give account for having written this book. It is before Him that you will one day stand and give account for decisions you have made after having read it.

Our message is not negative but positive for when the western church has moved this far away from the ways of the Lord and departed from His Word, we must look to Him to begin a new thing. We thank God for those churches and ministries who have remained faithful to Jesus and the true teachings of the Bible.

May the Lord bless you.

James Jacob Prasch

Appendix

Jesus Said "beware"

The real dangers of dominionism and triumphalism are that they suggest that Christ returns to the Church before He returns for the Church—that the latter rain is somehow the beginning of the return of Christ in itself—as opposed to the harbinger of it. That it will not be as Daniel chapter 7:21-23 says: "the Ancient of Days will finally defeat Satan and give the Kingdom to the saints". But rather that the saints achieve a great victory without the coming of the Ancient of Days. That is to say, for them Daniel chapter 7 refers to the first coming of Christ, not the second, and that the millennium is already being realised in the Church, and that Satan is bound.

As believers we must question how anyone who reads the newspapers, much less the Bible, can possibly believe that Satan is bound and that the Church has full dominion now. None the less, let us look at how the dominionists and triumphalists arrive at their over-realised eschatology.

In the Olivet discourse, Jesus repeatedly warned about falling prey to the suggestion that His return would happen in any way other than the way in which He left.[1] Kingdom Now theology is not simply a game played by unbiblical rules, it is a dangerous game leading people into potentially catastrophic unbiblical beliefs, of the precise nature against which Jesus warned.

The Three-fold Error

The first method of mishandling scripture which accounts for the errors of the triumphalists and restorationists is that they confine themselves to a preterist and historicist view of prophecy and eschatology. As we have already seen, biblical eschatological

---

prophecy is simultaneously preterist, historicist, polemicist, and futurist. Thus, we may now understand the error of restorationist David Chilton, who views the Olivet Discourse of Matthew chapters 24 & 25 as having been totally, instead of partially, fulfilled in the destruction of the temple in 70 A.D.

One need only look at Matthew chapter 25 to see that the Master has certainly not returned to settle accounts.[2] The Master has cast no worthless slave into the place of weeping and gnashing of teeth.[3] He has not come as a Shepherd to separate sheep and goats in the final judgement,[4] and He has not yet pronounced formal sentence on anyone to either eternal punishment or eternal life.[5] Yet, such texts which are integral components of the Olivet discourse are text portions which Chilton and his misguided followers, such as Rick Godwin, must somehow either ignore or over-spiritualise in order to make them fit into their restorationist error.

The second way of mishandling scripture, which accounts for how triumphalism and restorationism arrives at its Kingdom Now conclusions, is again by Gnostic hermeneutics—the most obvious example of which can be found in the late John Wimber and the Vineyard.

The third error in handling scripture is *eisegesis*—distorting scripture by reading into it something it does not say or mean.

I believe it is not too much to say that these errors truly bear the signature of Satan. It is precisely what he did in his temptation of Eve[6] and what he also attempted to do in his temptation of Jesus in the wilderness[7]—taking verses and passages out of their context and subtly altering their inherent meaning.

This is not to suggest that those engaging in such practices are wilful deceivers themselves, but rather that they themselves have been subtly deceived and—perhaps with the most noble of intentions—are being deceived into deceiving others.

An example of eisegesis can be viewed in Kevin Connor's book "The Church in the New Testament". Connor (who seems to be an oddity among pre-millennialists holding to a dominionist eschatology) states that: "We know the Church will be triumphant over Satan because of Genesis chapter 3:15—'And I will put enmity between you and the woman, between your seed and her seed. You will bruise him in the heel and he will bruise you in the head.'"

Connor's mistake is, of course, that in its first context, the woman (Eve) first of all represents Israel as much as she does the Church. More importantly, however, it is the seed of the woman—Jesus the Messiah, and not the woman herself who crushes the serpent's head—as we read in Romans chapter 16:20: "The God of peace will soon crush Satan under your feet". Again, it is Jesus—the Ancient of Days, who subdues the enemy and then gives dominion to the saints after the enemy first prevails against Him for a season.[8]

Error begets error and it is a combination of these three styles of bad exegesis combined with the errors of replacementism, post-millennialism and reconstructionism, that are setting the stage for perhaps the greatest deception perpetrated against Bible-believing Christians since the early centuries of the church.

Gnosticism and Montanism wrought havoc on the Christian Church in its early years, and they now look ominously set to cause similar damage today. It is sad to see the degree to which they are already doing so, particularly as they have been wedded to the related errors of faith-prosperity teaching.

However, in the early Church there were leaders like Irenaeus who refuted such false doctrines without throwing the baby out with the bathwater; that is to say he did not reject the place of signs and wonders, he simply rejected the absurd theologies of those who used signs and wonders to propagate expectations that were devoid of biblical basis but which were in turn greatly amplified by arrogant voices driven by spiritual pride.

The question is not "Will Kingdom Now theology come to nothing?" As with the Montanists, Joachim of Fiore and the Prophets of Zwickau, it has always come to nothing and it always will come to nothing.

The real question is—how much damage will it do to the Body of Christ in the meantime? How many congregations will it manage to destroy with the disillusionment that will surely follow its false predictions and ridiculous expectations before it comes to nothing? How many Christian lives will its heavy shepherding lead to ruin before it finally ruins itself? And how many of God's people will Satan use it to suck into serious spiritual deception and dangerous doctrinal error before it dies? These are sobering questions which demand answers.

Notes on Appendix
1. Matthew 24:23, 26, 27.
2. Matthew 25:19-29.
3. Matthew 25:30.
4. Matthew 25:31-46.
5. Matthew 25:46.
6. Genesis 3:1-6.
7. Matthew 4:1-11/Luke 4:1-13.
8. Daniel 7:21-23.

Index

A-millennial 49
Abraham 21-22, 41, 78, 83, 121, 205
Aeolina Capitolina 39
Akiva Rabbi 16, 73
Albigenses 43
Alpha 146-147, 168
Ambrose 43
Anabaptist 43
Anabaptists 49
Antichrist 16, 76-77, 201-202, 211
Antiochus Epiphanes 38
Archbishop of Canterbury 123-124
144-145, 151
Ariel 62
Augustine 43-45, 47, 216, 219
Authority of Scripture 5, 25, 43
50-51, 88, 96, 103, 171
Avanzini 17, 184, 191

Bakker 32, 125-127, 189, 191, 202
230
Baruch Maoz 62
Ben Zakai 73-74
Bill Bright 234
Bill Hybels 179
Bohemian Brethren 43
Bridges for Peace 61
Brownsville 220, 226, 228
Bryn Jones 157, 169
Bunyan John 236
Calvary Chapel 225
Calvin 44-47, 149, 167
Calvinism 43, 48
Casey Treat 184
CBN 49, 200
Cessasionist 23
Charles Capps 184
Chilton 162, 200, 244
Chosen People Ministries 62
Christian Broadcasting Network 49

Christian humanism 23
Christian Science 209, 211
Christian Witness to 62
Chuck Colson 234
Church's Ministry to the Jews 62
Cochba Simon Bar 73
Colin Chapman 122, 156, 169
Colin Dye 128-129, 132-133
Constantine 42, 44-45, 47, 233
Copeland Kenneth 17, 53, 61, 82, 134
166-167, 177, 184, 194-195, 200, 209
211, 222, 226, 231
Counter-Reformation 46
Covenant 21, 24, 40-41, 44-46, 48
64, 80, 82, 91, 118, 173, 177
Cyprian 43
Daniel 38
Dave Hunt 81, 207, 221, 223
240-241
David and Jonathon Project 65
David Chilton 99, 157
David Pytches 92, 100, 111, 128
David Shearman 52
David Wilkerson 99, 106-107, 126
136, 143, 225, 230
Derek Prince 63
Deuteronomic 48
Dominionism 14, 16, 20, 37, 49, 86
97, 112-114, 118, 143, 158, 160, 210
218, 243
Domitian 39
Dr Arnold Fruchtenbaum 62
Dr Harold Sevener 62
Dr. Michael Harry 61
Dualism 209, 211-212, 222
Dualistic 209
Duckering 53, 200
Ebenezer Fund 61, 65
Ecclesiology 47
Ed Cole 17, 94

Election 47, 122
Elim 128-133, 136-137, 165, 221
Ephesus 39
Erasmus 43, 221
Erastian 155
Eusebius 38-39, 41
Evangelism 60-61, 72, 76-77, 80
115-116, 130, 145, 147, 151, 156
163, 165-166, 168, 189, 232, 237
Feast of Dedication 38
Feast of Tabernacles 66
Frederick Price 17
Fredrick Price 139, 181, 209
Fuller 219, 237, 239
Futurism 38
Gamaliel 19, 72
Garry Noth 113
George Eldon Ladd 113
George Whitfield 48, 116, 126, 135
150-151, 197
George Wood 230
Gerald Coates 95, 103, 107-109, 115
128, 137, 164
Gnosticism 6, 25, 88-89, 94, 113-114
162, 209-212, 214-216, 218-219, 245
Graham Kendrick 92, 115-118, 144
Great Tribulation 16, 57, 65, 69, 79
Gustav Schiller 65
Hadrian 39
Hagin 17, 61, 81-82, 94, 165, 177
181, 184-185, 191, 205, 209, 211, 222
Hanegraaff 82, 99, 163, 166-167
207-208, 226, 229, 241
Hanukkah 38
Healing 15, 81, 132-133, 142, 171
185-188, 197-198
Hindu 53, 123, 174, 200, 215, 218
Hinduism 53
Hinn Benny 15, 17, 99, 125-126
133-134,136, 141, 146, 164-167
175-176, 191, 199, 202, 204, 207
211, 229
Historicism 38, 40

Hobart Freeman 185
Holocaust 16, 58, 65, 67, 121
Holy of Holies 39, 41, 73
Holy Trinity Brompton 93, 100, 124
128, 135, 146-147, 153, 226, 229
Hooker 45
Humanist 26, 44, 54, 219, 221

Ian Bilby 128, 130, 137
Icthus Movement 114
International Christian Embassy 57
60-63, 65, 67-68, 81-82
Islam 55, 76, 78-79, 92, 123, 131
139, 147, 156, 163, 174, 215
Israel 10-11, 21-22, 33, 40, 46-47, 55
57-70, 75-82, 91, 98-99, 106-107
110-111, 120-122, 141, 146, 156-158
162, 169, 173, 177, 188, 191, 217
245
Israel Harel 62
Jack Deere 216
Jack Hayford 194-195
Jamnia (see also Yavne) 72
Jan Huss 43
Jan Willem Van der Hoven 60, 68
Jay Rawlings 68
Jerry Saville 17, 94
Jewish Agency 66
Jews 11-17, 23, 29-31, 34-37, 44-45
48, 55, 57-65, 67-71, 74-79, 81, 98
102, 106, 113, 121-122, 130, 137
156-157, 173, 178, 202, 204, 217, 235
Jews for Jesus 62, 77
Jill Austin 184
JIM 127, 165, 237
John Arnott 82, 134, 167, 224
John Colet 43

John Wesley 116, 126, 135, 138, 151
197, 218
John Wimber 91-92, 94, 100, 110
119, 141, 144, 147, 158, 216-217
219, 223, 231, 244

John Wycliffe 43
Joseph Chambers, 227
Josephus 38-39
Judaizers 45, 113
Justinian Weltz 43
Justification by faith 43
Kevin Connor 135, 200, 244
Kilpatrick 225-229
King of the Jews 76
Kundalini Yoga 53, 200
Lance Lambert 63
Larry Lee 17, 199
Laughing experience 61
Lausanne Consultation on Jewish 62
Lefevure 43
Lollards 43
Luther 44-45, 59, 149, 155, 157, 218
241-242
Maccabees 14, 38, 41
March for Jesus 115-117
Marilyn Hickey 17, 134, 184, 221
231
Martyn Percy 167, 232
Mary Baker Eddy 209
Max Weber 47
Merril Watson 63
Michael Brown 228
Midrash 5, 17, 19-20, 22-23, 25-26
29, 37, 97, 209, 213
Mike Sullivan 224
Minus to Plus 165, 237, 240
Mission London 60
Montanism 113-115, 162, 245
Montanist 112, 115, 245
Morris Cerullo 17, 60-61, 81,
128-130, 132-133, 165-166, 193
204, 210, 221
Moshe Rosen 77
New Age 6, 52-53, 92-93, 115, 117
119, 122, 129, 135, 148-149, 153-154
164, 218-219, 231, 238-239
Nicky Gumbel 146-147
Nomians 45

Norman Vincent Peele 222
Olivet discourse 20, 37-38, 97, 108
243-244
Operation Mobilisation Israel 62
Oral Roberts 17, 94, 165, 177
184-185, 194, 202, 207-208
Orde Dobbie 61, 63
Palm Sunday 12-16, 35-36, 54, 173
177, 204
Pat Robertson 49, 200-201, 233-234
Paul 19, 25-26, 40-41, 44-45, 68-69
72-74, 86, 89, 109, 115, 118, 142-143
149, 175-176, 178, 180, 182-184
186-188, 190, 195-197, 199, 202, 205
210, 213, 216, 233-234, 238, 241
Paul Cain 92-95, 100, 103, 107-111
144, 158, 164, 169
Paul Crouch 17, 94, 99, 185
Pensacola 53, 100, 146, 192, 200, 220
223-230
Pentecostal Romany Gypsy 53
Phil Pringle 52
Philip Foster 53
Polemicism 38
Post-millennial 49
Pre-millennial 12, 49, 51, 125, 137
244
Presbyterian 47
Pretorism 37, 39
Promise Keepers 93-94, 163
Prophets of Zwickau 112, 245
Protestant 19, 23, 25, 40, 43-49, 52
76, 112, 124, 137, 140, 149-150, 174
218-219, 221, 235-236, 240
Protestantism 48
PTL club 230
Rabbi Ben Zakai 73
Rabbi Shaul of Tarsus 73
Rabbi Yochannon Ben Zakai 72-73
Rabbinic Judaism 72-77, 81
Rabbinic School of Hillel 72
Randles Bill 167
Randy Clark 134, 167

Ray Macauley 17, 212
Reconstructionism 46, 49, 112, 158
162, 167, 233, 236-237, 245
Reformation 23, 25, 43-44, 46-47, 49
149-150, 157, 163, 216, 218, 239
Replacement Theology 46, 157, 173
Restorationism 6, 16, 20, 37, 86,
88-90, 99, 112, 136, 144, 157-158
190, 211, 216, 218, 237, 244
Rick Godwin 17, 67, 82, 99, 128
141, 157, 169, 190, 212, 244
Robert Schuller 179, 222, 224, 231
Robert Tilton 184, 191, 199, 202
Roberts Liardon 184
Rodney Howard-Browne 53, 135
166, 200, 226
Roger Forster 92, 115, 117-118, 144
Roman Catholicism 25, 45, 47-48, 56
117, 123, 148, 154, 175-176, 214-215
221-222, 231, 233-236
Rushdooney 113, 137, 200
Sandy Millar 100, 111, 124, 128, 146
Sanhedrin 31-32, 86
School of Hillel 73
School of Shammai 73
Shakers 100
Shearman 51, 158, 203-204
Singing Watsons 61
Sorko Ram 81-82
Soteriology 47, 64
Spurgeon 236
Steve Hill 226
Surrat 39
Swaggart 125, 202, 230
T. Austin Sparks 114
Temple of Jupiter 39
Tertullian 114
The Apostle 73
The Trumpet of Salvation 63
Theocratic 45
Theonomic 49
Theonomy 48
Thomas Chakko 53

Thomas Trask 229
Titus Emperor 39
Toronto 34, 53, 61, 82, 100, 115
128-131, 134-135, 146-147, 165, 167
192, 200, 208, 220, 223-226, 228-230
Triumphalism 14, 17, 50, 52, 112
118, 124, 126, 144, 160, 201, 216
243-244
Ulf Eckmann 61
Vineyard 91-94, 107, 114, 119-120
163, 167, 218-219, 224, 226, 231-232
239, 244
Wagner Peter 179, 225, 237, 239
Waldenseans 43
Warfield B.B. 221
Whitfield John 236
William Carey 43
William De Artega 220, 231, 241
William Nunley 230
Willow Creek 237
Wings of Eagles 61
Yacov Dhamkani 62
Yavne (Jamnia) 72-73
Yonggi Cho 115, 135, 211
Zwingli 44-45, 149